Leading Academics

Fiona Steple

SRHE and Open University Press Imprint
General Editor: Heather Eggins

Current titles include:

Sir Christopher Ball and Heather Eggins: *Higher Education into the 1990s*
Ronald Barnett: *Improving Higher Education*
Ronald Barnett: *Learning to Effect*
Ronald Barnett: *The Idea of Higher Education*
Tony Becher: *Academic Tribes and Territories*
Tony Becher: *Governments and Professional Education*
Robert Bell and Malcolm Tight: *Open Universities: A British Tradition?*
Hazel Bines and David Watson: *Developing Professional Education*
David Boud *et al.*: *Using Experience for Learning*
John Earwaker: *Helping and Supporting Students*
Heather Eggins: *Restructuring Higher Education*
Roger Ellis: *Quality Assurance for University Teaching*
Gavin J. Fairbairn and Christopher Winch: *Reading, Writing and Reasoning: A Guide for Students*
Oliver Fulton: *Access and Institutional Change*
Diana Green: *What is Quality in Higher Education?*
Gunnar Handal and Per Lauvås: *Promoting Reflective Teaching*
Vivien Hodgson *et al.*: *Beyond Distance Teaching, Towards Open Learning*
Jill Johnes and Jim Taylor: *Performing Indicators in Higher Education*
Ian McNay: *Visions of Post-compulsory Education*
Robin Middlehurst: *Leading Academics*
Graeme Moodie: *Standards and Criteria in Higher Education*
Jennifer Nias: *The Human Nature of Learning: Selections from the Work of M. L. J. Abercrombie*
Gillian Pascall and Roger Cox: *Women Returning to Higher Education*
Kjell Raaheim *et al.*: *Helping Students to Learn*
John T. E. Richardson *et al.*: *Student Learning*
Tom Schuller: *The Future of Higher Education*
Geoffrey Squires: *First Degree*
Ted Tapper and Brian Salter: *Oxford, Cambridge and the Changing Idea of the University*
Kim Thomas: *Gender and Subject in Higher Education*
Malcolm Tight: *Higher Education: A Part-time Perspective*
David Warner and Gordon Kelly: *Managing Educational Property*
David Warner and Charles Leonard: *The Income Generation Handbook*
Susan Warner Weil and Ian McGill: *Making Sense of Experiential Learning*
David Watson: *Managing the Modular Course*
Sue Wheeler and Jan Birtle: *A Handbook for Personal Tutors*
Thomas G. Whiston and Roger L. Geiger: *Research and Higher Education*
Gareth Williams: *Changing Patterns of Finance in Higher Education*
John Wyatt: *Commitment to Higher Education*

Leading Academics

Robin Middlehurst

The Society for Research into Higher Education
& Open University Press

To the memory of
John and Rieteke Tomlinson

Published by SRHE and
Open University Press
Celtic Court
22 Ballmoor
Buckingham
MK18 1XW

and 1900 Frost Road, Suite 101
Bristol, PA 19007, USA

First published 1993

A catalogue record of this book is available from the British Library

ISBN 0 335 09988 2 (pb)   0 335 09989 0 (hb)

Library of Congress Cataloging-in-Publication Data
Middlehurst, Robin, 1954–
    Leading academics / Robin Middlehurst.
        p.   cm.
    Includes bibliographical references (p.   ) and index.
    ISBN 0-335-09989-0. — ISBN 0-335-09988-2 (pbk.)
    1. Universities and colleges—Great Britain—Administration.
    2. College administrators—Great Britain.   3. Educational
    leadership—Great Britain.   I. Title.
    LB2341.8.G7M53   1993
    378'.1'00941—dc20   93-14563
                                                 CIP

Typeset by Inforum, Rowlands Castle, Hants
Printed in Great Britain by St Edmundsbury Press Ltd, Bury St Edmunds, Suffolk

Contents

Acknowledgements

Thanks are due to a large number of people who have offered advice and inspiration in the genesis of this book. The university staff who have given of their time to respond to questionnaires and to be interviewed deserve a particular vote of thanks. I would also like to extend my thanks to Professor John Adair for our many leadership discussions, to the consultants who steered the second DES-funded project, to my fellow researchers who contributed to the success of the projects, to my students who sharpened my ideas and to my colleagues in the Centre for Higher Education Studies, who supported this book and allowed me time to write. Dr Ronald Barnett, who read and commented on my manuscript and who spurred me on when energy and enthusiasm were flagging, has earned my sincere gratitude. My family have also been endlessly tolerant of a wife and mother who has spent many evenings and weekends chained to the computer. Edmund, Sam and Tom, I thank you all.

Introduction

Focus

Leading Academics is an exploration of the concept and practice of leadership within academic institutions. The book represents a staging post in a quest to find answers to a puzzle, namely is the concept of leadership appropriate and useful for non-profit, professional organizations such as universities? Do their traditions of individual autonomy and consensus decision-making allow for the successful exercise of leadership? Are models and images of leadership developed in other contexts of relevance to academe, or is there something distinctive about the nature of leadership in the academic context? Where in the academic environment might leadership be identified and how might it be developed?

These questions, of course, raise other issues. The concept of leadership itself is not uncontroversial; systematic study of the subject over the past sixty or more years has produced several schools of thought and numerous definitions and descriptions of the phenomenon. These will be considered. The context in which leadership is exhibited is likely to have an impact on the way in which leadership is practised, so that the nature of academic institutions and their external environments will need to be explored. Recent studies of leadership have begun to identify still finer distinctions in the concept and operation of leadership: at different levels of an organization; in relation to individuals and groups; and within different sociological paradigms. All these themes will be addressed. Finally, some clarification will be attempted in order to tease out differences between leadership and other concepts with which it is frequently associated, such as management, power and motivation.

Purpose

The purpose of this book is to increase the level of interest and understanding of leadership within the academic context and to demonstrate the relevance of leadership for contemporary universities. The book is not a leadership manual or a scholarly treatise on leadership, although it contains elements of each of these. The premise on which the book is based, however, does reflect an important academic principle, namely that greater awareness and a deeper understanding of this subject not only will aid reflection on pre-suppositions and past experience, but will also increase the range of strategies available in practice. The content of the book is intended to capture the imagination of readers in order to encourage improvements in leadership. Some of the tools and conditions for change are identified and detailed background information and ideas about leadership are offered. The book is thus directed towards all 'reflective practitioners'.

Origins

If one looks into the distant past for the germination of ideas and interests that lead to a book, then a childhood exposed to naval traditions of leadership must be the starting point. The ideas sown in me then were further shaped through formal schooling in the archetypical leadership training arena of the English public school. The study of history, the experience of living in different cultures and working in a variety of organizations, heightened my intellectual curiosity about leadership, drawing attention to variables of time, place, circumstance and individual psychology and behaviour.

The opportunity to translate amorphous ideas into serious study arose in 1986 through engagement in a research project led by Professor John Adair, formerly Professor of Leadership Studies at the University of Surrey and currently Visiting Professor of Leadership Studies at the University of Exeter. The evaluation and development work associated with his programme of national leadership seminars for senior university staff gave access not only to Professor Adair's leadership ideas, but also to those of others within the various schools of leadership thought. Observation and discussion of the programmes with participants and tutors, as well as day-to-day work within the academic environment, drew attention to some of the problems, paradoxes, frustrations and opportunities that leadership generated, both in theory and in practice.

The Department of Education and Science, which funded the evaluation of the 'Action-centred leadership' programmes led by Adair, provided me with a chance to delve further into academic leadership by supporting a research project on the changing roles of senior university staff and the implications of a changing external context for leadership preparation and development. The data collected in the course of these two studies, the first of which focused particularly on the level of heads of academic departments, and the second on leadership at institutional level, form a major part of this book.

Note

The empirical studies were undertaken between 1986 and 1988 and between 1989 and 1991. The data were collected from the 'old' university sector, through questionnaires and interviews. In the first study, all those who had attended a leadership course were contacted by questionnaire (175 individuals). An 81 per cent response rate was achieved. Subsequently, interviews were conducted with 33 Heads of Department in 14 UK universities.

In the second study, interviews were conducted in ten institutions, spread geographically across the UK. Sampling took account of size, location, structure, age and subject spread. Some atypical institutions (Oxford, Cambridge, Buckingham, Ulster) were not included in the original population from which the sample was drawn. All members of the 'senior management team' or its equivalent were interviewed individually in each institution, as well as key lay members of Council or Court. Interviews with a cross-section of staff in four of the ten universities (Deans and Heads of Department in single interviews; academic staff, academic-related staff, clerical, technical and ancillary staff in group interviews) were also undertaken. A total of 90 senior staff were interviewed, as well as 166 other staff in groups of six or eight.

As part of both studies, comparative visits were made to training establishments in other sectors, for example in local government, the Health Service, the Civil Service, some private sector companies, and in further education and the compulsory education sector. A short survey of management and leadership development within higher education overseas was also undertaken. The full reports, containing the findings of both studies, can be found in *Collected Original Resources in Education*, volume 16, no. 1, March 1992.

Readers may notice the lack of comment about gender differences in leadership, both in the studies mentioned above and in this book. There are two reasons for this. First, the respondents in our studies were a relatively homogeneous group, the vast majority of whom were male (particularly at senior levels). Second, until recently, the mainstream leadership literature, has not highlighted gender differences in leadership. Most studies (which emanate largely from the USA) have concluded that there is no greater difference between women and men in relation to leadership than between women as a population (Alimo-Metcalf, 1993). In this book I have worked with these conclusions, assuming that what is said about leadership applies both to men and women. In the text, I have used 'he' or 'she' throughout. In further work, these assumptions will need to be tested.

Overview

This book is divided into three parts: Part 1: Thinking about Leadership, Chapters 1–4; Part 2: Practising Leadership, Chapters 5–8; and Part 3: Developing Leadership, Chapters 9–10. The first three chapters set the scene for later discussion and elaboration. In Chapters 1 and 2 the concept of leadership is examined, both in popular and in analytical terms. In Chapter 3, the idea of leadership is explored within an organizational setting and several images of academic organizations are considered.

Chapter 4 is a pivotal chapter since it is here that the central arguments about the nature and relevance of leadership in universities are presented and developed.

In Chapters 5 and 7 two key leadership roles at institutional and departmental level (that of the Vice Chancellor and the Head of Department) are examined in order to shed light on formal leadership in practice. This theme is also part of Chapter 6, which considers collective leadership in the context of the 'Senior Management Group'.

Having concentrated upon both formal leadership and group leadership, the focus shifts, in Chapter 8, to the individual and a discussion of 'informal' aspects of leadership. Here the spotlight is not on designated roles but on the opportunities for leadership at the individual level among all members of staff. The conditions that impinge on the emergence or identification of individual leadership are also considered.

Chapter 9 brings individual and group perspectives together by examining the relationship between leadership and learning and by discussing the issue of leadership development in universities. Finally, Chapter 10 offers a synthesis of earlier ideas and arguments and presents a number of themes that will present challenges for academic leadership in the future.

Audience

This book is written for academic managers and leaders in particular, but should also be of interest to others engaged in trying to understand, to practise or to develop leadership within the academic environment. These 'interested others' may include internal constituents, such as administrators, chief technicians, public relations or library staff, researchers, lecturers, students or lay governors, staff developers and personnel managers, as well as external groups, such as those working within other professional or public sector organizations.

A bolder hope may be realized if the book attracts an even broader readership within the private or voluntary sectors. The environment in which different kinds of organization must now operate is raising similar problems and opportunities, and the nature of managerial responses across sectors appears to be causing a convergence in management structures and processes between previously dissimilar businesses (Handy, 1989; Pollitt, 1990). Some influential management thinkers, such as Peter Drucker (1988) or Tom Peters (1991), suggest that companies in the future may adopt some of the central organizational features of universities. For such a suggestion to become a reality, business managers would need to understand the context in which these features operate and the ways in which universities are more, or less, effective. This book might help to develop such an understanding.

Part 1

Thinking about Leadership

1

What Is Leadership?

Introduction

The idea of leadership is complex, difficult to capture and open to numerous definitions and interpretations. Neither in common parlance nor in the literature on the subject is there consensus about the essence of leadership, or the means by which it can be identified, achieved or measured (Bennis and Nanus, 1985). Although spoken about as a concrete and observable phenomenon, it remains an intangible and elusive notion, no more stable than quicksand. As with beauty, the existence or absence of leadership is largely dependent upon subjective judgement by observers with different interests and perspectives. Again like beauty, leadership is likely to consist of a number of separate elements, which only in combination can be said to represent the whole.

Leadership is difficult to predict in advance and is usually recorded with hindsight, inferred from a combination of observed events and behaviour and reported through the perceptions of interested parties. Leadership as a concept is therefore unlikely to be value free, being dependent upon individual or collective perceptions and beliefs. This makes leadership a difficult subject to research since it is prone to 'contamination', as much through the perceptual frameworks of researchers as through those of their subjects.

Researching into leadership is further complicated by the difficulty of disentangling 'real leadership' from other social influence processes, such as power or authority (Bryman, 1986). The study of leadership is also an area that has interested scholars in a number of academic disciplines (for example, sociology, psychology, politics or history). Different disciplinary perspectives have influenced the assumptions that underpin theory and research into leadership. The variety of conceptual lenses that have been brought to bear on the subject add richness but also complexity to the task of decoding and analysing leadership.

Despite the difficulties, the challenge of trying to understand leadership is worth facing since it is a subject of considerable interest and importance in many contexts. In this chapter, therefore, the idea of leadership will be examined from the perspective of everyday associations and from the standpoint of different schools (and eras) of leadership thought. A number of issues will emerge as the ideas about leadership are presented; these will be discussed in the final section of the chapter.

Popular conceptions of leadership

Being in charge

Leadership is commonly associated with 'being in charge or in command' of people, activities or events. The designation of 'leader' (carrying with it the right or expectation to exercise leadership) can be formally or informally assigned. In this sense, leadership is at the same time identified with the occupation of a position of authority by an individual and with a course of action that is related to the discharging of the responsibilities of that position. Examples of this notion of leadership might be a conductor of an orchestra, chief executive, cricket team captain, mother superior or youth gang leader. In a formal sense the authority to exercise leadership is conveyed by virtue of legal or constitutional arrangements, while in the informal sense authority is likely to arise from peer group recognition, achieved by virtue of particular skills, expertise or personal characteristics that are of value to individuals or to a group. From this perspective, leadership is viewed as both a static and a dynamic concept. Some of these ambiguities can be seen in this newspaper headline: 'As Whitehall encourages local leadership in its approach to inner city regeneration, council leaders have come to realise the need to work with the grain of government policy' (*Financial Times*, 18 September 1992).

In this quotation the term leadership is used in several ways. It is used to denote a process of influence (working with the grain . . .), a form of authority (local versus national), a symbol (representation of local interests) and a role (responsibility for inner city regeneration). Below, we shall see further examples of the associations that are linked to 'leadership'.

Direction-setting

Beyond the right to exercise authority, leadership is seen as guidance towards an ideal or as the directing of events. Direction-setting may be achieved by means of personal example or by giving incentive to others to reach particular objectives or attainments. This idea has two faces. The first is associated with being 'at the forefront', where the leader is first to move in a particular direction or is further ahead in achieving a desired outcome. Examples might include leadership in the field of physics, in poetry or in art.

The second face of direction-setting refers to an activity that explicitly encourages others to move towards certain goals. In the first instance, the accolade of leadership is given to individual achievement – which may *inci-*

dentally offer a standard or guiding light for others to emulate. In the second case, there is a consciousness about the will to exercise leadership in order to encourage 'follower' achievement. Once again, leadership can be viewed as a symbol, as an active process or as a formal role. An example of leadership as direction-setting comes from an article about politicians and their ability to raise people's sights above the level of the mundane:

> The unmentionable Margaret Thatcher may have been wrong a dozen times over but she had a vision of the kind of country she felt would be great. For or against her, there was at last a sense that the country was going somewhere . . . What we are talking about is leadership. The great leader can lift our sights even higher. Perhaps not quite as high as Ronald Reagan's 'shining white city on the hill' – but certainly in that direction.
>
> (*Evening Standard*, 11 March 1992)

Influence over outcomes

When we talk about leadership as a role and a responsibility, as a symbol or a guide to action, we usually associate it with causation. In other words, the exercise of leadership has an influence either upon people or upon a course of events such that things happen. In explaining the source of this influence, particular capacities, characteristics or interactions that set the individual or group apart from others, enabling them to take charge, achieve great feats, or produce collective success, are often highlighted. There is considerable disagreement among people as to whether such capacities are innate or learned through social interaction and experience. There has also been debate about whether the kind of interactions involved are common to all contexts and situations, or specific to different settings. The research studies presented below provide evidence that seeks to answer such questions.

Commanding a following

As was implied above in the notion of leadership as an activity that encourages others to move towards certain goals, leadership is commonly associated with 'followership'. Whether leadership is acknowledged on the basis of individual achievement, after the event, or whether it is the proactive exercise of influence over people in order to reach particular ends, it implies a capacity to form and command a following. A distance is anticipated between leaders and followers. This distance is usually depicted as a vertical or hierarchical relationship between those above and those below (those above exercising greater power over others below). However, distance may also be seen on a horizontal plane: leaders may be seen as being ahead of others on a journey, or as having the task of enabling others to follow or, in a third sense, as shepherding a group forward, perhaps from a position at the rear. To the ideas of leadership as symbol, action and role, then, can be added the idea of leadership as a relationship between leader and others.

A question of style

It has long been recognized that there is infinite variety in the ways in which influence is exerted, authority exercised or followers' dreams fulfilled. Here the idea of what leadership is differs according to the context or environment (the style of leadership in a situation of crisis – war, a fire, an accident – is likely to be different from that exercised or expected in more settled circumstances). The individual leader, the nature of the group or the task in hand may also shape the style of leadership.

Differences in leadership style can be seen in the popular literature on the subject, represented in such diverse titles as *The Tao of Leadership, The Leadership Secrets of Attila the Hun* or *Servant Leadership*. The range of styles that can be observed or that has been recorded in biographies and elsewhere both suggests that leadership is a complex image to get a grip of, and raises the question of whether one style and not another truly captures the essence of the concept.

Up to this point, an attempt has been made to describe leadership in terms that are, as far as possible, value free. However, within these descriptions lurk the elements that can attract values, as iron filings are attracted to a magnet.

Set apart from others

Where leadership is associated with being first, being at the forefront or being set apart from other people, a differential element is introduced that distinguishes the leader from others in some qualitative way. The characteristics that are often attributed to the leader or that he or she may possess include charisma, exceptional energy, intelligence, a particular personal style of behaviour or level of experience and expertise. In each case, the characteristics that are identified with leadership in a particular setting are likely to reflect the values of that context and the groups of people concerned. One can say both that the leader is likely to personify the values of the group, society or organization and that the particular concept of leadership in operation will represent the prevailing values of that social context.

There is a further aspect of values that is often related to leadership. This is the link to moral values. Here the discussion usually focuses on whether, for example, the actions and behaviour of Hitler or Stalin in the 1940s can be described as leadership. Can the expert use of techniques and processes of power and influence, in a particular social setting, be identified as leadership, or are the purposes to which these skills are put of relevance in the attribution of leadership? Is there a distinction to be made between 'good leadership' and 'leadership for good'?

In organizations today, as ethical questions are raised relating to both the internal conduct of business and the external impact of business on the human environment, the moral dimensions of leadership are coming increasingly to the fore. Leadership is linked, for example, to qualities such as integrity, honesty and trust and is promoted as a means of releasing the creative talents and energies of staff for the achievement of exceptional levels of performance or even for the fulfilment of higher purpose (Kouzes and Posner, 1987; Badaracco and Ellsworth, 1989).

Summary of popular images

To summarize the discussion so far, it is useful to draw out the underlying characteristics of these ideas about leadership.

There are three dominant conceptions of leadership in use in everyday life. The first is that of leadership as an active process. This conception includes within its domain particular forms and styles of behaviour, relationships and interactions with others. The second perspective highlights leadership as role or function – 'the leadership' – within which a particular mantle of responsibility and authority is worn by those who are designated leaders. The third conception views leadership as symbolic, whether of intangible elements like power or excellence, or in more concrete terms of representation and public visibility. The last two leadership perspectives are often associated with particular attributes or characteristics, for example charisma, technical expertise or gravitas.

The boundaries between the conceptions are blurred and are in any case linked by some common elements, such as the attribution of particular values and expectations. It is the simultaneous use of these different conceptions that makes leadership a difficult subject to investigate; its constituent characteristics are likely to be clustered tightly together so that it is difficult to isolate, for example, the exercise of leadership from the personal attributes of the leader, from his or her social role as leader, and any of these from the context in which leadership takes place or from the expectations of interested others. An analogy can perhaps be drawn with certain kinds of diseases that may occur because of a particular cluster of viruses combining to produce an effect which is different from the effect of any of the constituent viruses in isolation.

On the other hand, the three conceptions of leadership described above may not in practice be intimately connected to each other. A lack of interconnection would account for the dissatisfaction that is recorded in the popular press, for example, with those who are designated leaders by virtue of their selection or election to high office, but who are subsequently regarded as falling short as leaders. They are perceived to be inadequate either in terms of expected leader behaviour or in terms of appropriate leadership qualities. The position of leader may thus be separate from and produce no certain guarantee of the existence of leadership. This would suggest that conceptions of leadership that link the concept to particular qualities or identify it as a process of social influence and interaction between followers and leaders are closer to the essence of leadership.

In order to examine leadership in greater depth and to cast more light on the subject, we must turn to the fruits of leadership research in the twentieth century. It should be recognized, however, that our current understandings of leadership are also coloured by the questions, insights and reflections of historians, philosophers, politicians and military theorists from past centuries. Many of the 'myths' that surround leadership can be traced to the writings of Plato, Xenophon, Tacitus, Machiavelli, Lao Tsu and others or to cultural traditions which in the West stem from tribal, classical and biblical sources (Adair, 1989).

Leadership theory and research: an overview (circa 1920–1980)

As Warren Bennis, a noted American writer on leadership, has said: 'Leadership is an endless subject and endlessly interesting because you can never get your conceptual arms fully around it . . . I always feel rather like a lepidopterist chasing a butterfly' (1992). The elusiveness of the concept of leadership has encouraged researchers to view the subject from different perspectives, drawing insights from a range of disciplines and utilizing a variey of investigative techniques. This brief overview, which is intended to be illustrative rather than comprehensive, will highlight the major themes in leadership research and draw attention to some models that are of potential practical relevance in the academic context. Since the field is large and has recently undergone a considerable metamorphosis, this chapter will concentrate on leadership research from (approximately) the 1920s to the late 1970s, and the following chapter will consider more recent work.

There is considerable overlap between the various 'schools' of leadership thinking, different authors choosing to subdivide the field in slightly different ways. The classification adopted here is that offered by Bensimon *et al.* (1989). Six different perspectives on leadership will be considered: trait theories, behavioural theories, contingency theories (in this chapter); power and influence theories, cultural and symbolic perspectives and cognitive approaches (in Chapter 2). Together these different themes represent a historical view of twentieth-century thinking and research about leadership. Table 1 provides an overview in diagrammatic form.

Academic research into leadership has largely been concentrated in the field of psychology and more recently in the burgeoning field of organizational behaviour, which draws upon the disciplines of psychology, sociology, anthropology and political science. As Adair (1989) and others (Symons, 1991; Hunt, 1992) have shown, there is still scope for further cross-

Table 1 Overview of twentieth-century thought

Period	Theories/approaches	Theme
Up to late 1940s	Trait theories	Leadership is linked to personal qualities
Late 1940s to late 1960s	Behavioural theories	Leadership is associated with behaviour and style
Late 1960s to present	Contingency theories	Leadership is affected by the context and situation
Late 1960s to present	Power and influence theories	Leadership is associated with use of power
1970s to present	Cultural and symbolic theories	Leadership is the 'management of meaning'
1980s to present	Cognitive theories	Leadership is a social attribution

Adapted from Bensimon *et al.*, 1989; Bryman, 1992

fertilization between disciplines in order to include insights from history, literature or philosophy. However, since the bulk of leadership research is psychological and because many of the new developments in leadership thought have emerged from this field, I shall concentrate mainly on psychological studies.

Trait theories

Early psychological studies of leaders focused upon the investigation of the essential qualities or traits assumed to be linked to leadership, building on previous 'great man' theories of leadership. The idea that 'leaders are born not made' is still a powerful theme in popular views of leadership.

Trait theories are based on several assumptions: (a) that leadership is a personal quality, usually a natural endowment or a characteristic that some individuals have developed; (b) that there are certain qualities which set leaders apart from other people; (c) that these special qualities contribute to the personal power which leaders are able to exert over others in order to influence their actions; (d) if these special characteristics could be isolated through research, then potential leaders could be identified through the screening and selection process within organizations.

Despite the attractiveness of the notion of specific leadership traits and the continuing commitment to this theme in the selection processes of many organizations (including higher education institutions), decades of research have so far been unsuccessful in providing conclusive evidence that general qualities or abilities can be discerned in relation to leadership or are firmly associated with effective leadership (Bennis and Nanus, 1985; Bryman, 1986; Bensimon *et al.*, 1989). Although trait research within psychology waned in popularity in the 1950s, it can be found in the management literature and is making a comeback now, albeit in a more sophisticated form, associated particularly with studies of leaders' mental predispositions or preferences (Hunt, 1992).

There are three broad types of trait that have been investigated: physical features, such as height, weight, physique, energy level, appearance and age; individual abilities, such as intelligence, fluency of speech, knowledge and expertise; and personality characteristics such as dominance, self-confidence, introversion–extraversion, interpersonal sensitivity, emotional resilience and control. Although some traits (such as assertiveness, decisiveness, dependability, persistence, self-confidence and creativity) and some skills (such as verbal fluency and persuasiveness) appear to be characteristic of successful leaders (Bass, 1981), possession of the traits does not guarantee success nor their absence proscribe it (Bensimon *et al.*, 1989). While possession of certain traits may be a necessary condition for leadership, it is not a sufficient condition.

In the academic world, trait theories still have some currency. Successful academic leaders have been described in terms of personal attributes, interpersonal abilities and technical management skills (Kaplowitz, 1986). The personal attributes include: courage, humour, judgement, integrity, intelligence, persistence, hard work and vision. Interpersonal abilities cover such areas as being open, building teams, empathy and being compassionate. Technical management skills include an orientation towards goal achievement, problem-solving skills, diagnostic and evaluative skills, and the ability to resolve conflicts and to shape the work environment. Our own recent study of institutional leadership in the UK also noted the importance of certain characteristics and abilities in perceptions of leadership: professional and technical competence; interpersonal skills; intellectual and conceptual abilities; communication skills; and information-processing skills (Middlehurst *et al.*, 1992).

One of the main problems with trait theory, apart from the difficulty of establishing which traits are most significant, is that people do not always exhibit the same traits over time, and indeed the same traits may not always be required since circumstances do not remain constant (Bensimon *et al.*, 1989). Traits by themselves, representing a somewhat static and unidimensional view, are therefore not an adequate indication or explanation of the phenomenon of leadership.

Behavioural theories

In the late 1940s, the focus of leadership research changed. The lack of consistent research findings supporting a correlation between the possession of certain traits and the existence of leadership was one reason for the shift; the emergence of the 'human relations' approach to the study of organizations was another (Bryman, 1986). Attention now concentrated upon the behaviour of leaders: what leaders did and how they did it – their actions and the style in which these actions were performed. The notion of particular attributes and abilities associated with leadership did not disappear altogether, as leadership style is often seen as a manifestation of personality (Stogdill, 1948; Fiedler, 1972), but the focus of attention moved primarily to behaviour. This alternative focus also opened the arena to notions of leadership development, since the idea that leaders could be 'made' challenged the view that leadership was purely a gift of birth.

One of the most influential research programmes in the behavioural tradition was conducted by an interdisciplinary team of researchers and is known as the 'Ohio State Leadership Studies'. Of major importance was the identification by the researchers of two aspects of leadership behaviour: 'initiating structure' (or an orientation towards the task) and 'consideration' (namely an orientation towards relationships with people) (Stogdill and Coons, 1957). Task-orientated behaviour included such activities as directing, coordinating, planning and problem-solving; while an emphasis on consideration included behaviour that was supportive, friendly and consultative. Researchers then tried to link each type of behaviour to effective outcomes, but this proved more problematic; although different conditions might call for different approaches, the precise mix required was unclear.

In parallel with the Ohio Studies, another large research programme, known as the Michigan Studies, was being conducted (between the early 1940s and the middle 1960s). An enduring and distinctive feature of this programme of studies was the awareness of the possible importance of informal leadership, in contrast to the formal leadership associated with those in designated positions of power and authority. Another contribution was the distinction made between 'peer and managerial leadership behaviour'. In other words, the group-related leadership functions (such as the development of teamwork or mutual support) may be carried out either by the formal leader or by one or more members of the work group. These ideas presage the work of Meredith Belbin (1981) and his categorization of team roles linked to effective teamwork and group productivity, or the work of Kakabadse and his colleagues (1992) on senior management teams.

The findings of the two research groups were eventually summarized by Bowers and Seashore (1966) and showed that there was considerable overlap between the studies. Four underlying dimensions of leadership seemed to emerge, as follows:

1. Support, behaviour that enhances the followers' sense of worth.
2. Interaction-facilitation, the building of close, mutually satisfying group relationships.
3. Goal emphasis, the stimulation of commitment to the achievement of goals, including high levels of performance.

4. Work facilitation, providing the technical and organizational means for goal accomplishment, that is planning, coordination and organization.

These dimensions have continued to be regarded as important in relation to an understanding of leadership, but in both sets of studies certain problems were present; for example the difficulty of establishing cause-and-effect relationships between leadership and successful outcomes and the lack of attention paid to the context in which leaders were operating (Bryman, 1986).

Three models, developed on the basis of the research findings from these two series of studies, have been particularly influential.

The managerial grid

The first model is presented in the form of a grid with two nine-point scales, as outlined in Figure 1 (Blake and Mouton, 1964, 1981, 1991). The vertical axis of the scale refers to a leader's degree of concern for people (relationship-orientation), while the horizontal axis relates to a leader's orientation towards a concern for effective outcomes (task-orientation). A person's leadership style can be identified by locating his or her degree of orientation towards both dimensions (with a possible total of 81 combinations). In most of their writing, Blake and Mouton concentrate on five combinations:

(a) 1,1: 'Impoverished management' (where scores are low on both dimensions), in which context conflict is likely to be rife and leadership is either non-existent or pathological.
(b) 1,9: 'Country club management' (with a high score on concern for people only). Here camaraderie and group spirit may be high, but people are not pressured to be productive.
(c) 9,1: 'Task management' (characterized by a high score on the concern for production dimension). The key orientation for leaders in this category is towards controlling and directing the activities of subordinates or towards planning their work.
(d) 5,5: a middle position in which there is some support for both orientations, although only sufficient to encourage satisfactory, rather than exceptional performance.
(e) 9,9: 'Team management' (where scores are high on both scales), which represents the most desirable style, with emphasis equally on productivity and people. It is described as a participative style with ultimate success being achieved when individual and organizational goals are congruent.

The model has been criticized since it points to 'one best style' which is appropriate for any context and circumstance, without paying attention to the nature of the environment, the task itself or the characteristics of leaders

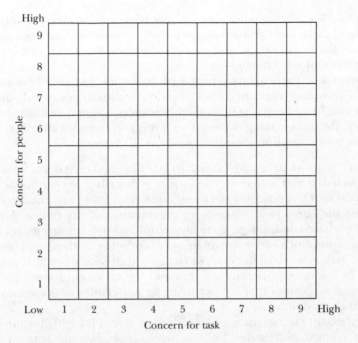

Figure 1 Leadership style: task and relationship orientations
(after Blake and Mouton, 1964, 1981)

and led. It also offers no explanation as to why a leader's style should fall into one part or another of the grid. Despite these difficulties, the grid has been adapted for use in the academic context and has been widely used in programmes for department chairpersons in the USA.

Likert's four systems of management

Likert's four systems are based on the assumption that group relationships, employee-centred concern and general supervision were important aspects of leadership. Likert (1961, 1967) proposed four systems of management:

(a) System 1 – 'Exploitative-authoritative', in which leaders are highly autocratic, have little trust in subordinates, motivate people largely through fear and punishment and only occasional rewards, engage in downward communication and limit decision-making to the top.

(b) System 2 – 'Benevolent-authoritative', where leaders have a patronizing confidence in subordinates, rewards as well as some fear and punishment are used to motivate, a degree of consultation over decisions is permitted along with some delegation of decision-making, but close policy control is retained by leaders.

(c) System 3 – 'Consultative', where subordinates are more readily consulted, threats are avoided as motivators, communication flows up and
down the organization, and there is a greater degree of trust between
leaders and subordinates.

(d) System 4 – 'Participative' (proposed as the ideal style) where leaders
have complete trust and confidence in subordinates, ideas and opinions
are sought and constructively used by leaders, a variety of incentives are
used, decision-making occurs at all levels and includes all group members, and communication flows easily in all directions.

In later years (Likert and Likert, 1976), two further systems were proposed: System 0 and System 5. The former is described as 'permissive' with
large areas of discretion over decisions residing at lower organizational levels, while the latter looks towards an organization of the future in which
authority is based on intra-group relationships and overlapping group memberships, instead of a hierarchy: an image of collective leadership. These two
'systems' reflect some of the current changes in organizations that are happening in the wake of decentralization and the creation of fewer management layers – changes that are occurring in universities or are in any case
part of their traditions.

An important characteristic of Likert's work is that it highlights the influence of context and makes links between organizational structure and
leadership style. However, again, the emphasis is on one best style, regardless
of circumstances. Much of the research was conducted within small groups
and at relatively low organizational levels – although the results have often
been applied, with little evidence to support them, to the total organization
(Bryman, 1986).

Functional or action-centred leadership

Where the previous models were American, a widely used model in the UK has
been Adair's three-circles model (Adair, 1968, 1983). Influenced by a range of
American work on leadership, group dynamics and motivation as well as by
the work of early management theorists, such as Fayol (1949), Barnard (1938)
and Urwick (1944), Adair proposed that people working in organizations had
three interconnected needs (represented by three overlapping circles; see
Figure 2): the need to achieve the common task, the need to be kept together
as a working group and the need to achieve individual satisfaction at work.
Leadership (that is, the particular actions of leaders) was concerned with
achieving satisfaction in relation to each of these needs.

Adair went further and defined nine functional responsibilities for
leaders, based on their awareness of what was happening in the work group,
their understanding of what action was required and their degree of skill in
carrying out the necessary functions. The success criteria for leadership
included a change in direction of the group, achievement of the task and

| Setting objectives |
| Briefing |
| Planning |
| Controlling |
| Informing |
| Supporting |
| Reviewing |
| Setting an example |

Figure 2 Action-centred leadership
(Adair, 1968, 1973)

the development of a high-performance team, characterized by high levels of individual motivation and intra-group support. The nine functions of leadership were: defining the task (setting objectives), planning, briefing, controlling, communicating (informing), motivating (supporting), organizing (coordinating), reviewing (evaluating) and setting an example; the labels vary slightly in different editions of the author's work. Adair defined each function in relation to the task circle, the team circle and the individual circle, giving leaders clear guidance as to the actions they needed to undertake.

In his later writing, Adair recognizes the potential importance of context and climate, arguing first that the three circles were in dynamic tension and that circumstances would (at least in part) dictate the level of attention that should be paid to each circle at particular times. Second, in relation to climate, Adair lists five conditions that will encourage the spread of leadership development in an organization: the direction and source of power and authority (centrifugal as opposed to centripetal), tolerance of mistakes, a forward-looking management orientation, teamwork and more equality within the organization.

Adair's work leaves several issues unresolved; for example, the impact of the external environment on leadership and the degree of reciprocal influence between leader and led. There are also problems with the nine functions since they do not differentiate clearly between leadership and management; with the hierarchical connotations of the model; and with the model's limitations in either explaining or predicting differences in leadership at different organizational levels. In his seminars (for universities and other organizations), Adair does acknowledge the reality of leadership differences at different organizational levels, but claims the value of the three-circles model in relation to all levels, without specifying the precise nature of leadership differences between, for example, supervisory, middle, senior and top management levels.

Despite these problems, the Adair model is well-established in numerous leadership awareness and development programmes, inside and outside the academic world, both in the UK and internationally. The approach is simple and accessible, relevant to appointed, elected or emergent leaders. It also provides a bridge between the qualities or traits approach to leadership and behavioural approaches since Adair (following Maslow, 1954) describes leadership as both instrumental and expressive. In other words, leadership is viewed as an activity which enables task, team and individual needs to be addressed while also being an expression of personality and character.

Behavioural approaches to leadership have continued to attract attention; research studies have increased the number of categories of behaviour investigated (see for example, Bass, 1981, Yukl, 1981) or have adopted a micro-skills approach to the study and training of leadership behaviours (Alban-Metcalfe, 1984; Wright and Taylor, 1984). Unfortunately, identifying ever more detailed behavioural variables, while extending understanding about leadership, gave no more definitive answers about effective leadership than had emerged from the earlier 'trait school'. Greater complexity in research design, the difficulties of achieving consistent results across studies and the problem of identifying the direction of causality, particularly across organizational contexts, again caused a shift in the focus of research (Bryman, 1986). New investigations took greater account of the context in which leadership was being exercised. Studies in this later tradition have been labelled 'contingency theories'.

Contingency theories

The third perspective on leadership emphasises the importance of situational factors (i.e. 'contingencies') – such as the nature of the task, the type of external environment, or abilities of followers – on the emergence or effectiveness of leadership. The theories are based on at least three assumptions: (a) that different circumstances require different patterns of behaviour (or qualities) for a leader to be effective; (b) that a dynamic interaction between leader and context will shape the nature of leadership, in other words that leadership is not unidimensional; (c) that context and circumstances place different demands, constraints and choices on leaders (Stewart, 1976, 1982).

A wide range of contingencies have been investigated by researchers. They include: the position of the leader in a heirarchy (leaders at lower levels, for example, have less discretionary authority); the functions performed by the organizational unit (leaders in a production unit, for example, can be more directive than leaders of research units); the characteristics of the task and the technology used (leaders of low complexity tasks tend to be more authoritarian); size of the organizational unit (leaders of large units engage in less support behaviour); subordinates' competence (effective leaders emphasize performance with weaker subordinates); and presence of a crisis (leaders are expected to act more decisively in crises) (Bensimon *et al.*, 1989). In some cases leaders may also encourage a feeling of crisis in order to justify or legitimize their actions. A case study of Aston University in the UK (Glendon, 1992) highlights this phenomenon.

Recent contingency models, for example that of House (1984, 1988), advance as many as sixty variables which can shape or constrain leadership style and behaviour. Given this variety, the interesting question concerns the precise nature of the interaction between leadership and context. This path has led researchers towards new areas of investigation into the thought processes which guide leaders' actions and direct their choice of style and behaviour.

Before examining these more recent research traditions in the next chapter, it is worth outlining some prominent contingency theories since they have again influenced contemporary thinking about leadership.

Fiedler's contingency model

Fiedler's model (1967, 1971, 1978) suggests that leaders are likely, personally, to be either task or relationship orientated. However, the degree of influence that the leader can exercise depends on 'situational favourableness', that is, on three factors: the quality of relationships between the leader and members of the working group, the degree of task structure (the leader's position will be assisted if tasks are clear and unambiguous), and the position of the leader within the organization, that is, the ability to reward or punish and so to enforce compliance.

The importance of Fiedler's ideas (despite the difficulties of verifying his research results) lies in their movement away from the notion of individual behaviour being the sole cause of the effectiveness, or failure, of leadership. Instead, effectiveness is deemed to depend upon the leader's personality and degree of control over the situation at hand; for the most productive results, leaders should be matched to a particular context and set of circumstances in keeping with their personal leadership orientation or should seek to mould the situation to fit their particular strengths. In the academic world, these ideas are practised to some extent. For example, considerable time and effort is expended within the search process for new Vice Chancellors on the task of matching candidates to the specific contexts of individual institutions (as perceived by those on the search committee). However, less attention seems to be paid to team relationships, despite their importance at senior management level (Middlehurst *et al.*, 1992).

Path-goal theory

Where Fiedler still relied on leader personality as a variable in effective leadership, later contingency theories focused upon other factors.

House's theory (1971, 1973, 1984) proposes two contingencies related to effective leadership: that subordinates must understand how to achieve the leader's goals, and that their own goals must be achieved in the process. These ideas build on earlier 'expectancy theories' of motivation (Vroom, 1964). In other words, effort is expended by people in relation to the rewards available and expected by them, rather than in relation to the need to satisfy their internal drives (as Maslow's, 1954, motivation theory suggests).

The path-goal theory, as House has labelled it, suggests that the leader's task is to choose the appropriate leadership style to suit the task environment and the characteristics of the subordinates. The leader can motivate followers by increasing the personal satisfaction to be gained in achieving the groups' goals, by clarifying the task and by removing barriers along the path towards goal attainment. In later versions of the theory, four styles of leadership are identified: instrumental, which emphasizes the clarifying of roles and expectations, as well as the structuring of the work process; supportive, in which concern for subordinates' well-being and status is paramount (demonstrated by friendliness and approachability); participative, where consultation and involvement of subordinates in decision-making are the key features of the leader's style; and achievement-oriented, in which high standards are set and high performance is expected of individuals.

The choice and effectiveness of any one style, the author argues, is dependent on the characteristics of subordinates (in terms both of abilities and personal qualities) and environmental factors such as the kind of task to be achieved, the nature of the work group and the authority structure within the organization.

Although tests of the path-goal theory have not provided conclusive support for its propositions (the direction of causality between subordinate performance and leader actions again proving problematic: Bryman, 1986), the theory has clearly influenced other models which have been widely used by trainers and personnel managers in a range of organizational contexts within the USA and the UK.

Hersey and Blanchard's situational leadership model

One prescriptive model which shows similarities to the path-goal theory has become very popular. In academic as well as other organizational contexts, the approach offered by Hersey and Blanchard (1969, 1977) and Hersey (1984) appears to generate considerable practitioner support.

These authors' 'situational leadership' model is based on two dimensions of leadership style or behaviour: task behaviour (which is primarily directive) and relationship behaviour (which is primarily supportive). One 'environmental' variable is also included: follower maturity or readiness, which is based on the degree of ability and willingness of subordinates to engage with the task.

Hersey and Blanchard's model proposes that a leader's style should vary to match a subordinate's 'maturity' or 'readiness'. When subordinates are 'immature', that is unable, unwilling or insecure in relation to the task at hand, a directive style is appropriate, which establishes clear objectives, standards and procedures. As the maturity/readiness of followers increases (that is,

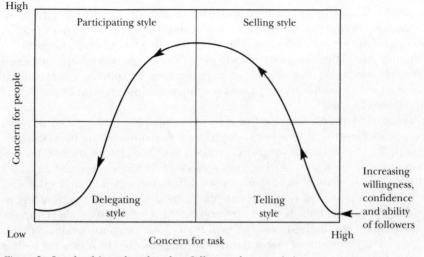

Figure 3 Leadership style related to follower characteristics
(after Hersey and Blanchard, 1969, 1977, Hersey, 1984)

they may be unable but willing or confident; able but unwilling or insecure) so the leader's style should change to be more supportive, with less emphasis placed on directing and organizing the individual's work. When subordinates are very mature, responsibility for work design can be delegated so that subordinates exercise considerable autonomy in their own areas. By using the appropriate style, 'follower maturity' can be encouraged by leaders. Hersey and Blanchard's model is represented in Figure 3.

Although aspects of the model have been criticized (such as the potential for disaffection caused by varied behaviour towards different individuals in the work group, or the problem of retaining integrity while operating different styles) the model has none the less been influential. Its main contribution has been in emphasizing the importance of flexibility in a leader's behaviour towards individuals and their work tasks, in contrast to earlier searches for an all-purpose leadership style. The model is particularly useful in highlighting the needs of newcomers to an organization or project, illustrating the benefits of managerial coaching and support in increasing the competence of staff, whether in the academic environment or elsewhere. The ideas are also readily understood, appearing to make sense to a broad range of practitioners; like Adair's action-centred leadership model mentioned above, situational leadership offers managers and supervisors a framework for reflecting on and practising leadership.

The Vroom–Yetton decision-making model

Vroom and Yetton's work (1973) concentrates on the relationship between leadership actions and decision-making. The aim of their approach is to assist the leader in enhancing both the quality of the decision (that is, those aspects of the decision that affect the group's performance) and its acceptability to subordinates (that is, the degree of commitment to implementing the decision effectively). These outcomes are achieved through specifying the degree of participation by followers that should occur in the decision-making process – when taking account of particular situational factors.

Vroom and Yetton propose five levels of participation along a continuum from autocratic through consultative to joint decision-making by leader and group; the approach has much in common with the classification of leadership styles to be found in the earlier work of Tannenbaum and Schmidt (1958). Where Vroom and Yetton's work differs and extends earlier theories is in their analysis of the 'decision environment' and its relationship to leader behaviour. Aspects of this environment include: whether it is important to obtain the highest possible quality decision or subordinates' acceptance of it; the amount of relevant information possessed by either the leader or the subordinates; the amount of disagreement about preferred alternatives. Depending on the situation, the model proposes a series of rules for determining the most effective decision-making style in a given setting. Leadership training associated with this model encourages leaders to gain insight into the nature of their leadership styles and to analyse the appropriateness of particular styles for the circumstances they face.

The model has received some support although it is still too complex to be a useful practical tool. The problem of identifying simple yet accurate representations of leadership makes the gap between theory and practice often a difficult one to bridge. The 'reality' of leadership, namely the range of factors that impinge upon it, is likely to be highly complex (as research studies suggest) yet practitioners instead often seek straightforward, practical tools and frameworks with which to operate.

Vroom and Yetton's model can none the less be helpful in stimulating leaders to analyse their own behaviour in particular situations and may yet prove valuable in the development of 'expert systems' which could recommend an appropriate match between leader behaviour and decision-making when supplied with relevant contextual information (Bryman, 1986).

In summary, contingency approaches have highlighted the relationship between leadership behaviour and a range of situational factors which are likely to impinge in different ways on the effectiveness of leadership. They have drawn attention to the need for flexibility in leadership style and have also demonstrated a requirement for diagnostic and analytical abilities on the part of leaders so that style and circumstances can be appropriately matched. Most importantly, these approaches have opened the way to concentrating far more closely on the nature of the organizational context and the kinds of individuals working in that environment (for example, their personalities, their social class or professional background, and their organizational level), as factors which are likely to shape leadership. This recognition is of importance in relation to academe.

However, there are other aspects of the theories which are less satisfactory. Once again, there are problems with the directions of causality – is it leadership style that affects performance or performance that impacts on style? – and with the consistency of research findings. Conceptions of leadership style still focus largely on the dimensions identified in earlier studies, that is, relationship or task orientation and degree of participation in decision-making. Leadership is also primarily identified with formal rather than informal or emergent leadership. Little account is taken of conflict (either between leader and subordinates or between different situational factors), or of perceptual differences between leaders and subordinates; and, finally, the direction of influence is still assumed to be predominantly from leader to followers (Bryman, 1986).

The models also seem to imply both a high degree of rationality and adequate planning time in which leaders can identify and adopt the appropriate style. Observations of managers' behaviour in the workplace do not support such assumptions (Mintzberg, 1973; Stewart, 1976). In addition, the particular contingency theories outlined above may have less relevance for organizational leadership, where contact between leaders and followers is limited or indirect, than for supervisory or operational levels where contact between leader and subordinates is frequent and where groups are smaller. Subsequent developments in the study of leadership attempt to redress some of these imbalances.

Before we leave contingency theories, it is worthwhile to consider a rather different model which may have more significance in the academic context and in other professional organizations.

Substitutes and neutralizers for hierarchical leadership

Where other contingency theories focus upon situations in which either task or relationship-orientated leadership improve a group's performance, the Kerr and Jermier (1978) model examines the nature of situations in which neither of these styles has any effect on followers' satisfaction, motivation or performance. In some organizations, there are elements within them which 'substitute' for or 'neutralize' leadership. Substitutes render the leader's behaviour redundant or unnecessary; these variables might include the nature of the task (which may be intrinsically motivating), the characteristics of the followers (perhaps autonomous professionals) or the structures and norms of the organization (where roles are clear and communication operates freely). Neutralizers, on the other hand, prevent the leader from acting in particular ways or counteract the effects of leadership; these might include lack of control over rewards, the competence and training of subordinates, inflexible organizational policies or procedures (Bensimon *et al.*, 1989). As Bensimon and her colleagues (p. 20) point out:

> While organizational leadership is important, it may be a mistake to believe that all leadership must come from *leaders*. In many organiza-

tions – and it would seem particularly true in professional organizations – much of the guidance and support may be provided by the participants, the nature of the task, or the characteristics of the organization itself.

This model provides a useful antidote to the notion of a leader's omnipotence. In the academic context, it may provide an explanation of why top-down, 'command and control' models of leadership are not sustainable: within the norms and practices of academic organizations, there are numerous potential substitutes and/or neutralizers for leadership of this kind. Kerr and Jermier's ideas may also be relevant to the implementation of management philosophies such as total quality management (Oakland, 1989) – whether in the academic environment or elsewhere – which appear to advocate the design of systems and processes that integrate some leadership functions (such as standard setting or feedback on performance) into the fabric of the organization rather than relying on their delivery through the behaviour of individual leaders.

Concluding comments

In the discussion of trait, behavioural and contingency theories of leadership above, it is possible to detect the influence of some of the popular conceptions of leadership mentioned at the beginning of the chapter. Of course, the direction of influence will also operate in reverse, as theory informs – and eventually transforms – practice.

The ability (or the earned right) to be in charge, to command a following, to influence a group's direction or the achievement of the group's task, is explained with reference to the qualities of an individual leader, to individual leadership style and behaviour or to the fit between context, situation and leadership character and style. All these explanations emerge from a frame of reference that is broadly similar: that leadership can be discovered through rational and objective analysis of leaders. The explanations also assume that ideal leadership exists since the search is generally set in the context of effectiveness. The ideas contained in the models are often appealing, either in emotional or practical terms, and they have provided some enduring insights into the nature of leadership. The balance between task and relationship orientations, the need to give attention to participation-levels in decision-making, the nature and strength of the variables that impact on leadership, and the connections and trade-offs between individual and group needs remain important issues in the idea and practice of leadership.

However, these theories by themselves do not offer a completely satisfying account of leadership at either conceptual or empirical levels. Little account is taken of leader–follower interactions, of follower influences on leadership or of differences in leadership at various organizational levels: the contrast between diffuse leadership influence (for example political or system leadership) and direct or face-to-face leadership influence is ignored. The theories also fail to isolate 'leadership' from 'headship' (that is leadership as process from leadership as position) since the focus of most researchers has been on detecting signs of leadership from those who have been designated leaders, usually by their organization. In more recent theories, subjectivist perspectives, the impact of power and culture within organizations and the idea of leadership as process and as symbol are explored more deeply. These form the subject of the next chapter.

2

The New Leadership

Introduction

Alan Bryman in his recent work on charismatic leadership (1992) has coined the term 'new leadership' for the collection of recent research studies which have focused upon some previously neglected or more elusive features of the subject. These features include: the use and nature of power within leadership, the impact of organizational culture on leadership, the connection between leadership and change (at individual and organizational levels), leadership and vision, and the nature of charisma in relation to leadership. In most cases, a dynamic perspective has been adopted in research designs so that assumptions about the direction of causality between leadership and other variables can be examined more closely and in more complex ways. The 'new leadership' ideas have been influenced both by advances in psychology and by cross-fertilization between disciplines such as sociology, organization and management sciences, anthropology, political science, linguistics and biology.

While using Bryman's umbrella term, this chapter will be subdivided with reference to Bensimon and her colleagues' classification (1989) mentioned in the previous chapter. The three main sections will include a consideration of different approaches to leadership: power and influence theories; cultural and symbolic theories; and cognitive approaches. As was the case in the previous chapter, the distinctions between the different schools or approaches to leadership are somewhat arbitrary and there is considerable overlap between them. None the less, for the sake of clarity, it is worth drawing out the distinguishing characteristics of each approach. Following these three sections, there will be a general discussion of some of the issues that emerge from leadership theory, particularly those which are relevant to the academic or professional context.

Power and influence theories

An exploration of power in relation to leadership is not new. Studies of individual leaders, such as Alexander the Great of Macedonia or Napoleon I,

Emperor of France, have raised the question of personal power, often termed charisma, while philosophers such as Macchiavelli have drawn attention to the machinations of political power. In writing about the academic world, in much more recent times, the question of power and authority has also been addressed (Moodie and Eustace, 1974; Fisher, 1984) although its association with leadership has not always been made explicit. In this section, attention will be given to two distinctive views of the nature of power and influence in conceptions of leadership: those that consider leadership in terms of the effects of the leader on 'followers', and those that focus upon the mutual influence and reciprocal relationships between leaders and followers. However, as a preliminary to the discussion, it is useful first briefly to clarify the terms power and influence.

Handy (1985) sheds light on the matter when he identifies the differences and connections between the terms power, influence and authority. He argues that power and influence make up 'the fine texture of organizations and indeed of all interactions' (p. 118), where influence is the process through which one individual modifies the attitudes or behaviour of another and where power is the force that enables him or her to do so. In other words, influence is identified as the use of power, and power is the resource behind it. Thus we can talk about different sources of power (from personal loyalty to technical expertise) and different methods of influence (from coercion to mutual exchange). The term authority is used when the power is seen as legitimate or has some official support. To quote Handy: 'To say that someone has influence is therefore . . . a shorthand way of saying the power to influence. To say that someone has authority is a shorthand way of recognizing and accepting his or her power source' (p. 119).

A rather different conception is put forward by Moodie and Eustace (1974) (based, in part, on the writing of Lord Beveridge). It is a conception which is specifically associated with the academic context. In this case, power and influence are seen as different degrees of a common phenomenon (power is stronger than influence); they can be distinguished by identifying the means through which they are exercised in practice. Hence, power is viewed as the ability to give orders enforced by sanctions, by punishment or by control of rewards, while influence is seen as the ability to change the actions of others by persuasion, through reasoned argument or by appeals to emotions other than fear or greed – where the instruments of influence are words, spoken or written. Influence (for good) is expected to rest on knowledge and to be greater if it rests in part on a measure of power (p. 62). Authority is once again defined in terms of legitimacy.

Moodie and Eustace's description is particularly relevant to universities since power in the academic context seems often to be interpreted as an 'ultimate' currency. Influence, on the other hand, is widely perceived as the normal (and culturally appropriate) currency of day-to-day interactions between groups and individuals. Moodie and Eustace's interpretation provides a good illustration of the way in which the meaning of terms and concepts is likely to be shaped by the norms and practices that pervade in different settings. Ideas such as these will emerge more clearly in the section on 'cultural and symbolic leadership' that follows, but their essence is captured by Smith and Peterson (1988) when discussing leadership and power: 'the leader's exercise of power resides in the ability to transmit influence by way of the network of meanings which constitutes the organization's culture' (p. 130).

Both interpretations of power and influence discussed above have their uses and should be borne in mind when considering the models and theories set out in the forthcoming sections. Whether we use Handy's definition (in which power is the resource and influence the vehicle for its exercise) or Moodie and Eustace's perspective (where power and influence are stronger or weaker methods of persuasion) leadership can be viewed as a particular kind of social influence. In different contexts, it will rest upon different resources and will be exercised through a range of mechanisms that are likely to be culturally determined. In the following section, the way in which this special influence process works is described in a number of ways.

Social power approaches

Bensimon *et al.* (1989) have clustered together a group of theories that share a common focus on the way in which leaders use power to influence followers. There is an underlying assumption in these approaches of unidirectional influence from leader to led.

In an early and influential study into the nature of authority, Max Weber (1947) identified three different kinds of authority on which a leader's power might be based: traditional authority, which rests on established beliefs and time-honoured practices within a particular social system (for example, tribal leadership or hereditary kingship); rational-legal authority, where leaders are formally entitled to exert influence by virtue of their assigned responsibilities within a system of rules and regulations (for example, the position of managing director in a modern corporation); and charismatic authority, which rests on a belief in the exceptional personal qualities or 'supernatural' powers of a leader.

Subsequently, different authors have drawn upon Weber's classification. Distinctions have been made between formal (or official leaders) who rely on social power to influence followers by virtue of their official position (the term 'headship' has also been used in this connection) and informal (or emergent) leaders who influence others through their personalities (Etzioni, 1961, 1964). A widely used and more elaborate classification proposed by French and Raven (1968) identifies five bases of social power as follows:

1. Leaders can influence followers through their positions because of the legitimacy provided within social or legal systems (legitimate power).

2. Leaders can exert influence through their ability to provide rewards (reward power).
3. Leaders can exert influence through their ability to threaten punishments (coercive power).
4. Leaders can influence others through their knowledge and expertise (expert power).
5. Leaders can influence others by means of their personalities and the extent to which others like them or identify with them (referent power).

More recent theories by House (1984, 1988) identify four types of power used by leaders, three of which are similar to those of Weber or French and Raven (charismatic, expertise and authority) but one of which is different: political influence. This is described in terms of an indirect process of influence whereby leaders may accomplish their ends through the mobilization of resources (for example, through contacts with 'influential others') and through controlling the flow of information. This is a potentially more Machiavellian approach and one which is recognized within the depictions of universities as 'political organizations' (see Chapter 3).

Although these various classifications are useful in identifying the sources of power that may be available to leaders (the most likely sources of power for academic leaders being expert and referent power), they do not fully explain the nature of the leadership process. Insufficient attention is given to the ways in which power is received (or perceived) by followers. On the basis of our recent research in universities, reported in more detail later in this book (see Chapters 5–7 particularly) it is clear that the 'follower' dimension cannot be ignored.

Attention to the interaction between leader and followers is addressed in the work of Kipnis (1976) through his analyses of power-holders. The author argues that the method of influence selected by power-holders is a product of their individual power needs, their perception of the target of influence and the history of previous transactions with the target. Kipnis allows for interaction in the use and impact of power, although control of the process is still assumed to rest largely with the leader. Some support for this notion from within the higher education context emerges in Birnbaum's study of 'The implicit leadership theories of college and university presidents' (1989b). In the latter study, the majority of presidents described leadership as a process of influence, the purpose of which was to persuade others (the target) to follow or accept the leader's directives and initiatives. Birnbaum does not refer to Kipnis's other variables, namely the President's personal need for power or the history of previous interactions, both of which may also shape a leader's style.

For a different view of the interaction between leaders and followers – and one which gives more prominence to followers – a second group of ideas needs to be considered. These are loosely collected here under the heading of social exchange theories.

Social exchange theories

Where social power approaches assume one-way influence from leader to led, social exchange theories depict a reciprocal relationship between leaders and followers based on an exchange of valued things (Blau, 1964).

Leaders provide services to a group in exchange for the group's approval or compliance with the leader's demands. These 'services' may be financial rewards, political visibility, social approval, administrative or psychological support. In order to reach or to continue in a position of leadership, leaders must take account of follower expectations and be responsive to their needs. Although leaders may accumulate power on the basis of their personalities, positions or expertise, their power is constrained by followers' expectations (Hollander and Julian, 1969; Hollander, 1985). The positive response of the group to the leader provides his or her legitimacy and enables the process of leadership to occur; in other words, the practice of leadership cannot be separated from the expectations of followers. As Bensimon *et al.* (1989) explain it, 'In essence, the group agrees to collectively reduce its own autonomy and to accept the authority of the leader in exchange for the rewards and benefits (social approval, financial benefits, competitive advantage) the leader can bring them' (p. 10).

The maintenance of the leader's power and authority rests on his or her continuing ability to fulfil follower expectations. Some variants of exchange theory go further still in arguing that leaders can increase their own power (by what may appear to be ceding power) through empowering their followers (Kanter, 1983; Peters and Austin, 1985; Kouzes and Posner, 1987). In this case, the leadership process is conceived as facilitating the personal growth or task achievements of individuals or groups, a process which in return brings increased loyalty to the leader.

Social exchange theories are of particular interest within the academic context where the notion of group and individual autonomy is strong and where power and authority is widely spread across different interests and constituencies. In Birnbaum's study of university presidents, mentioned above, constraints on presidential authority were recognized by some presidents, causing them to view leadership as an interactive process. This view was also present in our research (Middlehurst *et al.*, 1992), where the institutional leadership role was sometimes described in terms of 'interpreting and articulating collective goals' or as 'shared responsibility for institutional outcomes'.

In recent writing, social power and social exchange theories have been re-examined, a distinction being made between the acceptance of follower expectations as they exist (that is, leadership as the fulfilment of follower expectations) or the challenging of follower expectations (that is, leadership which changes or reshapes follower expectations). These distinctions are captured in two influential approaches to leadership which will be discussed below: transactional and transformational leadership.

Transactional leadership

The term 'transactional leadership' was coined by the political scientist James McGregor Burns (1978) to contrast with a different form of leadership which he described as transforming leadership. Others have termed the latter, transformational leadership. Burns saw the two forms as opposite ends of a spectrum. The transactional leadership approach is in essence a social exchange approach whereby follower compliance is 'bought' by the leader through the provision of benefits such as wages or prestige. This kind of implicit contract between leader and followers may result in adequate performance, Burns argues, but will only have limited impact since the aspirations of leader and led are not touched. The key motivator in transactional leadership is self-interest, as pay or status is exchanged for work effort. In contrast, transforming leadership seeks to build on people's altruistic motivations and personal ideals to achieve greater things.

Other writers and researchers have built on Burns's distinctions, using his analysis within the context of business organizations. Notable among these writers is Bass (1985), who attempts to delineate the elements of 'transformational' and 'transactional' leadership more closely. The elements of the latter approach include: the achievement of actual or promised rewards contingent on reaching specified levels of performance; and management by exception where action is taken by the leader only when matters are not proceeding as planned. Such action may be based on one of two forms: either an active search by the leader for deviations in performance or passive reaction to deviations when they materialize.

Bass differs from Burns in seeing transactional leadership as a separate dimension from transformational leadership (rather than as two ends of a spectrum), the implication being that a leader may employ both approaches at different times. This argument has been used to explain why different kinds of leadership will be needed to suit different organizational circumstances. For example, transactional leaders may be required for the maintenance of a steady-state situation but may not be suitable for a crisis. In the latter case, a transformational style which creates a new set of aspirations and sense of collective purpose may be necessary. Different leadership approaches might also be required within different organizational contexts. Some authors, for example, argue that transactional approaches are better suited than transformational approaches to the values and culture of academic institutions and other professional organizations (Bensimon *et al.*, 1989).

The separation of the two dimensions of leadership has raised questions about the differences between leadership and management, since transactional leadership closely resembles traditional definitions of management. The characteristics of the leader have also come under scrutiny in the debate, as researchers try to identify whether it is personality, behaviour or experience that produces transactional or transformational leadership.

Before looking at the issues raised above in more detail, it is first necessary to describe transformational leadership more fully. The distinction originally drawn by Burns has provided an opportunity to develop new perspectives on leadership which also tap traditional (and popular) conceptions, such as charisma, inspiration and vision. The idea of transformational leadership has led to a flowering of leadership studies during the 1980s and 1990s as attempts are made to chart and explain the more ephemeral aspects of leadership.

Transformational leadership

At the heart of transformational leadership is the notion of higher-order change (at individual and organizational levels). Transformational leadership, according to Burns (1978), goes beyond meeting the basic needs of followers for security or recognition and beyond base emotions such as fear, jealousy or greed. Instead, it entails both leaders and followers raising each other's motivation and sense of purpose by appealing to ultimate values such as liberty, justice or equality. In the process, collective and individual behaviour and aspirations are transformed.

In Burns's view, transformational leadership has strong moral connotations. The sense of high purpose held out by the leader is one in which the aims and aspirations of leader and followers become fused, rather than being separate as in transactional leadership. The focus of this kind of leadership is on the whole person, addressing higher order needs and motivations, such as Maslow's self-esteem, affiliation and self-actualization. Through the pursuit of these goals, leaders and followers engage in a mutually stimulating and elevating relationship that may transform followers into leaders (for example, through the notion of 'empowerment' mentioned above) and leaders into 'moral agents' (Burns, 1978: 4).

Many writers have expanded on Burns's ideas and in the process some elements of his transforming leadership have been lost. Transformational leadership has become synonymous with inspirational or innovative leadership (and with 'real leadership' in contrast to management), losing some of the high moral connotations that were part of the original conception. The inspirational elements are visible in the work of Bass (1985) Bennis and Nanus (1985) Peters and Austin (1985) among others, and can be seen from this description of a leader as: 'cheerleader, enthusiast, nurturer of champions, hero finder, wanderer, dramatist, coach, facilitator, builder', which is achieved through 'passion, care, intensity, consistency, attention, drama . . . the implicit and explicit use of symbols' (Peters and Austin, 1985: 265).

Through their empirical work, Bennis and Nanus (1985) and Bass (1985) have drawn attention to some of the components of transformational leadership. The former authors noted four strategies employed by top leaders:

1. Attention through vision (having a clear agenda and being oriented towards results).
2. Achieving meaning through communication (interpreting reality in

order for action to take place by using metaphors, images, models to convey meaning and explanations).

3. Gaining trust through positioning (acquired by demonstrating account-ability, trust, predictability, reliability, constancy).
4. Gaining recognition or attention through positive self-regard (emphasiz-ing strengths and minimizing weaknesses).

In more recent work, Bennis (1989) has expanded these strategies and related them to leadership development.

Bass (1985) linked transformational leadership first to the individual, whom, he suggested, is led through increased confidence and high aspira-tions to levels of performance that are beyond what was expected and whose range of needs and wants is altered and expanded in the process. Second, Bass related the idea to organizations, where the transformational leader is said to invent, introduce and advance new cultural forms.

The elements of transformational leadership outlined by Bass (1985, 1990) include: (a) charisma (which generates emotional arousal, a sense of excitement, instils pride, gains respect and trust); (b) inspiration (which is sometimes seen as part of charisma and sometimes as separate, involving the setting of an example or model of behaviour, the communication of high expectations, the expression of important purposes in simple ways, the artic-ulation of a vision); (c) individualized consideration (where each individual is given personal attention according to their needs, is treated with respect and trust, is encouraged and stimulated to grow and develop through the creation of appropriate learning experiences); and (d) intellectual stimu-lation (where the leader challenges old ways, encourages new ideas and enables problems to be refocused and resolved).

Bass and his associates (Avolio and Bass, 1988; Hater and Bass, 1988) have found transformational leadership to be related to higher performance rat-ings, higher-performing groups, higher potential for advancement, and more satisfied followers. These authors' work has been continued by others who have also identified the 'exceptional performance' benefits of transfor-mational approaches (Kouzes and Posner, 1987), attempting in the process to delineate those aspects of transformational leadership which are part of personality traits and those which are behavioural patterns that can be learned. Other writers have preferred to adopt an alternative perspective whereby the attribution of transformational leadership arises from followers' reactions to the leader's behaviour rather than being the result of the delib-erate efforts of the leader (House *et al.*, 1990).

In the academic context, there have also been calls for transformational leadership (Kauffman, 1980; Fisher, 1984). Yet despite the appeal of trans-formational leadership, Bensimon and her colleagues (1989) express scepti-cism about the ability of institutional leaders to bring about the kind of radical change either in individuals or in the institution that is envisaged by transformational leadership models. They point out that within the transfor-mational approach it is assumed that leadership will emanate from a highly visible individual, that followers are motivated by a need for organizational affiliation and that leadership depends on visible and enduring change. These conditions are not necessarily present in universities, where dual authority exists (administrative and professional); where loyalty is as often to the discipline or department as to the institution; where motivation is intrinsic to the nature of academic work, not needing to be created extrinsically through presidential acts of leadership; and where positive responses to radical change are unlikely to be present.

Instead, these researchers suggest that transformational leadership in higher education may refer more appropriately to the inspirational role of the leader – a factor recognized as important by both leaders and 'followers' in our research study (Middlehurst *et al.*, 1992). Bensimon *et al.* none the less recognize that under certain conditions transformational leadership may be achieved or may be necessary: for example, in small institutions where direct contact with institutional leaders is possible and where a strong institutional identity can be formed, or in a crisis when either the financial viability or academic quality of the institution is perceived to be in jeopardy. The current British context, where changes in mission, activities and individual roles are being called for, may present a further condition in which transformational leadership is required.

Cultural and symbolic approaches to leadership

It will by now be apparent to the reader that many of the 'new leadership' ideas contain further iterations of earlier models. For instance, setting an example is part of Adair's action-centred leadership model, individualized consideration is close to conceptions in the Ohio Studies of the 1940s, while charisma has been associated with leadership for centuries (Adair, 1989; Bryman, 1992), although it has been neglected in research designs until recently. Cultural and symbolic approaches to leadership, while breaking new ground, also echo earlier contingency theories. However, in certain ways these approaches to leadership are significantly different.

To a greater or lesser extent, the earlier models and theories assume that leaders exist in a world that is essentially rational, certain and linear, and that leadership as an entity can be discovered through the application of scientific analysis and reasoning. By systematic and careful study, leadership can be identified, explained and improved.

In contrast, cultural and symbolic approaches suggest that leadership does not exist 'out there' waiting to be discovered, but is part of the interactive process of sense-making and creation of meaning that is continuously engaged in by organizational members; leadership can therefore only be understood in relation to these shared, invented meanings or 'cultures'. Some important elements of these ideas as elaborated by Bensimon *et al.* (1989: 21) are:

1. Organizations are not concrete entities, but instead represent an attempt by humans to impose meaning upon an equivocal, fluid, complex world. They are invented and enacted according to different images and beliefs about how people behave, how things work, or how successful outcomes can be achieved (Morgan, 1986).
2. The importance of facts, descriptions of events, or cause-and-effect relationships is not their existence, but their interpretation. In other words, 'truth' or 'reality' is relative, filtered through perception and subject to individual cognitive bias.
3. Participants in organizations, over time and through their interactions, develop shared meanings that influence their perceptions and their activities. These shared meanings represent the prevailing values, norms, philosophy, rules and climate of the organization, that is, its culture. Such common meanings also reflect the self-image held by organizational participants and their interpretation of their environment. Culture can be seen in the way language is used, power is distributed and decisions are made and particularly in the symbols, rituals, stories, legends and myths that infuse specific organizations with meaning (Deal and Kennedy, 1982; Tierney, 1988; Harman, 1990).
4. Leadership operates within this complex social and psychological system by offering a way of finding meaningful patterns in the behaviour of others and by helping to develop common understandings about the nature of reality both within and outside the organization. Such common understandings may reflect existing circumstances or a new set of understandings, developed in response to change.

Several roles for leadership in relation to organizational culture are possible. At one level, leaders can articulate and influence cultural norms and values and can reinforce consistent values. At another level, leadership can mould, reshape and transform culture in line with institutional objectives. Leadership is thus defined as 'the management of meaning' (Smith and Peterson, 1988) and may be associated with different stages of organizational development: the establishment of culture in a new unit or organization, the maintenance and reinforcement of culture in a thriving operation, the transformation of culture at a time of organizational stagnation or decline or in response to new situations. At each stage of institutional development, different styles of leadership, encompassing a different balance of elements, will be required. In many ways, these cultural and symbolic models are revisiting earlier ideas about leadership which focused on face-to-face interactions between a leader and followers, and recasting them with reference to the indirect leadership process at institutional level.

The extent to which culture can be manipulated or managed by leaders is far from clear since, as Bensimon and her colleagues point out, it is created in many different parts of the organization through a myriad of day-to-day interactions and activities. Nor is culture likely to be monolithic, although some overarching elements may characterize a particular institution.

Universities will contain a variety of cultures created by students, academics, administrators and others; and these cultures themselves will be further subdivided, as Becher (1989) has shown. Partly because of this variety and partly because of the strength of tradition in universities, culture is more likely to act as a constraint on leadership.

None the less, leaders can *influence* culture by affecting people's sentiments and commitment to the unit or organization. Leaders may help to make sense of events that would otherwise be perplexing or chaotic. They can direct attention to issues relevant either to the maintenance of values or to changes in values and activities. Leadership can also play a political role by signalling through symbolic and ceremonial activities (particularly to external audiences) that the organization is functioning as its sponsors believe it should, even if such activities have little tangible or direct effect on the achievement of organizational goals (Bensimon *et al.*, 1989). In Britain, the recent spate of institutional visions and missions developed at the behest of funding councils often represents just such symbolic activity.

Within the academic context, an understanding of colleges and universities as cultures was originally introduced by Clark (1970) and has since been developed by many others in relation to institutions, departments and disciplines (Chaffee, 1984; Chaffee and Tierney, 1988; Becher, 1989; Harman, 1990). Chaffee's work is particularly important in considering both the substantive and the symbolic role of leadership in institutions suffering financial difficulties which were then successfully turned around.

Chaffee's examination of presidents' managerial techniques revealed three alternative strategies: linear, adaptive and interpretive. Linear strategists were concerned to direct the institution towards specific goals, adaptive strategists were concerned to align the institution with its environment (that is, to be responsive to external demands) and interpretive strategists were concerned to discover how people saw, understood and felt about their lives so that leadership could be targeted at the values and emotions that influence behaviour. The use of adaptive and interpretive strategies in combination was most effective in turning institutions around (Chaffee, 1984). Some support for the need to recognize the impact of culture in relation to leadership and to change strategies can be found in the British context in Shattock's (1988) analysis of the financial problems of the University College of Cardiff. Shattock pointed to the inability of the leadership to shift the culture of the institution as a major factor in the college's financial decline. His conclusion (p. 112) is worth reporting:

> The real lesson to be drawn from the Cardiff experience is that organizational culture is a crucial element in the management of an institution. Good financial management is dependent on a positive organizational culture and an ineffective organizational culture will not easily be changed quickly either by removing a few senior individuals, or by external exhortation through the medium of efficiency reports or governmental pressure. An effective organizational culture

needs to be developed and maintained over many years: there are no short cuts.

Where change is required, cultural and symbolic ideas should alert leaders to the need to be culturally sensitive. In order to see the institution through a cultural lens, comparative awareness must be developed, and contradictions and inconsistencies between values and structure should be identified. Clues to culture can be unearthed in the metaphors embedded in the language of the institutional community, in the ways in which status is conferred and through analysing the nature, scope and strength of university operations and networks (Bensimon *et al.*, 1989). Leadership styles themselves may also be examined by exposing the symbols and myths contained in the language and behaviour of leaders and, in particular, by raising awareness of contradictions between words and deeds. To quote Dill (1982: 304), 'the techniques of managing meaning and social integration are the undiscussed skills of academic management'.

Cognitive theories

Like cultural and symbolic theories, cognitive approaches (Cohen and March, 1986; Smith and Peterson, 1988; Hunt 1992) concentrate on the ways in which meaning is created in the social context of organizations through the perceptions and interactions of organizational members. However, within these approaches, greater emphasis is placed on the ways in which individuals construct reality than on the nature of their reality. Under these conceptions, leadership is seen as 'a social attribution – an explanation used by observers to help them find meanings in unusual organizational occurrences' (Bensimon *et al.*, 1989: 23), and therefore 'leaders are individuals believed by followers to have caused events' (p. 49).

The essential distinction between the two approaches is that cultural and symbolic approaches stress the role of leaders in 'inventing' reality for followers, while cognitive models emphasize the importance of followers in 'inventing' leaders. If one took a sociological rather than a psychological perspective, one could say that leadership is as much a social construct of those being led as it is an indication of influence exerted over followers by 'leaders'.

This kind of transference occurs towards those in positions of leadership (Chief Executives, Vice Chancellors, Prime Ministers) for a number of possible reasons: because of the human and social need to impose order and control or to seek causes for otherwise inexplicable events; because of the prominence of these individuals and the emblematic nature of their roles; or because of the leadership 'myths' that surround what leaders are expected or imagined to be, both by followers and by themselves. These images and allegories may be extremely powerful, as can be seen in popular or media reactions to perceived indecision, lack of integrity, lack of conviction or competence from those in senior positions in the nation or in organizations.

Cognitive dimensions can be useful when considering the issue of leadership effectiveness. Perceptual bias of the kind described above (where individuals or groups see what they are expecting, or wish to see) may cause leaders to claim or followers to attribute successful outcomes to leadership ability and effort, when no such evidence exists. In the same way, failure of organizational goals may be attributed to environmental factors, internal difficulties or bad luck. This may be sensible for, as Pfeffer (1977: 110) proposes, successful leaders will be those 'who can separate themselves from organizational failure and associate themselves with organizational successes'.

On the other hand, conceptions of one-way rational and directive leadership (where the leader has control of the organization, sets goals and priorities, makes decisions and issues edicts) are likely to be both inappropriate and unwise in certain contexts – such as academic or professional organizations – potentially causing serious errors of judgement. Birnbaum's work on presidential leadership in the US university context demonstrates some of these dangers (1989b, 1990).

Recent interest in cognition has concentrated both on the individual (Hunt *et al.*, 1990) by trying to examine leaders' thinking in relation to leadership, and on the issue of social cognition in organizations, or the way in which leadership is 'negotiated' in the constructed reality of organizational participants (Smith and Peterson, 1988).

The focus on the individual has revived interest in the contribution of individual traits to the development of leadership concepts and behaviours. Aspects such as individual background factors, psychological preferences and predispositions, the development of conceptual maps and schemas, the nature of leadership skills in relation to the above and the nature of leaders' self-management abilities are all being investigated (Smith and Peterson, 1988; Bennis, 1989; Hunt, 1992). These are discussed more fully in Chapter 8.

Of great importance in this context is the notion of cognitive complexity or cognitive power, which has been described in different ways by researchers but includes some or all of the following: the ability to differentiate and integrate large numbers of elements (for example, to differentiate between conflicting views of university purposes and to integrate these into the range of current and potential university activities); the ability to adapt to different task and situational demands; and the scale and complexity of what an individual can pattern and construe mentally. This last element relates to the amount and variety of information that a leader can process and the time-scale in which leaders can operate with this information (their 'time-orientation') (Jacques, 1982; Hunt, 1992).

Cognitive complexity may offer a key to differences between effective and ineffective leaders since more complex leaders will have the flexibility to understand situations through different and competing scenarios and to act upon these simultaneously while paying attention to different organizational needs. Ineffective leadership, by contrast, is often characterized by rigidity, narrow conceptions and limited perspectives of organizational needs (Faerman and Quinn, 1985; Whetton and Cameron, 1985). Different degrees of cognitive complexity are also likely to be required at different organizational levels so as to match the complexity in the critical tasks of leaders, the complexity of the internal and external environment and the time-scale of the organization's operations (Hunt, 1992).

As Birnbaum (1988) argues, cognitive complexity is particularly important in the academic context since the institution contains multiple realities and should therefore be viewed through different lenses. By so doing, leaders can develop appropriate behaviours to deal with the often mutually inconsistent requirements (at institutional level) to act as chief executive, colleague, public official, symbol or community representative.

In terms of organizations, research into cognitive processes has considered areas such as performance appraisal, problem-solving, decision-making and leadership perception. As was mentioned above, followers' implicit theories have been the focus of attention, although some studies have also considered implicit theories of successful organizational design (Downey and Brief, 1986). The relationship between implicit theories and high performing groups, leaders' behaviour or the selection of leaders suggests that a fit between followers' expectations of leadership and leaders' behaviour can influence organizational effectiveness, individual performance and satisfaction (Hunt *et al.*, 1990). Moreover, the schemas held by top leaders may have implications for the different phases of an organization's development or life-cycle, with the notion of appropriate fit again being important (Hunt *et al.*, 1988).

One comprehensive model of leadership in an organizational setting is that offered by Hunt (1992) in his 'extended multiorganizational-level leadership model'. The model takes into account elements of both past and present research and integrates various dimensions that have concerned researchers over time. These elements include: the nature of individual personality characteristics, skills, behaviours, experience, attitudes, values, beliefs and mental abilities; the nature of followers, in groups, in different cultures and organizational circumstances; the nature of the organizational context, internally and externally; different levels of leadership and different kinds of critical leadership tasks.

Although complex, the model provides a much needed synthesis of psychological research on leadership with fieldwork undertaken within management and organizational studies. In particular, the model attempts to explain differences between face-to-face leadership, which usually operates in small units, in teams and at lower levels of the organization (where direct contact between leaders and followers is possible), and indirect leadership processes at the top of organizations. The latter are likely to be mediated through culture and language as well as through organizational systems and designs. To some extent, the distinctions are represented by the division between 'old' and 'new' leadership approaches as described in Chapters 1 and 2 of this book.

Some unfinished business

In considering popular conceptions of leadership, early leadership studies and more recent research, a number of issues arise. Some of these are general and some specific to the academic context. The issues include difficulties in distinguishing leadership from other closely related concepts (such as power or management), the problem of identifying and separating substantive from symbolic aspects of leadership and the differences between objectivist and subjectivist perspectives on leadership. They will be discussed briefly below under the headings of: leadership and power; leadership and motivation; leadership and position; leadership and management; leadership as attribution or action? However, the issues will also re-emerge in various guises in later chapters of this book.

The range of definitions of leadership in general use, which include leadership as a process of social influence, leadership as a role or function, leadership as goal-oriented, leadership in relation to a group of followers (team, unit, institution, nation), all cause difficulties when one tries to identify the essence of leadership as distinct from other closely related concepts. For example, power or motivation are also classed as social influence processes – to what extent is leadership different? How can leadership be distinguished from the incumbency of a position or the occupancy of an organizational role? How far can leadership be separated from management, which is also linked to the completion of tasks and the achievement of goals in organizations? What is the balance between leadership as it exists in the eyes (or mind) of the beholder and as it is exercised through the thought processes and actions of leaders? These questions are not easy to answer, but I shall attempt to do so below.

Leadership and power

Turning first to power, Handy's distinction mentioned at the beginning of this chapter is useful. Power of various kinds (expert, referent, legitimate and so on) provides a resource for leadership, while leadership itself is the medium through which such power is exercised. The shape of leadership then takes different forms according to the nature of the power source and the nature of the circumstances and context in which it is exercised. In this way, leadership and power are inextricably linked but none the less distinct.

Other writers have tried to distinguish leadership from power by drawing attention to the *shared* influence between leader and led, the *common or compatible* goals between leaders and followers (Gibb, 1969), or by suggesting that leadership *changes the preferences* of those being influenced (Etzioni, 1965), in contrast to power, which may act upon others but without any such necessary inferences of mutuality or willing participation. Within the academic context, where the degree of autonomy has traditionally been high, the notion of shared influence is likely to be important.

Leadership and motivation

It is the link between leadership and voluntary compliance that relates leadership to the motivation of followers. The motivational drive resides within individual followers, but leaders can tap into this energy through the attention they give to individual needs, to the structuring of a task or to the articulation of collective values. Leadership is seen here as the means by which the motivational drive of individuals is translated into achievement, in terms of actual performance or levels of emotional, psychological or spiritual satisfaction. Individuals and groups, according to cognitive or symbolic theories, may attribute their own successful achievements to effective leadership; and leaders may assume that their leadership style and actions caused high levels of performance among followers.

Within academe the relationship between leadership and motivation takes on a particular cast since the work of academics has traditionally been regarded as intrinsically motivating, not requiring the external influence of leadership to encourage exceptional performance. This issue is dealt with more fully in Chapter 4. Suffice it to say here that the form and elements of leadership that will be appropriate in academe – for different individuals and groups and under different circumstances – are not likely to be identical to those emphasized in other contexts and cultures. For example, the symbolic aspects of leadership which are concerned with creating a culture and a climate conducive to productive work and relationships may be more important (most of the time) than the face-to-face inspirational elements which are emphasized in other contexts as part of a transformational process.

Leadership and position

The problem of distinguishing leadership from the mere incumbency of a position is easier to clarify. A senior position carries with it the expectation that leadership will be exercised. The norms of the organization, as well as the legal authority attached to the position, will define the nature of the legitimate power appropriate in that particular context. These elements in turn will shape the form of leadership that is likely to be acceptable. However, it is not the passive act of occupying the position that denotes leadership, but the active exercise of this special process of influence, which is then interpreted and given the accolade of leadership by others. Indeed, if leadership is not perceived to be occurring – in terms of guidance, goal achievement, creation of climate or motivation of followers – then those occupying such senior positions are likely to be regarded as deficient in their role.

Distinguishing 'leadership' from 'headship' is made easier because of the different terms: formal, informal or emergent leadership. The first of these is normally associated with the legitimate exercise of leadership from the vantage point of senior positions in organizations; the second with the informal exercise of leadership outside formal positions; and the third with the 'spontaneous' exercise of leadership in any context. In recent studies, as distinctions have been made between transactional and transformational leadership, researchers have become increasingly interested in identifying those elements which lie at the heart of leadership, or which denote 'real' leadership. These elements are assumed to be common to formal, informal or emergent leadership and thus clearly to differentiate the exercise (or attribution) of leadership from formal status and position in organizations. Leadership is then seen as an influence process that is separate from the domain of formal, or legal, power and authority. However, the power which surrounds 'headship', such as that vested in the status of chief executive or king, will provide an additional resource for leadership. This distinction is likely to apply within the academic context as much as elsewhere.

Leadership and management

As leadership has become more central to the interests of organizational researchers, the question of whether it is synonymous with management, a subset of management or entirely distinct from management, has become an issue for researchers and practitioners alike. These matters are relevant to the training and selection of leaders and managers as well as in understanding the role and function of leadership and management within organizations.

Management has long been associated with the classic organizational functions outlined by Fayol (1949) and others, including planning, organizing, staffing, budgeting, controlling, coordinating, decision-making, while leadership has been linked to the 'people-aspects' of management, including communication and motivation. With the work of Mintzberg (1973), Stewart (1976, 1983) and others whose research involved the observation and tracking of the actual work routines of managers, a broader and far less clearly structured view of management and managing has developed. It was recognized that the 'leader role' within the interpersonal domain overlaid many other activities that fell, for example, into Mintzberg's 'informational' and 'decisional' domains of management.

Early leadership researchers took as their focus those who were executives or managers in organizations and investigated them and their behaviour for signs of leadership. It is therefore often difficult to disentangle leadership from management in the research findings of trait or behavioural approaches. The work of Zaleznik (1977) signalled a change when he attempted to forge a distinction between the types of individuals who occupied the separate roles of leaders and managers, arguing that the latter were concerned with the complex routines of the organization and with essentially short-term objectives, while the former were actively engaged in challenging the status quo, in creating new ideas about the direction of the organization and thus in changing what people believed was desirable and possible.

While Zaleznik mapped out this path, work on organizational culture highlighted the place of values, norms, beliefs, symbols and vision in the successful functioning of organizations. Tom Peters and Warren Bennis were influential here, while biographies or autobiographies of visionary industrial leaders (Iaccoca, Carlzon, Kay, Harvey-Jones) illustrated connections between leadership and organizational change. With the arrival of Burns's and Bass's distinctions between transformational and transactional leadership (as well as Bass's classification of '*laissez-faire*' as non-leadership) the earlier, rather blurred distinctions between leadership and management have become clearer. 'True' leadership is now linked largely to transformational approaches (where changes in practice and values are sustained by high aspirations and ideals) while management is associated with transactional approaches (where reward is contingent upon specified levels of performance). Some writers, such as Bennis in his later work (1989) have gone further still in arguing that leaders and managers are different psychological types, but there is as yet insufficient evidence to sustain this proposition (Bryman, 1992).

Perhaps the most useful contribution to the continuing debate is that offered by Kotter (1988, 1990) in his differentiation of leadership and management as two separate but complementary systems of action. Leadership, he argues, is required to effect or to cope with change, while management is needed to handle complexity within and around organizations. For Kotter, leadership encompasses the direction-setting, inspirational and motivational capacities necessary for effective organizational development, while management includes the planning, coordinating and financial capacities which enable a complex organization to operate efficiently on a continuing basis. The charismatic features often present in transformational approaches are not included in Kotter's model, although the elements of vision, motivation and inspiration come close to these; and Kotter's management elements echo many analyses of transactional leadership. The model is useful for its clarity and for its recognition of the need for both leadership *and* management in today's complex and fast-moving world. Kotter has also managed to avoid some of the negative overtones that have come to be associated with management in the writings of those who extol the virtues of vision, values and empowerment.

Within the academic context, the distinction between leadership and management has other connotations since the traditions of academe have for long upheld a separation between leadership and policy-making on the one hand and policy implementation and administration on the other. The distinction has been manifested clearly in the traditionally separate roles of academics (whose domain included academic leadership and policy formation) and administrators (whose domain included advice on policy and the responsibility for policy execution). Handy (1984) traces the origins of these distinctions to the nature of professional practice and the traditions of professional groups. He describes the distinctions as follows:

> In professional organizations the leadership function has to be carried out by the senior professionals – to hand it over to an outsider would be an abrogation of responsibilities. The administrative function, on the other hand, can be delegated . . . because it is under the direction of professionals.
>
> (Handy, 1984: 292)

Handy continues by illustrating the nature of policy-making in professional organizations as

> a joint activity, led by the senior professionals but in which all professionals can participate – it is a collegial activity based on consent. The executive side of things, on the other hand, requires hierarchy and a formal structure of oversight. Professionals are more likely to accept an executive hierarchy if it is part of an agreed policy in which they participated.
>
> (Handy, 1984: 292)

As Handy and others have pointed out, this form of pure collegiality has become adulterated as institutions have adapted to changing internal and external circumstances. None the less, these traditions are still recognized in the hearts and minds of many academics (and some administrators) as interviews in the course of our two studies (Middlehurst, 1989; Middlehurst *et al.*, 1992) well demonstrate. By maintaining a distinction between leadership and management, for example in the roles of senior administrators and Pro Vice Chancellors, important aspects of academic culture are recognized.

Leadership: attribution or action?

Perhaps the most difficult issue to clarify or reconcile is that of whether leadership resides in the eye of the beholder or in the actions of leaders, since the two views are associated with alternative perspectives on reality (or different sociological paradigms: the subjectivist/interpretivist and the objectivist/functionalist) (Morgan, 1991). Although reconciliation between the two paradigms may not be possible, the use of alternative perspectives to analyse an event or problem may provide a key to understanding.

Hunt (1992) argues for the adoption of an attitude of 'critical pluralism', which tolerates and is non-judgemental about alternative views while being harshly critical of dogmatic positions in either camp. He advocates this approach for all those who are concerned with gaining, using and assessing leadership understanding. Hunt goes further in suggesting that it is both necessary and useful to be able to consider leadership from different perspectives in order to understand, think and act more effectively in relation to the assumptions, purposes and definitions of leadership that are associated with different stakeholders.

Hunt's argument is linked to the logic of cognitive complexity: that one is likely to be a more effective leader if one can hold, project and test different perspectives on leadership. These different perspectives reflect different assumptions about human nature, human activity and human relationships; about the nature of reality, truth, time and space; and about the nature of the organization and its environmental relationships. This position is obviously valuable in the context of a multicultural society or a multinational company, but is perhaps less well recognized in more apparently homogeneous contexts. The exercise will none the less prove worthwhile in an organization containing as many diverse interests and activities as a university.

It may also be useful to think of leadership as having two faces, which are exercised simultaneously. Leadership roles are both symbolic and functional; the office of Vice Chancellor as well as the actions of the individual occupying the position are important in the understanding and exercise of leadership. This notion has some similarity with Becher and Kogan's (1992) distinctions between normative and operational aspects of higher education. The idea is taken further by several scholars, some of whom advocate the development of a 'Janusian' leader able to face in several directions simultaneously (Quinn, 1988). Others have used the idea in relation to leaders' thinking and behaving, which has been observed to occur simultaneously or intuitively among those described as 'expert leaders' (Weick, 1983; Isenberg, 1984); and still others have applied the concept to leadership development, which is seen as combining knowledge aspects, a skills emphasis and intuitive/judgemental aspects (Hunt, 1992). Whatever the area of concentration – whether on behaviour, thinking, learning, interpretation or meaning in relation to leadership – a pluralistic approach that attempts to accommodate alternative paradigms would seem wise. As Heider (1986: 21) says in the *Tao of Leadership*: 'To become aware of what is happening, I must pay attention with an open mind.'

3

Organizational Images

Introduction

While some aspects of academic leadership are not associated with the governance of the institution – the domain of disciplinary leadership, for example – most current discussions about leadership in the academic context are concerned with formal leadership in a particular organizational setting. As we saw in Chapter 2, early contingency theories highlighted the importance of the environment in which leadership is exercised; since then, more sophisticated analyses have demonstrated the reciprocal impact of the organization and leadership (Hunt, 1992). In these depictions, researchers point to a match between leadership and its context, such that leadership is shaped as much by the nature and requirements of the organization as the organization is deemed to respond to the leadership exercised within it.

In this chapter, we shall be looking at different images of academic organizations and the relationship of these perspectives to the practice of leadership. It will become apparent that there is a third dynamic which is relevant to the complex equation of leadership in academic institutions: that of the external environment in a particular time-frame. This dimension will form the focus of Chapter 4, while the present chapter is concerned largely with the internal 'norms and operations' of the institution (Becher and Kogan, 1992). The different images presented provide a kaleidoscopic lens through which to view academic institutions. No one image is likely to represent an institution in its entirety, instead these images will illustrate different parts of the institution and different conceptions of organizational reality. The images that have been selected are drawn from a number of sources. They are by no means exhaustive (see Morgan, 1986, for a wider selection) but they represent the most widely known perspectives. The cybernetic and entrepreneurial images are of recent origin.

The collegial perspective: the institution as a community of scholars

The collegial image, historically the oldest depiction of universities, has exerted a powerful influence on the culture and functioning of academe even though many of its significant features are now more symbolic than real. Central to the vision of a community is the idea of a group of scholars who work together to their mutual advantage within a self-governing collective. The image carries other associations: of consensus decision-making and academic autonomy, of democracy and cohesion based on a limited hierarchy of seniority and expertise, a common heritage and shared ideals. The chief organ of government in a collegial institution is the committee system.

In Britain, the archetypical collegial institutions are the universities of Oxford and Cambridge. As recently as 1989, Cambridge, prompted by external political and economic pressures, sought to restructure its machinery of government in the interests of greater efficiency. The university was also clearly concerned to protect some fundamental collegial values: 'The University of Cambridge must conduct its business efficiently, and it must be prompt and decisive in its dealings with outside bodies. It must also remain, as it is now, a self-governing community of scholars' (Report of the Wass Syndicate, Cambridge, 1989, quoted in Tapper and Salter, 1992: 38). As Tapper and Salter observe, it may prove difficult to reconcile the pressures of efficiency with the desire for consensus decision-making across the full academic community. Later images illustrate the organizational accommodations that have occurred in academe in response to such modern pressures.

Despite the disciplinary and structural heterogeneity of modern academic institutions, the present managerialist and market pressures of the external environment, and the conflicts of territory and interest present within institutions, the 'community of scholars concept remains as a myth of considerable strength and value in the academic world' (Harman, 1990: 32). The ideal is manifested in various ways: in language, where fellow academics are addressed as 'colleagues'; in the teamwork of research and, more recently, teaching groups (course teams) where expertise rather than position is the key to participation; and in the obligation of academics to engage in administration at both departmental and institutional levels as part of their shared responsibility for governance. Although weakened by the pressures of competition during the 1980s and 1990s, collegial behaviour between academics can be seen in the sharing of information, ideas and tasks, and in the professional critique of each other's work before it enters the public domain. Finally, the tug of the community ideal is also evident in such unusual organizational roles as that of the Pro Vice Chancellor, which combines elements of collegiality with executive authority, reflecting 'the dual systems of hierarchy and collegium' that run through traditional universities (Becher and Kogan, 1992).

Leadership within a collegial perspective is based on consultation and persuasion, where leaders are seen largely as servants of the group (rather than its masters) bearing a particular responsibility for articulating the purposes of the group – its collective direction – and representing the group's interests. Leaders are described as 'first among equals' and are likely to reach their position because others see them as embodying the group's aspirations and achievements. The leader's role is to facilitate and encourage individual and collective performance, to promote consensus within the community, to communicate widely and to use consultative and democratic processes for decision-making. Leaders are likely to exist at many levels within the organization. The words of a Deputy Vice Chancellor from our study (Middlehurst *et al.*, 1992) express the essence of collegial leadership: 'Leadership involves representation, conciliation, being articulate, being accessible, developing a consensus. It takes political skills, demands flair and a sense of direction'.

Universities as professional organizations

Where the key feature of the collegial image is 'the community', the chief focus within the image of the university as an organization of professionals is on the characteristics of the staff. Although there is still disagreement among scholars over the precise range of features that characterise professionals and 'professionalism', some characteristics which are often quoted include: a lengthy period of education and training; apprenticeship and socialization into the norms and procedures of the professional group; a licence to practise on the basis of specialist knowledge and skills; the offering of a service to clients; autonomy in directing one's own work; and adherence to the standards and codes of practice established by the professional associations – where they exist (Johnson, 1972; Jarvis, 1983; Downie, 1990).

Although able to operate as sole practitioners, in the current competitive climate professionals will often combine in partnership with others in order to share resources and to gain a greater segment of the market by offering a range of specializations within a professional field. A feature of modern organizations and of Western economic life is the increasing numbers of professionals who are employed in specialist roles in large companies; a further development is the expanding range of occupations that are labelled professional (Watkins *et al.*, 1992).

As in the collegial image, expertise is an important source of influence and authority in professional organizations. This technical expertise is based on the competence and experience of individual 'stars' whose influence can be manifested in the form of a personal following (of clients or more junior professionals). Individualism of this kind can be seen clearly, for example, in one of the early traditions of the legal profession, where the partners of a solicitor who was retiring from a practice, or an incoming partner, had to buy the 'goodwill' of the exiting professional in order to acquire their personal client base.

There are other areas of overlap between the collegial and professional images. Although the notion of community is not as strong within the professional perspective, it still exists in terms of shared norms and common interests. These are represented collectively, for the purposes of self-protection, regulation, political lobbying and development of the profession, in the form of the professional bodies (the Law Society, Royal Institution of Chartered Surveyors, British Medical Association). Within the professionals' business organizations, the working relationship is conceived as a partnership of independent individuals, rather than an interdependent community where some individual freedoms are foregone in the interests of the group as a whole. In practice, this distinction is ephemeral, since a sense of community may well develop out of the experience of an effective working partnership, and the legal and practical requirements of running a modern professional practice will necessitate a degree of interdependence perhaps not required in earlier times.

Besides the similarities between collegial and professional images at the level of values and social interaction, there are also analogies in their modes of governance. Again, autonomy in this arena is highly prized, professionals playing a key part in policy-making and decision-taking, often through committees. The form of authority exercised in governance – that based on seniority and expertise – mirrors the kind of authority that is valued in the technical/professional domain.

Universities can be identified as organizations of professionals in a number of senses, although they may fall short in other ways. To quote Harman (1990: 33),

> Universities are seen as extreme cases of professionalised organisation as they create and transmit specialised knowledge and skills; their members are granted a great deal of autonomy once their qualifications and competence have been certified, and their bases of authority are determined by professional expertise as opposed to bureaucratic hierarchies.

Thus universities have 'professional' characteristics through the nature of their work (in teaching 'professional' subjects and in training professionals, as well as in undertaking research and scholarship which underpin professional practice), in the way in which academic work is carried out and in their structures of governance. They also employ other groups of staff who, through their separate professional expertise, support the functioning of the university. These groups of professionals – librarians, accountants, surveyors and personnel staff, for example – owe allegiance to and are in part regulated by their own professional associations.

Where universities currently fall short in displaying the full characteristics of a professional organization is in the area of certifying professional competence in the pedagogical domain and in the representation of professional interests, with their regulatory and lobbying powers, through a common professional association. The disparate professional and political interests of academe are represented in various arenas, from disciplinary groupings and professional associations to the CVCP or the trade unions; and regulation is partly achieved by institutions themselves and partly through external agencies, such as the funding councils, the Division of Quality Audit (formerly Academic Audit Unit) and the Public Accounts Committee.

Leadership in an organization of professionals shares many features with leadership in a collegium. These include an emphasis on negotiation and persuasion, the development of consent – if not consensus (see Handy, 1984) – and an emphasis on the facilitation and encouragement of group achievement. Leaders are expected to articulate and explain the group's activities to others and to alert the collectivity to external opportunities and threats. They are likely to be involved in the development of broad goals, the setting of standards and the monitoring of performance, in part because of their long experience as successful practitioners, sensitive to informal codes of professional practice, and in part as 'representatives' of formal codes of practice. Leaders are likely to be involved in the creation of an appropriate working climate and also in the acquisition of external resources.

The emphasis placed on individual and group autonomy in both collegial and professional perspectives results, in practice as well as in theory, in considerable ambivalence about the place of leadership (and management) within these kinds of organizations (Middlehurst, 1989). For some, the combination of professional norms and the nature of academic activities carry internal controls and self-directional forces without requiring the external foci of leadership and management (Barnett, 1992). These arguments will be dealt with more fully in the next chapter, but the style of leadership represented in this image and described above already acknowledges the issue of professional autonomy.

The political image of universities

Neither the collegial nor the professional perspective is entirely satisfactory in providing a descriptive model of modern universities. Baldridge (1971) has offered an alternative scenario. This image concentrates on features of difference and competition within the institution, in contrast to the emphasis on homogeneity and cooperation within collegial and professional images.

By viewing the university through a political lens, many of the assumptions and ideals that underpin 'the collegium' are challenged, while some of the features of the 'professional' image (for example, individual autonomy) may be accommodated. The internal heterogeneity of universities and their multiplicity of interests is freely acknowledged, making notions of collegial 'solidarity, intimacy, and kinship' (Harman, 1990: 33) as difficult to imagine as to achieve. Current efforts to establish a sense of corporateness at institutional level are also having to cope with these realities.

Instead of ignoring or underplaying the differences of interest, values and norms of individuals and groups within the university, the political perspective emphasizes such differences as a key feature of the organization and assumes that the task of governance is in large part to mediate between this diversity. Differences in interest and values also give rise to power, status and resource differentials, which are augmented by separate working territories and their perceived relationship and relevance to the organization's primary purpose. Thus, in universities, traditional distinctions have been maintained between academics and administrators, between professional and lay members and between staff and students as members of the community. More recently, other differences have emerged: between management and staff, between researchers and teachers and between 'income-generators' and 'non-income-generators'. To add to these differences, there are also hierarchies of disciplines, departments and institutions. Some of these have emerged without obvious planning (or rather, as a result of the internal dynamics of academic life), while others are part of the intended or unforeseen consequences of deliberate external planning (Elton, 1988).

Differences of interest, value, power, status and territory lead almost inevitably to the possibility of conflict. When resources are scarce, the potential for conflict is still greater. An emphasis on scarce resources and on conflict is central to the political perspective. Because of the focus on interest groups, their relative power and the likely conflicts between them, the political image assumes that the goals of the organization are unstable, often ambiguous and contested, and that decisions emerge after complex 'processes of bargaining, negotiation and jockeying for position among individuals and groups' (Bolman and Deal, 1984: 109). The organization itself is seen as no more than a coalition of different individuals and groups, kept together in dynamic tension, but with the potential to break asunder as resources and power become unbalanced, or as dominant groups choose to strike out independently (Kerr, 1963).

It is clear that for many the political perspective presents a powerful view of institutional reality. Yet as Bush (1986: 85–6) argues, the political interpretation of the institution has a number of limitations:

1. In focusing chiefly on power and conflict, usually at the level of policy formation, policy implementation is given insufficient weight. Other aspects of daily organizational life, such as formal authority structures and routine bureaucratic procedures, are accorded only limited attention, yet may directly impinge on or even upset the political process.
2. The political perspective assumes the fragmentation of the organization and the dominance of sectionalism as departmental/college influence vies with institutional influence on the direction and development of the university. Although many Vice Chancellors acknowledge the constraints on their authority arising from the departments as well as other internal sources of influence, there have been recent moves in the USA and Australia, as well as Britain, to strengthen influence at the institutional level. The managerial emphases of the 1980s and 1990s have promoted corporate identity at the expense of departmental sectionalism.
3. The emphasis on conflict in the organization ignores the variety of

professional collaboration that takes place. The political perspective thereby underplays the capacity of individuals and groups to work in harmony with each other for collective and altruistic purposes and to engage in genuine debate about alternative perspectives. Individuals do not always pursue selfish interests at the expense of their colleagues, although competition for scarce resources (students, grants and contracts, promotions) will doubtless increase the potential for conflict and thus the validity of the political perspective on institutional life.

4. Finally, a political perspective is not one that should be promoted, even though it may describe aspects of reality which must be managed. As Bolman and Deal (1984: 146) argue, 'the amorality that often characterises political perspectives raises questions of values. To what extent does the political perspective, even as it purports to be simply a description of reality, ratify and sanctify some of the least humane and unsavoury aspects of human systems?'

The political perspective raises two rather different conceptions of leadership, which share similarities with McGregor's (1960) 'Theory X' and 'Theory Y' views of human nature. Under Theory X, managers assume that employees, who inherently dislike work, will resist management's performance objectives and therefore must be coerced, controlled, threatened or bribed to perform. These assumptions give rise to systems of management control which result in conformity, mistrust and conflict – and which are also costly to administer. In contrast, Theory Y assumes that a desire to work is natural, that self-direction and self-control can be expected from committed people and that creativity is widely dispersed in the organization. Management systems which are linked to these assumptions emphasize the gaining of commitment to collective objectives, participation in decision-making, encouragement of individual autonomy and responsibility for work performance.

If a Theory X view is taken, then leadership within a political frame will involve controlling information and resources and making use of status and power differentials to divide and rule. Conflict and confusion between different interests and goals are seen as opportunities to gain competitive advantage over other groups. Within a Theory Y conception, legitimate differences of value and interest between groups are recognized and the leadership task is to work towards acceptable goals through joint problem-solving, negotiation, mediation and compromise. Conflict is recognized as a potentially creative rather than a destructive force and is managed accordingly. Diplomacy, persuasion, the establishment of networks and a keen sense of timing are important skills.

Universities as bureaucracies

Max Weber (1947) regarded the bureaucracy as the most efficient organizational form for the coordination, regulation and control of work activity (see

Handy, 1985). As a complex and diversified organization, the university requires a means to coordinate and regulate the whole enterprise. The political perspective in particular, but also the collegial and professional images, ignore certain key dimensions of the university that fall within the bureaucratic image of the organization.

A central feature of bureaucracy is a hierarchical structure of formal chains of command aimed at providing order and method out of the potential for chaos present in large, complex organizations, which none the less exist to achieve a common purpose. In order to reduce the emphasis on individuality and the potential for individual discretion, the bureaucracy is based on a division of labour with carefully defined and circumscribed responsibilities. Positions in the hierarchy (each carrying different levels of decision-making authority) are divided into roles which can be filled by any individual who fits a pre-arranged role-specification and who subsequently meets organizational requirements. Beyond individual roles, groups are also organized according to functional areas, which are linked through a combination of managerial activity (planning, organizing, decision-making) and rules, procedures, rewards and punishments that guide behaviour in appropriate directions. Impersonal relationships between staff and clients are characteristic of bureaucracies; and recruitment and career progression are on the basis of merit.

Bureaucracies share certain features with other 'formal' models of organization, such as structural models, systems or rational approaches (Bush, 1986). Within all these models, organizations are seen as hierarchical systems in which managers use rational means to pursue agreed goals. Organizations, according to this perspective, exist to pursue official purposes and are accountable to their sponsors for the achievement of these purposes. In order to control and coordinate organizational activity, relationships between organizational members are structured, formal and regulated.

Each of the formal models emphasizes one or more of these features over others. The structural approach, for example, is most concerned with the pursuit of official goals by means of specialized roles and through the exercise of impersonal authority within a formal hierarchy of coordination and control (Bolman and Deal, 1984). Systems models (Moran, 1972; Latcham and Cuthbert, 1983) stress the interaction between component parts of the organization, introducing the notion of boundaries between the organization and its environment. In open systems, these boundaries are relatively permeable; in closed systems (the classic 'ivory tower' image of the university) they are not. Rational-analytic approaches (Cuthbert, 1984) emphasize managerial processes – processes that are ideally systematic, informed and rational – which take place within agreed objectives and bureaucratic structures.

As a model of organizational reality in universities, the bureaucratic or 'formal' perspective is relevant but still limited as either a prescriptive or an explanatory tool. The image has particular relevance for the administrative side of the university, with its structure of formal roles and positions, and its general *modus operandi*. The committee system, in its governance and administrative role, is also structured in a bureaucratic fashion, with terms of reference and regulatory procedures being specified. In addition, many large departments, particularly in scientific or technological disciplines, are organized internally on lines which reflect the formal perspective; and, indeed, the organization of many universities into departments, then faculties or schools, reflects both the specialized divisions of labour present in bureaucracies and a hierarchy of levels of decision-making authority. Recent external pressure to increase managerial efficiency in universities (Jarratt Report, CVCP, 1985; NAB Report, 1987; DES, 1987, 1991) have further encouraged the development of bureaucratic structures in higher education institutions.

The systems image, which differs from the bureaucratic perspective while sharing some common features, also has value in the university context. It offers a means to conceptualize the interactions between parts of the organization (as well as the organization in relation to its wider environment) and the ways in which the separate parts and activities of the university may be integrated and directed towards the achievement of institutional purposes. Although the notion of common organizational goals in universities is contested (Greenfield, 1973; Allen, 1988), recent emphases on accountability to sponsors and to clients have focused attention on the need to determine some common objectives and priorities – particularly those which meet the requirements of these sponsors and clients (for example, government, industry and students). As the external environment has impinged more directly on university operations, the systems image has become more potent, drawing attention to the nature of the boundaries between systems and subsystems, and the levels of dependency and integration of their transactions and interactions: open or closed, tightly or loosely coupled (Weick, 1976). The idea of 'boundary management' has gained currency as a consequence. This has relevance for leadership, since both institutional and departmental leaders must operate on the boundary between the internal and external worlds of the institution.

While there are useful elements, of both a practical and a conceptual kind within these formal images of organization, they also have limitations in the university context. As has already been mentioned, the ability to reach common goals is problematic since institutions contain many interests and serve many masters (students, government, research agencies, employers, society, the professions etc.). Yet the notion of common goals is central to formal models. The process of trying to reach common priorities is itself fraught with difficulties and is not achieved purely on the basis of rational decision-making processes at senior levels in the institution. Yet formal models stress such rational processes (Davies, 1985; Sizer, 1987).

Formal models depict the organization as a coherent entity, with power clearly located at the apex of the organization, a picture that does not take into account the power and autonomy of individuals and groups at different levels, the existence of devolved managerial responsibility and the importance of informal, personal interactions. Professional authority is also underplayed and in this way the tensions and conflicting demands between the hierarchy and the requirements of professionalism are given insufficient weight. Finally, the time required to pursue rational and linear decision-making processes presupposes both environmental and internal stability. Neither of these states currently applies in universities, and formal models are seen as inappropriate in the face of requirements for responsiveness, flexibility and change. However, the difficulties of changing large and complex organizations (Pettigrew *et al.*, 1992) to meet the needs of different environments, technologies or markets demonstrates the hold that formal structures and procedures have on institutions. As Clark (1983: 114) puts it:

> Academic structures do not simply move aside or let go: what is in place heavily conditions what will be . . . As systems grow larger and more complex, their internal structures acquire greater momentum, thrusting themselves powerfully into the future and snapping back with considerable resilience after imposed changes seemingly altered their ways.

The essence of bureaucratic leadership is depicted as making decisions and designing systems of control and coordination that direct the work of others so that compliance with directives is assured. Leadership is ascribed to the person at the apex of the hierarchy, who is assumed to set the tone of the organization and to establish its official objectives. The leader in a centralized, bureaucratic structure is often seen in heroic terms as the fount of authority, ultimate arbiter, chief problem-solver and defender of the enterprise against external threats. Influence and control over people and events is viewed as unidirectional and great expectations are held of the leader. A university example that identifies the role of institutional leader in this way can be found in the words of a departmental technician (Middlehurst *et al.*, 1992): 'The Vice Chancellor is responsible for the university. He has to keep within government guidelines. He has to increase the efficiency of the university and must maintain staff morale. He has to improve standards and must push the university forward.'

Some institutional leaders may believe or wish that power and control to achieve these goals rests entirely in their hands. However, many will recognize the messier and more constrained environment in which they operate, as well as the importance of shared leadership within the university.

Subjective and ambiguity perspectives on universities

Theory developed in the 1970s reflects a paradigmatic shift from a rational, linear perspective on organizations such as that featured in the bureaucratic image above to one that is non-linear and interpretive. Instead of organizations being seen as concrete entities, operating according to rational principles within clearly defined structures and conditions of relative stability, organizations seen through subjective or symbolic 'lenses' are depicted as 'systems of reality invented through the continued interaction of their participants' (Bensimon *et al.*, 1989: 31); and these interactions take place in a fluid, equivocal world. Within this uncertain and ambiguous environment, participants in organizations attach different meanings to events and so construe reality (and act on their constructions) in individual ways. These alternative perspectives of organizations mirror the cultural, symbolic and cognitive approaches to leadership outlined in Chapter 2.

Two models that broadly share the interpretive or symbolic approach will be outlined here: subjective and ambiguity models. Although the level of analysis is again the total institution, the perceptions and behaviour of individual organizational participants are a key focus.

Subjective models in the UK have been developed largely out of the work of Greenfield (1973, 1979) as a counterpoint to traditional, formal concepts of the organization. In the USA (where the various theories are categorized as featuring a 'symbolic' rather than subjective framework; Bensimon *et al.*, 1989: 31), the work of March and his colleagues has been influential (Cyert and March, 1963; March and Olsen, 1979; Cohen and March, 1986).

In subjective models, the emphasis shifts from structure towards a focus on perceptions and interpretations. A central concern is with the meanings placed on events by individual members of the organization. The structure of the organization is not seen as fixed or predetermined, but as a product of human interaction so that individuals influence structure through their own interpretations of action and interaction. Some writers recognize the differential amounts of power available to individual members of the organization (the Vice Chancellor and Registrar, for example) and therefore argue that these individuals have greater scope to impose their interpretations on the organization's structure:

> Structuring is typically the privilege of *some* organizational actors . . .
> The analytical focus then becomes the relations of power which enable some organizational members to constitute and re-create organizational structures according to their provinces of meaning.
>
> (Ranson *et al.*, 1980: 7)

Theorists who adopt a subjective perspective do not accept the notion of 'organizational goals' but see only socially constructed purposes. Again, through power differentials, the current preoccupations of a dominant organizational coalition may be interpreted as the goals of the organization, but in practice different 'goals' exist for clusters of academics, students or managers within institutions and these affect their perceptions of organizational reality and organizational objectives.

Ambiguity models, based on research in American universities, are primarily associated with the work of Cohen and March (1974, 1986). These models draw attention to the uncertainty and unpredictability present in organizations and the instability and complexity of institutional life. Like subjective theorists, researchers working with concepts of ambiguity regard the idea of clear organizational goals and structure as problematic. Institutional goals are seen either as so vague as to be unhelpful in guiding behaviour or to be open enough to justify any course of action. Some recent mission statements from British universities fall into this category. In the words of Cohen and March (1974: 3),

> The organization appears to operate on a variety of inconsistent and ill-defined preferences. It can be described better as a loose collection of changing ideas than as a coherent structure. It discovers preferences through action more often than it acts on the basis of preferences.

Structural ambiguity can be seen in the overlap between the power and authority vested in committees and that granted to individuals within a line-management structure. In recent times, further ambiguities can be seen in the relationship between new informal groups, such as the 'senior management team' and the formal committee structure.

Cohen and March draw attention to other areas of ambiguity within universities:

1. Their 'technology', arguing that key institutional processes such as teaching and learning are not properly understood and are open to different interpretations – a point brought into sharp relief in the current debates about the identification and assessment of teaching quality in British institutions.
2. Institutions are characterized by fragmentation where, despite internal coherence within sub-groups, the links between groups are tenuous and unpredictable. In recent times, top-down attempts to promote interdisciplinary activities or to create budget groups from cognate but still discrete disciplinary areas have had to contend with the ambiguities at unit level. These include strong degrees of individual professional discretion which may not match institutional objectives for efficiency and administrative clarity.
3. Decision-making within ambiguity models is not in the 'rational' form depicted within formal models since different individuals participate in decision-making at different times, in different arenas and with different levels of commitment to different topics. In this way, decisions may not be carefully planned according to managerial priorities; problems, solutions, participants and choices can become attached to each other for other reasons, emerging out of the mixture dumped in the 'garbage can' (Cohen and March, 1974: 81–2).
4. Finally, and importantly in the present economic and educational environment in the UK, the model takes account of turbulence and uncertainty in the external domain. If the organization is to survive and prosper, the environmental signals must be correctly interpreted and acted upon, but these are also ambiguous as current changes in funding mechanisms and in policies well demonstrate. Is it greater central control

of higher education that will determine institutional direction or the vagaries of the market economy – or neither, as the political complexion of the government or the pressures of the economy change?

The models identified here and loosely categorized as interpretive are useful in drawing attention to the complexity of universities. Subjective images recognize the values and motivations of individual organizational members, an element that is important for effective management. Ambiguity models, although exaggerating the degree of unpredictability in institutions, none the less illustrate the problems to be faced when relying on rational, bureaucratic managerial processes. These models also have value at a time of rapid change in the external environment, pointing to the difficulties of rational planning approaches when funding mechanisms, funding sources, research and teaching assessments, and income levels are unknown or at best uncertain.

Both subjective and ambiguity perspectives pose problems for leadership: within the former because of the emphasis on individual values, beliefs and perceptions; within the latter because of the problems of cause and effect relationships and the associated difficulties of control.

For subjectivists, the leader's formal position allows for a greater concentration of power as well as the ability to make use of institutional communication systems. Institutional leaders can therefore shape collective understandings and interpretations of the external world as well as the internal one. In this way, leadership may be a manifestation of a powerful individual's goals and vision or a more participative process whereby different interpretations of reality contribute to the articulation of institutional mission and purpose. Successful leadership will entail either influencing and aligning the views of others to match the leader's interpretations, or developing a consensus out of different perceptions and then articulating and presenting this collective view.

Cohen and March (1974: 195), representing the ambiguity perspective, point to the problems faced by leaders because of internal and external organizational uncertainties that strike at the heart of traditional interpretations of leadership:

> When purpose is ambiguous, ordinary theories of decision-making and intelligence become problematic. When power is ambiguous, ordinary theories of social order and control become problematic. When experience is ambiguous, ordinary theories of learning and adaptation become problematic. When success is ambiguous, ordinary theories of motivation and personal pleasure become problematic.

Taking account of these difficulties, the authors propose two alternative leadership strategies. In the first case, leaders are encouraged to maximize their influence on policy by being present to influence decisions, by persisting with proposals in different forums and by overloading the system with ideas to ensure the success of at least some initiatives. By dominating the institutional agenda, institutional leaders can exercise strong influence on university direction and operations.

In contrast to the tactical machinations of the first strategy, the second strategy involves forsaking direct involvement in the policy-making process in order to concentrate on areas of organizational design, such as structural and personnel matters. By seeking staff with compatible educational philosophies and organizational goals (either as new members of the institution or as members of working parties and task forces) and by restructuring organizational systems, procedures and roles, leaders may influence the organization by a mixture of subtlety and stealth, negotiating, nudging and encouraging institutional progress. It is likely that a combination of these two strategies will be adopted in practice, also integrating aspects from the other perspectives outlined above.

Recent perspectives

Morgan's work *Images of Organization* (1986) provides a wide spectrum of metaphors from which to capture the essence of organizational life in different milieus. At least two of his images have been adopted within the higher education literature to draw attention to new features of the university that have developed as a consequence of changing external circumstances. An important feature of these perspectives is the concern with the organization's ability to 'learn' or, if one takes a subjectivist stance, the ability of organizational members to learn by changing their behaviour to meet new challenges. The two images that will be described are the 'entrepreneurial and adaptive university' (Davies, 1987) and the university as 'cybernetic system' (Birnbaum, 1988).

The university as an adaptive system: the entrepreneurial image

Building on developments in organizational theory over the past fifty years, Davies (1987) uses the metaphor of the institution as a living system, existing in a wider environment on which it depends for the satisfaction of various needs (Morgan, 1986). The institution must maintain 'a state of creative equilibrium' (Davies, 1987: 15) with its environment in order to survive and prosper.

The particular environment of the 1980s and 1990s is one of political and economic turbulence, dominated by competition (for sponsors, contracts and students), by the requirements of industry and commerce and the model of business operations, and by public accountability. A concentration on these elements adds the entrepreneurial aspect to the adaptive core of this model. Davies notes that the European university has traditionally carried out two major roles, teaching and research, while the US university has also promoted the public service role. He argues, therefore, that conceptually

> the development of the EAU (Entrepreneurial and Adaptive University) sees a coming together of two traditions: the Providing tradition (of which the dominant operating metaphors are Collegiality, Bureaucracy, and Organized Anarchy) and the Client/Consumer tradition (of which the dominant operating metaphors are Consumerism, Business and Public Accountability).
>
> (Davies, 1987: 15)

Central to the idea of the EAU is its proactive and opportunistic stance, whereby it adjusts its activities and operations to take advantage of external developments. The university exploits its strengths in order to achieve maximum political and financial gains in the marketplace, relying on the initiative and risk-taking of individuals and groups in different parts of the institution and a clear managerial framework from the top. The organizational characteristics of the EAU are built upon an explicit, understood and visible university mission and a focused and relevant portfolio of activities. The organizational characteristics then include a core of academic disciplines organized into faculties and departments and beyond these a series of satellite units established for the purpose of achieving multidisciplinary research and teaching, and for exploiting the commercial potential of academic expertise through close client links. The university itself appears more as a 'holding company' for its decentralized units than as an integrated bureaucracy (Davies, 1987: 25–6).

The internal structures and processes of the EAU are also different from those of more traditional universities. Departments are grouped into budget centres led by academic managers and new posts mushroom at the central level as the university is linked more closely to its local context (e.g. Director of External Relations, Director of Research Contracts Office). Environmental scanning and market analysis, strategic planning and evaluation of institutional quality become key processes; and, ultimately, the move towards entrepreneurialism will demand a change in academic values and culture as new students enter the university, subjects are taught in different ways, and research is increasingly governed by external priorities and commercial deadlines.

Leadership within the EAU is split between an internal director of operations and an external politician and ambassador. The leadership task is to facilitate and regulate the delivery of services by the operating units through: the development and enactment of vision; political lobbying; business and market planning; incentive building and effective processes of staff selection, appraisal and development; and sensitive evaluation (Davies, 1987: 29). Although leadership at institutional level is emphasized, Davies and his colleagues also recognize the need for and widespread extent of 'dynamism and imagination at the level of dean, chairman [of department], and especially by heads of special centres' (p. 29).

At the time that the authors were undertaking their research into the idea of the 'entrepreneurial and adaptive university', the model seemed more acceptable and applicable to the culture and traditions of universities in the USA than in Europe. Six or seven years later, the image has considerable application in the British context as the former polytechnics are added to the university league and as the 'old' universities become more diversified in their missions and their funding sources.

The cybernetic image

Both the EAU and the cybernetic image use the metaphor of a 'living organism' to describe the university. The cybernetic perspective views the organization as a brain, capable of being flexible, resilient and inventive in relation to new situations (Morgan, 1986). For a system to be described as 'cybernetic' (taken from the Greek word for 'steersman', *kubernetes*), four principles of communication and learning must be achieved:

1. The system must have the capacity to sense, monitor, and scan significant aspects of its environment.
2. The system must be able to relate this information to the operating norms that guide system behaviour.
3. The system must be able to detect significant deviations from these norms.
4. The system must be able to initiate corrective action when discrepancies are detected (Morgan, 1986: 87).

If these four conditions are satisfied, a continuous process of information exchange is created between a system and its environment, allowing the system to monitor changes and initiate appropriate responses to maintain itself in steady state. Again, like the EAU, this model takes account of the constant need for awareness and intelligent action in the light of changes in the internal or external context of the institution, features which have strong currency in today's world.

The image of the university as a 'cybernetic system' builds on both subjective/symbolic and ambiguity perspectives in particular, but also incorporates aspects of other models; for example, the bureaucratic, collegial and political (Birnbaum, 1988). Through this lens, institutions are identified as self-correcting systems (using the metaphor of a thermostat):

> controlled in part by negative feedback loops created and reinforced in the institution's (bureaucratic) structure and negative feedback loops created and reinforced in the institution's (collegial) social system. The balance and relative importance of these loops are mediated by systems of (political) power and cultural and cognitive (symbolic) elements unique to the institution.
>
> (Bensimon *et al.*, 1989: 63)

The system works through the monitoring of institutional performance at senior levels and by taking corrective action on the basis of negative feedback. For maximum efficiency, Birnbaum argues, a combination of external constraints and internal self-direction is required, a pattern that is currently emerging in British institutions, for example in relation to the quality of educational provision. The key problem that faces cybernetic systems which are designed essentially to run themselves (and therefore operate best in conditions of relative stability) arises when drastic change is needed. Since the connections between parts of the institution are often loose rather than 'tightly coupled' and thus not direct and linear, change initiated through directive institutional leadership may not emerge in the ways intended. Instead, the style of leadership needs to work through the communication channels and feedback loops within the cybernetic system (or to alter the system through organizational redesign) in order to achieve desired change.

Under normal circumstances, leadership within the cybernetic institution consists of monitoring performance against priorities so that negative feedback is acted upon and potential imbalances are adjusted. The use of student feedback on academic programmes provides an example of this process; here course teams should respond to negative feedback and departmental leaders would be involved in monitoring faculty responses to student comment. Birnbaum argues that, in general, interventions from leaders (departmental or institutional, in our example) should be limited in order to allow the self-correcting mechanisms of the institution to operate effectively. Instead the leadership role should include the establishment of priorities, the design of appropriate early warning and communication systems, the coordination and balancing of the various subsystems within the institution and the directing of attention, symbolically and actively, towards the priority areas (Birnbaum, 1988).

Within modern cybernetic theory, the difficulties associated with swift and appropriate responses in times of turbulence or crisis have been addressed through the notion of 'single-loop' and 'double-loop' learning (Morgan, 1986: 87). Where 'single-loop' learning involves being able to detect and correct deviations from preset norms, 'double-loop' learning involves questioning the relevance of the operating norms, making adjustments to them as well as to the detailed operations, as different situations require (Morgan, 1986: 88). This process has been labelled 'learning to learn' and has entered the organizational literature through the idea of the learning organization (Garratt, 1987; Pedler *et al.*, 1991) and the learning university (Duke, 1992).

There are considerable strengths to the cybernetic image, particularly when it is linked to learning. Through such a linkage, the difficulties of addressing major change in institutions may be overcome as flexibility and responsiveness are built into the systems and processes of the university. The notion of adaptation to the environment is also included in the cybernetic perspective and takes into account not only changing external circumstances, but also the creative internal potential of information-processing technology which will ultimately facilitate new forms of organization

(Drucker, 1988; Handy, 1991). However, bearing in mind the earlier 'subjec-tivist' perspective, any move towards a learning institution requires major changes in attitudes and values, some of which are identified by Morgan (1986: 109) and include: 'emphasizing the importance of activeness over passiveness, autonomy over dependence, flexibility over rigidity, collabora-tion over competition, openness over closedness, and democratic inquiry over authoritarian belief'.

While some of these ingredients may be present in British institutions (and are reflected in collegial and professional organizational perspectives in particular) they also vie with countervailing forces of centralization, com-petitition for scarce resources and external assessment. Appropriate cultural change *within* institutions is likely to be insufficient without commensurate shifts in attitudes at system and government levels.

Use and value of organizational perspectives

As was mentioned earlier, the images outlined above may be the most well-known depictions of the university as an organizational form, but they are by no means the only perspectives in existence, nor are they uncontested (Schmidtlein, 1991). Other writers have drawn attention to the importance of ideology on behaviour and structures in higher education (Collier, 1982; Barnett, 1990; Tapper and Salter, 1992), while ethnographic approaches to organizational analysis have demonstrated the importance of the concept of culture in various domains and levels of the institution (Becher, 1989).

Cultural perspectives on the university have opened a rich vein of scholar-ship, extending the focus from global analyses of the institution to micro-analyses of various aspects of institutional functioning (Chaffee and Tierney, 1988; Harman, 1990). In particular, these analyses have drawn attention to the variety of institutional life, illustrating at group level alternative re-sponses to the tasks of higher education and to perceived external or inter-nal pressures (from government and community, from discipline and profession). Examples might include the growth of franchising in response to pressures to increase access to universities, developments in resource-based learning to cope with increased numbers of students, or changes in roles to cope with increased managerial pressures.

By highlighting internal heterogeneity, micro-perspectives provide a more useful practical tool for policy analysis and implementation than do more global images, since they focus on levels other than the institutional alone. None the less, global or macro-perspectives such as those offered in this chapter can act to sensitize leaders to some of the factors that will impinge on the appropriateness of organizational designs, for example: efficiencies and inefficiencies of different coordination and control systems (total quality management or the British Standards approach, perhaps); the strength of values, habits of thought and practice in different parts of the institution; the impact of the environmental context on higher education. In the previous chapter, the idea of 'critical pluralism' was advanced as a means to approach and make use of different views of leadership. There are likely to be similar benefits to be gained for policy analysis and system design in undertaking 'cultural diagnosis and critical evaluation' in the light of different perspectives of the organization (Morgan, 1986: 322).

The models outlined above are 'pure' examples of a particular image. Reality is considerably messier and no one perspective is likely to prevail. Furthermore, aspects of one or other image may predominate in different parts of an institution, linked to specific activities. Particular circumstances, or different stages of an organization's life-cycle, may also influence the organizational structure and culture that predominates (Baliga and Hunt, 1988). The central issue for leaders is a willingness to seek and an ability to 'see' and interpret alternative images, and then to use this facility to develop an appropriate fit between institutional tasks, purposes, resources, environment and stakeholder interests.

4

Leadership and Academe: Traditions and Change

Introduction

By looking both backwards and forwards in time, this chapter attempts to explore the idea of leadership within the university context. The literature on leadership, much of which is based on research undertaken in the private commercial sector, is examined in the light of academic traditions, culture and environment. Out of this examination, I argue that leadership is relevant in universities, especially at a time of considerable change in academe, but that its practice will take on a particular cast within this domain of autonomous professionals.

Conceptions of leadership

In order to examine the value of leadership within the academic context, the core features of the concept must be drawn out. This is by no means easy since, as we have seen in Chapters 1 and 2, ideas about leadership have not remained static but have evolved in response to a range of influences.

First, ideas about leadership have been (and continue to be) influenced by factors beyond the organization and the individual, such as the culture of a society, the political and economic context of that society and any prevailing religious or secular ideologies. Second, within an organization or group, the purpose and nature of the task as well as the structure and culture(s) of the organization will impinge on understandings and expectations of leadership. For example, both participants in and observers of a football team, an orchestra, a bank or an army will carry different conceptions of the nature of leadership within those settings. Third, the structure and development of the disciplines in which leadership studies are located has also influenced thinking about the topic as several writers have indicated (Bryman, 1986; Bensimon *et al.*, 1989; Hunt, 1992).

Given the fluidity of the concept, subject to changing intellectual fashions and traditions, perceptual bias, economic, organizational and historical circumstances, we may well ask whether the idea of leadership has retained any essential characteristics over time. If there are some consistent features to be found, we also need to consider which (if any) of these are relevant to universities. These questions provide the basis for this chapter.

A starting point is offered by Bryman (1992), who, analysing leadership research within organizations, points to three main elements contained in current definitions of leadership. These are: influence, group and goals. In other words, leadership is typically identified as 'a process of social influence whereby a leader steers members of a group towards a goal' (p. 2).

The association of leadership with influence – or power – has a long history, as we have already noted. However, the nature and sources of influence which have been regarded as relevant have differed over time and culture, as Adair (1989) suggests: for example, knowledge, skill and rationality (Socrates, Tacitus); humility, selflessness, compassion and mutual service (Lao Tzu, Jesus); political strength and acumen (Machiavelli); charisma, inspiration and personal example (Napoleon I, T. E. Lawrence, Alexander the Great); legal authority, hierarchical position and hereditary tradition (Weber).

Links between leadership and 'followership' are not new either (Kouzes and Posner, 1987; Heywood, 1989), although once again the delineation of 'following' varies. It may include the image of a group following an individual (generals and their army, conductors and their orchestra) or an image of a group or an individual following an idea or ideal (disciples of a prophet, students of a sage, supporters of a political party). In the former example, contact between leader and followers is generally direct and face-to-face, and in the latter case, engagement between leadership and following may be indirect. In both instances, the force that exerts influence upon the individual or group in order to promote action is identified as leadership, while the impulse towards action rests with 'the followers'.

The relationship between leadership and 'goals' is also long-standing, but here there is still more conceptual elasticity since goals can be interpreted to include direction, purpose, meaning or ideals, each of which may vary according to time and context. Adair (1989: 57–60) traces the association of leadership with movement towards an end-point by referring to the etymology of the word leader: the roots of the word lie in the Anglo-Saxon word *laed* meaning a path or road, and the verb *laeden* meaning to travel or go. Adair notes that the leader was the person who showed the way, whether as guide, steersman or navigator.

Adair points to similar etymological origins for 'leadership' in other languages (for example, Dutch, Scandinavian and Egyptian) and to differences elsewhere (for example, in French or Spanish), where an alternative image of leadership, as 'headship', is used (French *chef;* English chief). He suggests that the first image – of guidance on a journey – has no connotations of hierarchy, whereas the second image does. While it is difficult to imagine a complete lack of hierarchy in either of these images, the kind of hierarchy envisaged is likely to differ. For example, the hierarchy, or distinction between leader and followers, may be either tacit or overt and may be defined by the group themselves or by others beyond the group. Second, the source of authority upon which the exercise of leadership is based (knowledge of the terrain or divine right) is likely to vary. Third, the psychological distance between leader and led may also differ where leadership involves guidance or where it involves command. Since modern English has been subject to both Anglo-Saxon and French influences, it is not surprising that leadership carries these different associations within its conceptual baggage.

The above points serve as a reminder of some of the common themes which are linked to the idea of leadership and which were explored in more detail earlier. A further dimension that must be remembered is the distinction between the two paradigms of rational/objective and interpretive/subjective, each reflecting opposing assumptions about the nature of reality. Within the first paradigm, leadership is seen as an observable phenomenon that can be identified and measured. In the second paradigm, leadership exists only as 'a social attribution' arising out of individual perceptions and ways of constructing reality. Each paradigm is likely to have an effect on what is seen, understood or done in the name of leadership.

These key ideas provide a backcloth against which to examine leadership in the particular context of academic organizations.

Leadership and academe: traditional dimensions

Use of the term 'leadership' in academic settings has in the past been associated with one particular purpose of the university: that of education for leadership in society. A key function of British universities was to educate and train the next generation of leaders destined for government, the church, the professions and more recently for industry and commerce. In the words of Halsey and Trow (1971: 452): 'What we have seen as most distinctive of the British and especially the English universities was the strong organizational expression of careful and intensive education for scholarship and social leadership.'

Beyond this educational purpose, the term leadership did not have currency in relation to academic life either in the intellectual sphere (within disciplines) or in the administrative sphere (in relation to governance and administration), until the latter part of the twentieth century. However, this is not to say that leadership was not practised either collectively or individually. Opportunities existed for leadership to be exercised in a number of arenas. Intellectual leadership, founded upon individual endeavour, could be achieved in research, teaching and scholarship and recognized both within the university community and beyond it. Academic leadership (that is, influencing the direction of academic activities and areas of study) was also possible within departments, schools or faculties, usually under the direction of the professoriate. And at institutional, college and system levels, the potential to demonstrate administrative leadership was also present. Some examples will illustrate these points.

Flexner (1930) described the great teachers who inspired their students with 'stirring enthusiasm, directing and sustaining it by encouragement and guidance to create the zeal and equipment for seeking knowledge' (p. 283). He also noted how the Oxford and Cambridge system of well-endowed and loosely jointed colleges enabled individual genius to forge its own path, to train a succession and 'to open new vistas for men of talent to follow'. Although these examples were not described in terms of leadership, they reflect the elements of leadership outlined above.

Within organizations, leadership is often associated with policy and decision-making responsibilities (that is, with 'formal' social influence processes) or with the freedom to chart a direction and to take initiative within a particular operational sphere. Several authors (e.g. Halsey and Trow, 1971; Moodie and Eustace, 1974) point to the power of the professoriate in these respects – within their subject area, in academic decision-making and in university governance – from the late nineteenth century onwards. Prior to this period, greater authority or control over academic affairs, rested with laymen rather than scholars (Moodie and Eustace, 1974: 28–9).

Professorial authority had several sources: academic reputation and rank, the potential for entrepreneurship or command of independent research funds, and position and voice on policy-making bodies such as Senate. Moodie and Eustace (1974: 215) describe the status and formal expectations of the professoriate:

> Professors are still appointed in the belief that they are intellectually distinguished, some are appointed also because of their known administrative ability, and all are expected to be capable of bearing the responsibility placed upon them for guiding and developing research and teaching within their subject.

Where professorial rank was combined with the office of Head of Department, a still greater potential for leadership existed:

> although recent years have witnessed some diminution in his position of unchallenged eminence, he [the Head of Department] remains, nevertheless, *the* key figure in his own department and, largely as a result, *a* key figure throughout university government. To this day, he continues to wield a measure of real power as well as (in part consequentially) a pervasive influence.
>
> (Moodie and Eustace, 1974: 62)

To this potential can be added an explicit expectation of leadership in the headship role, according to Startup (1976: 234):

> the professorial head is the person who has been appointed to grasp as a whole the activities of his department. He is the one who is required to anticipate problems which may arise for the department as such and for its individual members. He must be aware of, and be ready to react to, changes in the environment of his department. The head is

required to formulate particular policies – however much these policies may subsequently be the subject of discussion among staff or subject to democratic processes of decision making. At the very least, it can be said that the departmental head has a duty to *lead* (Startup's italics).

The role of the Dean in budgetary allocations, as described by Moodie and Eustace (1974), can also be identified as a possible focus for leadership. It is interesting to reflect upon the different style that is depicted here in comparison with that implicit in the 'heroic' headship roles described above. The Deans 'are likely both to be the main spokesmen for their faculties or schools in making the main division of academic funds and, once a sum has been allocated to their units, to fulfill a "steersman's" role in securing agreement on the further subdivisions' (p. 181).

In all these examples, Bryman's three elements of influence, group and goals are evident, although rarely is leadership identified explicitly.

Turning to the administrative domain, the first question is whether those employed as administrators exercised a leadership function. Neither Halsey and Trow (1971) nor Moodie and Eustace (1974) credit senior (non-academic) administrators with the power or will to exercise 'leadership'. However, each set of authors recognizes that in their role as facilitators of university business, in the permanency of their tenure, in their access to information, their preparation of policy proposals, their responsibilities for decision implementation, and their guardianship of constitutional procedures and 'due process', senior officers were able to exercise considerable influence over university affairs.

Moodie and Eustace (1974) also point to the often close relationship between Vice Chancellors and Registrars/Bursars and between committee chairmen and committee secretaries, and to the considerable contribution made to 'moulding university policy' by individual officers. Like the contrast in the styles of Heads of Department and Deans depicted above, the issue may not be the presence or absence of leadership, but the nature of 'leadership' implied. The images of 'servant leadership' (Greenleaf, 1973), of facilitation, guidance and support as aspects of leadership (Adair, 1983) or of collective leadership in a shared enterprise (Belbin, 1992; Kakabadse *et al.*, 1992) may be more appropriate to the traditional role of senior administrators working with academics than an image of independent initiative and command exercised by senior officers.

The second question in the administrative domain is whether the Vice Chancellor exercised leadership. There seems little doubt among scholars that the Vice Chancellor's position created a potential for leadership at various levels (institutional, system, national and international), as well as in several domains (educational, academic and administrative). Szreter (1968: 17) in his study of 'an academic patriciate' describes Vice Chancellors as 'responsible to a considerable extent for the direction of activities of their individual institutions and generally of British higher education, upon which hinge both the material and non-material (or "ideational") development of our society'.

Guttsman (1963), in his study of the British political elite, lists sixteen elites among which 'the leaders of science and learning' are represented, that is, the members of the Vice Chancellors' Committee, the heads of Oxford and Cambridge and some London colleges, the heads of medical schools and chief officers of major learned associations. Whilst recognizing that Vice Chancellors are not the only scholars of prestige and eminence in the academic world, Guttsman argues that others are less influential since influence 'comes more readily to those who hold official positions than to many who are merely distinguished' (p. 327).

Separately, Halsey and Trow (1971: 161) and Moodie and Eustace (1974: 129) point to the special influence that is open to the Vice Chancellor:

> Vice Chancellors are distinguished from the rest of the university pro-
> fessions by the extent of the influence they can exert both on develop-
> ments within their own institutions and on the general pattern and
> direction of higher education in the country as a whole.

> Despite the unspecified nature of his positive activities, nevertheless the
> vice chancellor is normally the most important single figure in any
> university. He may, for better or worse, affect the whole climate of a
> university.

These authors trace the sources of Vice Chancellors' influence to their position as the main link between academic and administrative hierarchies internally, and to system and government externally; to their position as focal points of communication; to their chairmanship role on key university committees; to powers of patronage; to the opportunities for shaping financial and academic decisions; and to the expectation of ultimate decision-taking and arbitration which is laid upon Vice Chancellors by university members themselves. In Weber's terms, the Vice Chancellor has access to three sources of legitimate authority: traditional authority (which is built on formal and informal expectations of role incumbents, accumulated over time), charismatic authority (resting on the personal qualities, experience and competence of the individual) and legal-rational authority (which is associated with the rules and regulatory systems of the organization and which the role incumbent has a right to exercise). Clearly, the potential for leadership existed in the Vice Chancellor's role, and beyond this – on the evidence of university histories and individual biographies – leadership *was* exercised in practice at institutional and system levels.

The examples presented above suggest that the concept of leadership is applicable at various levels within the academic context, even if the term itself has not been widely used until quite recently. Why the term has not had wide currency in academe is the focus of the next section.

Constraints on leadership in the academic context

So far, this discussion has tended to assume that the idea of leadership is applicable to academe, even if its precise character is elusive. However, many would question the appropriateness or legitimacy of the concept within the university context. It is to these arguments that we now turn under the headings of values, structures and processes.

Values

At the centre of the traditional academic value system lie the ideals of academic freedom, critical reflection, rationality, democratic participation and autonomy. The ways in which academic work is conducted, authority is distributed and influence is exercised at least in part reflect these underlying values.

Academic freedom implies individual discretion to pursue (and promote in others) the quest for knowledge and truth in ways that are guided by individual choice within a framework of professional norms of conduct and behaviour. As the main vehicle for the pursuit of knowledge, scholarly enquiry carries with it a duty to question, to exercise independence of thought and judgement and to strive after creativity: in short, to reflect and to evaluate critically upon past knowledge and future premises. The results of such critical enquiry must then be presented according to the conventions of reasoned argument.

The activities of academic life – teaching, research, scholarship – although individual in terms of discretion, are also collective in that they take place in the context of disciplinary and organizational groups. The idea of democratic participation stems both from the assumption of individual expertise in knowledge areas and from the notion of community. Since it is possible to achieve expertise in intellectual domains independently of age and rank (although rank is usually accorded in recognition of intellectual achievements), all individuals, regardless of age and rank, have the right to a voice in relation to academic matters. The degree of weight or influence accorded to any individual voice will, at least in part, be related to the principles of rationality mentioned above. The right to a voice in academic affairs is also accorded on the basis of membership of a community with shared interests, ideals and activities. Individual contributions are expected and legitimated on the basis of democracy (equal rights within a community) and on the basis of reasoned argument. Finally, when the notion of autonomy in governance is added to the notion of community, the 'right to a voice' is believed to extend beyond the purely academic arena to the operations of the group as a whole.

At first glance, these values may pose problems of 'fit' when linked to leadership. First, the value placed on individual expertise, predicated as it is on the ways in which knowledge is created and disseminated, makes the individual supreme in his or her own area. There may be few others in the immediate academic community (department or institution) who can rival such individual expertise and who might, on the basis of their academic supremacy, be able to exercise authority or influence over others founded upon expertise. Many academic departments represent such collections of individual stars.

The importance of individual discretion is enshrined in the concept of academic freedom, which here implies the right to organize and shape the nature of one's academic activities without reference to a 'superior'. Licence to exercise such discretion is based on 'professionalism' and suggests a second constraint on the direction or control of activities by someone other than the individual academic.

Beyond the difficulties posed by individual expertise and professionalism, the notion of critical reflection and evaluation implies that 'authority' from any source is open to challenge (in this case, the authority of a leader). If we add to these constraints the democratic/egalitarian and rational ethics, further problems arise for the idea of leadership in that there may be neither justice nor logic in the separation of one individual (or even a group of individuals) from the other members of the community in terms of their power to direct the activities of others.

The picture that has been drawn here is ideal and, to an extent, exaggerated. Divisions of status and authority exist in the intellectual arena, granted on the basis of levels of expertise or achievement, that is, by greater or lesser contributions to academic purposes as recognized and acknowledged by the members of the community. Such authority is not, however, unassailable; it is always open to challenge and reputations sometimes dissolve.

Beyond the intellectual arena, in the interests of self-governance, divisions of labour have developed in order for the communities to operate effectively. Such divisions of labour may develop – indeed have developed – into differences of status and authority, for example in the roles of Vice Chancellor or Head of Department. Yet the authority of these individuals, particularly in academic matters, is still open to challenge in the collective arena of Senate or the departmental meeting. It is only in relatively recent times that a sharper distinction has begun to be forged between academic/intellectual matters and institutional/departmental matters that fall into the areas of governance and management. Such a distinction is likely to lead to a diminution in the area of discretion or individual authority open to the ordinary academic.

So what of the idea of leadership in this setting? The heart of the matter is that leadership can only be exercised effectively in the academic context – or in other professional contexts – on the basis of legitimate authority and influence and the willing compliance of organizational members. It requires individual assent to limit one's own sphere of discretion or to acknowledge the influence of another; this is unlikely to occur unless some benefit (whether psychological, professional or material) is perceived to accrue to those engaging in the self-restraint.

Within the academic environment, legitimate authority has to be accorded by the members of the community, individually and collectively, tacitly and overtly, because of the high premium placed on individual discretion. The sources of influence and authority are likely to reflect the prevailing values of the community or organization, in this case expertise, rationality and equality. In other words, leadership is defined by the ability to convince and persuade others to act on the basis of greater knowledge or competence, reasoned argument and fairness. Where authority has been conferred on an individual or group to act on behalf of the community's interests (as in the case of a departmental chairperson), a further source of influence is added. In all these instances, what emerges is that leadership is not likely to function solely as a unilateral or top-down process in the academic context. The 'right' to influence must be acknowledged by the individuals in the community and earned by those aspiring to leadership through exemplifying particular values, by providing benefits to individuals and groups that would otherwise be unavailable to them and by serving the diverse interests of the university community. If authority and influence are to be maintained, these values will need to be practised in word and deed, although once trust is established it is possible to go beyond them.

Structure

Becher and Kogan (1992) have posited a relationship between 'normative' and 'operational' domains, that is between the sphere of values and day-to-day activities in higher education. Both domains are reflected in the organization's decision-making structures, as we shall see below.

Many features of academic organizations have already been explored (see Chapter 3). Here it is only necessary to highlight those structural features which may be problematic in terms of leadership. There are three that stand out: the dual hierarchy of academic and administrative authority and activities; the use of part-time decision-makers; and the diffusion of authority within the university.

The dual hierarchy creates potential difficulties for the notion of 'solo-leadership' since there is an innate tension in the sources of authority and operational priorities of each area (for example, legal versus professional authority, financial efficiency versus academic freedom). An attempt at resolution is to be found in the position of Vice Chancellor, which provides a link between the two areas, according the status of 'chief' in respect of both academic and administrative domains. In the past, when resources were more plentiful and academic growth, determined on the strength of internal academic priorities, was more assured, the tension between the two domains was perhaps less noticeable than in recent times. The academic domain was in the ascendant and academic leadership was prominent. In the words of

Halsey and Trow (1971: 114): 'The administrative staff of the British universities appears, by contrast with the American universities, to be small in number and strongly conditioned to subservience to the academic will.'

The implication for leadership of a dual hierarchy again points to the need to have alternative images of leadership to the unilateral, top-down, command and control variety. Both administrative and academic domains serve the overall functioning of the institution and a balance therefore needs to be maintained between their separate claims and priorities. An image of leadership as steerage or negotiation is likely to be more appropriate.

The reliance on part-time or temporary decision makers within the committee system and in some senior roles, such as that of Dean, Pro Vice Chancellor or in rotating chairmanship roles, has served to diffuse authority, as well as to spread participation and responsibility for academic governance across the institution, faculty or department. Like many of the features of governance in traditional universities, the spread of authority provides a check on the concentration of power, a danger which might otherwise threaten the values of equality, the rights of individuals and also, perhaps, the principles of rationality outlined earlier.

Once more it would seem that this environment of checks and balances presents a challenge for leadership; and indeed it does for some conceptions of leadership. However, by spreading authority and by valuing individual and collective initiative at different organizational levels, there is potential for leadership in many quarters of the university. Yet such diffusion is not without its own problems: organizational fragmentation can readily occur and the difficulties of achieving and maintaining an overall direction for the university are considerable. Once again, the shape of leadership is likely to be distinctive and to vary at different points in the institution. At the centre, for example, the leadership task will involve the development of a cultural and operational framework that guides, facilitates and regulates the leadership approaches elsewhere in the institution (Birnbaum, 1988). To the extent that this framework is supported by existing norms and practice, the degree of direction from the centre will be minimal; however, where there is a need to increase cohesion or to change practice, the degree of central direction is likely to increase, as occurred in several British universities following funding reductions in the 1980s.

Processes

The issue of diffused authority has just been raised. A further reason for authority to be spread, which also adds to the potential for organizational fragmentation in the university, is the variety of academic interests that exist in the institution. Each interest group, in following its own path, can claim to be fulfilling the academic purposes of the university, while at the same time the pursuit of these specific interests may be limiting the 'corporateness' of the whole.

Closely allied to this problem of divergent interests is that of different, sometimes conflicting and often ambiguous goals that exist at basic unit and at institutional levels. Both these issues, it might be argued, pose difficulties for the concept of leadership insofar as leadership implies the establishment of a common purpose, direction and meaning for the activities of the whole enterprise. Yet the existence of ambiguity, a potential for conflict and for fragmentation, while making the leadership task more complex, more difficult and different in kind, does not necessarily imply that leadership cannot be exercised or that it has no purpose within the academic context. As Cohen and March (1974, 1986) have suggested, the implications of such a setting require the adoption of alternative conceptual frameworks and operational strategies. Emphasis should be placed on conceptions of leadership that acknowledge the significant features – and constraints – of academe. Political, symbolic and cultural images of leadership, in which the functions of negotiation, interpretation, reconciliation and alignment are of particular importance, provide a fertile source of ideas.

Beyond academics

So far, our discussion has focused on the particular characteristics of the academic environment and of academics as a group. Features of individual members of the university, as individuals (including their humanity and their personalities), have been ignored. General features of the university, such as the need for stability combined with change and development, characteristics which are shared with other organizations, have also been left out. It is time to consider these issues.

Both Becher and Kogan (1992) and Hunt (1992) in their conceptual frameworks (of higher education and leadership, respectively) point to the influence of external cultural, social and psychological factors on the norms and behaviours of individuals and of organizations. Following these authors, the peculiarly 'academic' shape of leadership, it can be argued, is likely to be modified both by individual perspectives and by external factors: the economic environment or the leadership myths and attitudes to authority which prevail in any society during a historical period. Several recent cross-cultural studies, although undertaken in private sector organizations, support the assumption that cultural and psychological factors affect the nature of leadership (Hofstede, 1980; Peterson and Smith, 1988).

A decline in deference to traditional authority combined with the continuing development of democratic and egalitarian principles in Western society is likely to have an impact on conceptions of leadership in the academic context and outside it (Stogdill, 1974; Bass, 1981). Since academic organizations contain many other constituencies beyond the academics and because the academics themselves are more tightly interconnected with society and the state than in previous centuries, these individual and external influences are likely to carry increasing weight within institutions. A recent CVCP report acknowledges these influences in its strategy for the management and development of university staff: *Promoting People* (CVCP, 1993). In the next section, some of these broader influences on the university and all its members will be discussed.

Change in academe

Given the longevity of some universities (seventy of them are among the oldest surviving institutions in the Western world; Kerr, 1982), identifying boundaries between tradition and change or delineating the continuities and discontinuities of academic life is not straightforward. None the less, the range of recent structural, legal and ideological shifts that have occurred across the education sector point to a major fault-line in the late twentieth century. Several eminent futurists, including Toffler (1970, 1980) Drucker (1988) and Handy (1989), argue that the focus of change goes far beyond education and educational organizations, as economies and societies across the globe grapple with a technological revolution, which, like earlier agricultural and industrial revolutions, is having profound effects on all aspects of life. Education is of central importance to this revolution since it simultaneously feeds the processes of change and assists adaptation to their consequences.

The changes that are affecting academic organizations emerge from several sources and have an impact on most aspects of organizational functioning. They will be considered in three sections before undertaking an examination of their implications for leadership: the macro-environment; the state, system and institution; the domain of the individual. While it is customary to see these domains in terms of hierarchical levels, it is more appropriate to view them as interlocking systems that exert reciprocal influence upon each other.

The macro-environment

Major changes within the macro-environmental domain include technological innovations, alterations in the patterns of economic power across nations (and across corporations), developments in socio-cultural values and shifts in geographical and racial territories.

In the technological area, for example, innovations in electronic communication and information technology have facilitated changes in institutional management, in teaching and learning strategies and in the size and location of institutions, making more feasible 'outreach' approaches, international links, decentralized decision-making and flexible patterns of working and studying. Other changes made possible by advances in technology, such as the contraceptive pill, have also had a significant impact on employment patterns, family relationships and individual aspirations, enabling more women to participate in and benefit from higher education.

As the worldwide recession of the late twentieth century bites deeply into the economies of the richer nations and has a reciprocal and immediately more serious effect on poorer nations, it is obvious that changing patterns of economic power have a direct impact on the resources available for education. As economies are squeezed by the twin pressures of reduced resources and ever-increasing demand, the economic ideology is advanced through state pressure on institutions to seek income directly from the market and to tie academic activities more closely to the wealth creation needs of society and economy.

Economic and technological possibilities are nurtured and launched within a particular social context but also give rise to further developments in social and cultural values as new opportunities emerge, new practices are established and new ways of thinking are cultivated. Education in general and higher education in particular, as creator and disseminator of new knowledge, and as defender, reflector or critic of current social and cultural values, plays a central role in this domain. For example, the ways in which access to higher education is defined and controlled and the ways in which the outcomes of higher education are determined and received have in the past (and will no doubt continue to have) profound effects on social and cultural status and beliefs as well as economic prospects (Ball, 1992; Tapper and Salter, 1992).

Where, in the past, strong influence in the socio-cultural domain has rested with institutions, particularly the universities, the balance of power is now shifting outside them so that institutions are obliged to become more responsive to external demands and requirements – from the state, industry, the professions, minorities, students or the public at large. Developments such as National Vocational Qualifications (NVQs), which shift the emphasis of learning from acquisition of knowledge to outcomes and levels of competence, Students' Charters, spelling out student rights as well as responsibilities, the Enterprise in Higher Education Initiative (funded by the Department of Employment) and the Education for Capability project (sponsored by the Royal Society for Arts) testify to the increasing pressure from outside the institution to effect changes in traditional curricula.

Finally, in this brief outline, changes in economic status, often in conjunction with technological developments and ideological shifts, have produced new territorial configurations across several continents, notably in Europe, Asia and Africa. Shifts of this kind have encouraged institutions to seek new markets for their talents, to develop innovative programmes and mechanisms for credit transfer or opportunities for educational exchange, and to build new international partnerships and networks (such as the ERASMUS and TEMPUS programmes).

From state to system and institution

Although direct signals are received from the macro-environment and are then acted upon independently by institutions, external signals are also received through a political filter. Thus, the state, through the Funding and

Research Councils and its own Departments, exerts influence over the operations of higher education institutions. The gradual but inexorable increase in the influence of the state on higher education in the twentieth century has been illustrated by several authors (Becher and Kogan, 1992; Tapper and Salter, 1992); it is paralleled by similar experiences in other public sectors (Pollitt, 1990; Willcocks and Harrow 1992). The process was given fresh impetus under the political philosophies of the New Right, whose period of ascendancy in the UK (from 1979) was long enough for the impact of their policies to be widely felt and to have a more than superficial effect on institutional practice. The translation of policy into legislation (Education Reform Act, 1988; Further and Higher Education Act, 1992) has increased this impact.

As described above, the economic imperatives of the state in the post-war period are reflected in requirements for institutions to become more responsive to national needs (while less dependent on public funds), and to produce greater numbers of scientists and technologists as well as a generally numerate and literate graduate population with a range of transferable skills. Numerous reports and government White Papers provide evidence of these concerns and aspirations (Stewart, 1989).

Closely allied to this economic dynamic has been the bureaucratic pressure exerted by the Department of Education and Science (now Department for Education) through the funding agencies, for institutions to become more accountable for their use of public funds, to seek increased value for money from their activities and to identify ways of increasing efficiency (Cuthbert, 1992; Tapper and Salter, 1992). Across the public services there has been a push, particularly from central government, for positive management, or 'a replacement of an administrative culture by a managerial culture derived from private-sector decision-making frameworks' (Harrow and Wilcocks, 1992: 50).

Increased centralist pressures from the DES/DFE have vied with the market philosophies of the New Right, sometimes producing strange conceptions such as 'the managed market'. Unsurprisingly, the institutional consequences of these conflicting views have produced neither the controlled efficiencies assumed of managed systems nor the full entrepreneurial opportunities associated with a free market, since the structures and attitudes required to operate each form of organization to its best advantage do not easily coexist. Indeed, as the organizational images in Chapter 3 imply, the nature of higher education and the governance structures that have evolved to fit its particular purposes do not fit neatly into either a bureaucratic or an entrepreneurial pigeon-hole. As many scholars concerned with public sector management are pointing out, the value base of 'managing for social [rather than financial] result' (McMahon, 1990: 16) extends the range of institutional concerns well beyond those of efficiency and enterprise.

None the less, institutions have responded as best they can to the inconsistencies of government policy and to the dual pressures – of market and of management – described by Gunn (1988) as the 'five Es' of economy, efficiency, effectiveness, excellence and enterprise. Since the late 1980s, these different imperatives have essentially been subsumed under the rallying cry of 'improving quality in higher education'.

Institutions have adapted to this external environment by effecting changes in internal infrastructure (for example, reshaping or creating new financial management and information systems), in planning processes (for example, by establishing better links between physical, financial and academic resources), in the organization of research, in teaching and learning strategies, and have developed new policies in the areas of quality assurance, equal opportunities, public relations and marketing. Institutional responses have differed across the former binary line, between polytechnics and universities (Cuthbert, 1992), as well as between institutions in any one sector (Middlehurst *et al.*, 1992). Such diversity of response is likely to develop further as the effects of legislation, resource constraint and changing state and public expectations of higher education continue to challenge and to influence the norms and operations of the post-compulsory education system (Becher and Kogan, 1992; McNay, 1992).

The individual domain

The impact of change is often felt most keenly at the level of the individual. At senior levels this may be felt as a buzz of excitement as managers rise to the challenge of negotiating mergers between institutions, or venture a large-scale bid for a contract or ear-marked fund, or tackle the task of changing a culture in order to reposition the institution or to introduce a major innovation. At other levels, the perception of change may not be experienced positively by individuals who see their autonomy, life-style, status or value systems threatened by the new developments.

The personal impact of change in organizations, in terms of the effect on self-esteem, performance and stress, has been explored recently by Carnall (1990) and earlier by other writers who have examined the stages involved in adapting to change (Adams *et al.*, 1976; Miller and de Vries, 1985). Within higher education, some of the trade unions have been active in highlighting the effects of recent change on individual roles and on levels of stress (Carroll and Cross, 1991; NATFHE, 1992). There are many points of similarity between individual responses as recorded in private sector or higher education contexts; critical factors which shape responses to change are determined by personality and emotional health, by status and power positions, by expectations and value orientations, and by leadership.

The brief survey above illustrates the range of changes and the wide source of influences which form the higher education operating environment. They are the context in which leadership is exercised and expected; it is time to consider their implications for leadership itself.

Change, leadership and academe

Leadership is closely linked to change in its broadest sense through the elements identified earlier: influence, group and goals. Most contemporary leadership scholars trace the current resurgence of interest in leadership to the prevailing concern with change – its scope, its pace, its duration and its consequences – across all economic sectors. Leaders are seen as creators of change, as innovators and initiators of action; and in times of change and uncertainty there appears to be both a heightened need for leadership and an expectation that those in senior positions will provide leadership. The academic world is no exception, as can be seen in the calls to strengthen institutional leadership in order to effect desired change – in numbers and kinds of students, in curricula, in the quality and diversity of provision – both in Britain and elsewhere (Fisher, 1984; Kerr, 1984; Lockwood and Davies, 1985; Sizer, 1987).

The kind of leadership which is often projected as necessary for the academic world in response to the changes identified above is, in essence, a transformational one where emphasis is placed on vision and a clear sense of direction, on building a corporate culture around common purposes, on political acumen, charisma and risk-taking. Top-down, proactive initiatives are seen as central to this process. Many of the environmental elements that affect the private sector, such as increasingly competitive markets, tight resource constraints and emphases on quality, are now reproduced in the higher education sector so that models of management and leadership drawn from the private sector are hailed as relevant and useful.

Yet leadership, if disconnected from the occupancy of position, is crucially linked to the idea of 'taking people with you' and of building commitment, enthusiasm and trust in the directions and strategies proposed. This aspect of leadership has often been ignored in the rush to increase managerial efficiency, or to respond to government initiatives such as large-scale expansion of the system (without increasing staff numbers and often without adequately supporting existing staff), as reports of low staff morale in some institutions, both old and new universities, bear witness (NATFHE, 1992). To use Davies's (1985) dimensions of leadership, there is a need in times of change and uncertainty to combine:

> strategic policies (which describe the shape, size, philosophy, and na-
> ture of the university); tactical or substantive policies (which focus on
> areas like curricula, personnel, finance, research, facilities); and clima-
> tic policies (which are designed to create an atmosphere of openness,
> trust and goodwill, without which policy formation in the other two
> areas is much more difficult).
>
> (Davies, 1985: 76)

Davies's three policy dimensions have much in common with Kotter's (1990) argument (outlined in Chapter 2) that in the current environment, organizations require management and leadership in parallel, as two complementary systems of action, in order to cope both with increased complexity within the organization and in its external environment, and with accelerating change. The leadership component of these twin organizational pillars consists of establishing vision and direction, building commitment through communication and negotiation about collective goals, and providing support and inspiration to address and overcome the barriers to change. The management component includes the familiar elements of planning and budgeting, organizing and staffing, controlling and problem-solving, which produce a necessary degree of predictability, consistency and order required both by internal constituencies and external stakeholders of the university.

Another important aspect of leadership is its relationship to values and to culture. The message from the literature is that leaders either recognize the existing culture and seek to interpret and represent its values through their words and deeds, or aim to change the organization's culture in order to achieve necessary shifts in attitudes and practices. However, there is some evidence (from within higher education in the USA) that university presidents in institutions in crisis who have operated initially by conforming to organizational culture have been more successful in achieving transformational *effects* than those who have operated in an entirely 'transformational' fashion from the outset (Bensimon, 1989). Where cultures are deep-rooted, as in many academic institutions, it would seem to be more profitable to work with the grain to achieve change than to work against it.

The environment in which universities currently operate is different from twenty years ago (and radically different from earlier centuries) in at least three major ways. First, higher education is perceived to be linked more closely to 'national security' than ever before (both at the level of the economic well-being of the nation as a whole and in terms of individual economic security). Second, and as a consequence of the first point, there are many more people who aspire or expect to participate in higher education, thus necessarily changing its character. Third, connected with both of these points, there is far greater external concern and interest, particularly from government, about the management and governance of higher education and in the nature of what is offered by higher education. The resource question is at one and the same time foreground and background to this picture.

The pressures of the external environment have implications for both the external and the internal face of leadership at all levels of the institution. In essence, the leadership task consists of reshaping the university in the light of the demands of the future while remaining true to what is of enduring value from the past. The task requires both symbolic and substantive actions, preferably in harmony with each other. For example, at institutional level, the rituals and ceremonies which express the values of the university need to be respected and reinterpreted for internal audiences while also being communicated appropriately to external constituencies. At the same time, funding opportunities need to be sought, political networks created, key appointments made, new policies drafted and new systems put in place to provide a framework in which the institution can reposition itself – as a tanker is slowly manoeuvred.

Inevitably, the leadership task will also involve challenging existing practices, modes of thought or academic areas that no longer fit the direction proposed. In order to generate the necessary momentum for change (whether that involves steaming ahead in line with the existing institutional direction or turning towards other compass points), a variety of constituencies must now be satisfied and a number of others challenged. To achieve this, signals must be sent or interpreted in a language that is appropriate to the concerns of each group. The language of cost-efficiency, value-for-money, audit, competition and performance indicators is not the same as that of intellectual development, value-for-life, professionalism, collaboration and reputation among peers. Leadership involves translating and interpreting these different languages (and the modes of thought and of practice which are attached to them) to those constituencies that must now communicate and cooperate with each other. It will also involve taking hard decisions about those values and practices which should be retained and those which will need adaptation.

Like learning, where new understandings are achieved by making links with existing knowledge, leadership requires an understanding of the present position as well as the future goals so that connections can be made with existing conceptual maps. To effect change, a sense of dissonance with the present combined with an excitement about the future must be created so that a debate can be opened in which the desirable and the possible are illuminated alongside the necessary and feasible steps to their achievement. Again like learning, a balance must be maintained between challenge and support. A 'push–pull' strategy, which is responsive to the needs of individuals and groups, and which is based on goodwill and mutual respect more than coercion or bribery, is likely to be necessary at different levels of the institution.

The leadership function will differ subtly at different levels of the institution. For example, at institutional level, establishing the boundaries and the ground-rules for the debate will be a key task alongside interpretation and questioning of the status quo, while for individual members of the university, the task will be to create and test new ideas, examine solutions to problems and provide feedback on successes and failures. The leadership responsibility at departmental level involves providing support and challenge in a number of ways: providing time and space for individual and group initiative, offering psychological and financial encouragement and acting as a conduit between institutional and individual levels. The push–pull notion is likely to apply at all levels of the university as collectively and individually the tides of independence (or autonomy) and responsiveness to the priorities of others ebb and flow.

Summary

The discussion in this chapter has a number of strands that need drawing together, not least because they provide a link between Part 1 of this book, which was concerned with ideas about leadership, and Part 2, which focuses on leadership in practice.

I have argued, first, that leadership is particularly associated with change and with values, and second, that change, as well as a struggle over values, is part of the higher education agenda in a number of areas. My third point is that leadership can assist the process of change, both by supporting and challenging individuals and groups and by developing academic opportunities to meet the expectations of a new era. The core of my argument is that universities operate in a changing environment where the boundaries of the known and the valued are no longer clear or certain: in a physical sense, where and how teachers and learners operate and with what resources; in a cognitive sense, what is taught, researched and learned, for what and for whose purposes; in an emotional sense, who I am as a teacher, learner, researcher or manager, what my role and my contribution are, what power I will have or lose, who will judge me and how, what I must protect or surrender. It is part of the responsibilities of leadership to address such questions and to seek appropriate answers.

A further strand in my argument concerns the approach to leadership that is chosen in response to change. In earlier chapters, differing conceptions of leadership and their organizational fit have been explored. In this chapter, I have suggested that although transformational *effects* may be required (in some though not all institutions, or in parts of institutions) a purely transformational approach may not be successful or necessary except in certain circumstances. Transformational approaches, though exciting, will experience difficulties in universities since the notion of corporateness is often problematic; because charisma – or hype – is likely to encounter scepticism among academics; and because high risk strategies adopted by publicly funded institutions are unlikely to be eagerly welcomed by 'the taxpayer' or his or her representatives.

Instead, leadership should aim to take people forward with their consent and commitment, while recognizing the existence of conflicting views and a range of different constituencies. Such an approach has been presented here in a variety of ways: in terms of attention to substance as well as symbolism in leadership; in terms of levels of policy formation, strategic, tactical and climatic; as a distinction between leadership and management action; and finally in terms of the scope of leadership at different levels of the institution. An analogy was drawn between leadership of this kind and learning, where support and challenge are needed in combination.

Overall, the importance of communication in its widest sense must be stressed. Attention needs to be given to the culture and language of different groups; to the messages sent by the policies and systems which are put in place; to the signals received through those areas of institutional life, or people, that are accorded priority status.

Highlighting communication and culture as essential features of leadership brings us back to the first part of this chapter, where the idea of leadership was examined against a background of some of the historic traditions of academe. While change dominates the university system today, it should not be forgotten that transitions must coexist with stability, particularly in universities where cycles of activity proceed over a lengthy timeframe. It was argued that leadership could be found in the academic world in earlier times and this argument can be extended to present-day academic life, where transactional leadership is required on a day-to-day basis, supplemented by elements of transformational leadership. Leadership is necessary for guiding and developing disciplinary and teaching directions; it is also relevant to the development and implementation of research programmes. Leadership is involved in the interpretation of values, in the representation of collective purposes and interests. It is also needed to facilitate, stimulate and focus individual and group effort in universities, as much as in other organizations.

Part 2

Practising Leadership

Part 2

Producing Educational...

5

Institutional Leaders

Introduction

The first part of this book has focused on the idea of leadership and its interpretation within a particular organizational setting. Now we turn to consider the practice of leadership, first at institutional level in this chapter and then at other levels in subsequent chapters.

The cast here is made up of senior academic leaders and managers, Vice Chancellors and Pro Vice Chancellors. The chorus is provided by other groups: lay members of Council, Heads of Department and Deans, academic and administrative staff, clerical and technical staff, who offer views about leadership from an internal institutional perspective. External expectations, although more diffuse, can be discerned from reports, government White Papers and Funding Council memoranda.

The evidence for this chapter was gleaned largely from a research study into the changing roles of senior university staff (Middlehurst *et al.*, 1992) conducted before the 'old' universities in the UK were joined by the 'new' through the Further and Higher Education Act 1992. The structures and cultures of the two kinds of universities are different so that examples drawn from the old cannot be matched exactly in the new universities. However, many of the underlying principles will be valid, and where they are not, the variations between the leadership practices of the two types of institution can provide useful comparisons and opportunities for reflecting on the causes of difference.

In our study, institutional leadership was investigated along four dimensions. First, we examined the responsibilities of senior staff within a formal structure, that is, those aspects of leadership that are closely associated with 'position'. Second, we investigated personal interpretations of senior staff roles held by those occupying the senior institutional posts, thus adopting a subjectivist perspective on leadership. This latter perspective was continued in our third strategy, when we explored the expectations of senior staff roles held by others (within and outside the institution). Our fourth dimension concentrated upon relationships between positions, both formal – within the committee structure – and informal, for example within the 'senior management group'. In each case, the data were drawn from individual and group interviews and from documentary material. Evidence from the first three dimensions are presented in this chapter, while the fourth perspective, which considers collective roles and their relationship to institutional leadership, is discussed in Chapter 6.

The four dimensions of our framework were based on different analyses of 'role' (Biddle and Thomas, 1966; Mintzberg, 1973; Ribbins, 1985), which also allowed us to take account of different interpretations of the organization. For example, by examining the formal aspects of a role identified in formal responsibilities, duties and structures, a bureaucratic perspective was revealed. A political or collegial perspective emerged through analysing the nature of informal interactions between individuals and groups at senior level, while a cybernetic or entrepreneurial perspective was evident when respondents discussed the day-to-day nature of their managerial and leadership tasks.

The chapter will be divided into sections that follow the lines of our enquiry: functions and responsibilities; personal interpretations of role; perceptions and expectations of leadership from interested 'others'. The cast and the chorus will be on stage here, commanding most of our attention. However, the lights will also be turned on to the background scenery in order to illuminate conceptions of university leadership in the late twentieth century. An understanding of these conceptions is integral to the successful performance of the whole play.

The Vice Chancellor

Responsibilities and activities

The charters and statutes of British universities (established before 1992) are similar in identifying and legitimising the position of Vice Chancellor as head of the institution. In recent appointment details (1987–90) for the post of Vice Chancellor, the position is described variously as chief academic officer, principal academic and administrative officer, or chief executive of the university, reflecting the jostling collegial/professional and bureaucratic/managerial perspectives of the traditional university. These are again visible in the formal responsibilities of the post.

Within the statutes, the Vice Chancellor's duties and authority are only briefly outlined. They include a general responsibility (to the University Council or Governing Body) for 'maintaining and promoting the efficiency and good order of the university'; various committee responsibilities – as Chairman or *ex-officio* member – and authority for admitting, disciplining and excluding students from the university. The appointment details come little closer to a job description, only highlighting some of the recent additions to the Vice Chancellor's role, recommended particularly in the Jarratt Report (CVCP, 1985), but also emerging out of a changing external context.

Reference is made to the Vice Chancellor's financial responsibilities as Chief Accounting Officer for the university, to his or her academic leadership role as Chairman of Senate and to the internal and external representative role, respectively: to Council on behalf of the academic interests of the university, and within the local region and at national level on behalf of the university and its interests as a whole.

The Jarratt Report stressed the importance of the institutional leader, arguing that the Vice Chancellor's effectiveness 'is absolutely crucial to the success of the institution' (3.55: 26). One of the Report's main purposes was to increase the formal authority vested in the role, a move which can also be seen in the USA, where the 1980s witnessed many calls to strengthen presidential leadership (Keller, 1983; Fisher, 1984).

When outlining their tasks and duties, Vice Chancellors in our research sample drew attention to their internal and external functions. Internally, the committees were seen as the main vehicles through which the Vice Chancellor exercised responsibilities for strategic planning; academic development and direction; consultation, communication and negotiation with a variety of constituencies; and monitoring, regulation and steerage of the university. At the same time, the committees were seen to represent the university's collective responsibility for particular areas of decision-making. A number of the organizational images that were outlined in Chapter 3 are reflected here: from bureaucratic, through collegial and political, to cybernetic.

Some committee responsibilities were common to all Vice Chancellors (although the titles of committees differed): for example, chairmanship of Senate, of the Planning and Resources Committee (the focus for integrated academic, financial and physical planning), the Establishment Board (staffing levels), Professorial Appointments and Salaries, and the Honorary Degrees committee. Beyond these, Vice Chancellors also attended – or had the right to attend – other key committees associated with policy-making and performance, such as Council and Court (governance functions), Finance and General Purposes Committee (resource allocation), Academic Planning (academic direction and development), Estates and Buildings (plant and fabric responsibilities), Joint Consultative Committees (industrial and constituency relations) and Staff Review Committees (personnel performance: policy and evaluation).

External duties, which have increased in scale and importance over the past fifteen years, are exercised on several levels. The first level incorporates activities which are linked closely to the material and academic needs of the individual institution. Here, the Vice Chancellor will engage in public relations and representation, political lobbying, fund-raising, negotiation (over contracts and endowments) and liaison (for example, with community groups, health authorities or other educational establishments). Many of these activities will involve the building of 'thick informal networks' to use Kotter's phrase (1990: 89) as well as the interpretation of external trends and the development of commercial and academic opportunities.

Within the Committee of Vice Chancellors and Principals (CVCP), Vice Chancellors exercise another aspect of external leadership as they play a part in the governance of the national university system. However, this level is often less straightforward than the first level above, since there are obvious tensions between the unique requirements of one institution and the collective needs of the system as a whole.

Third, for some Vice-Chancellors, the external role also involved 'educational leadership' on a broader front, through representation, elucidation and promotion of educational values on a national and international stage. And beyond this, some Vice Chancellors carried national and international consultancy commitments which they had acquired on a personal basis through their professional reputation as much as through their position as chief executive.

In their daily round, Vice Chancellors reported a full agenda. Apart from the chairing of committees and other formal gatherings, meetings of other kinds were part of the everyday routine: management meetings for exchanging information, for delegating and reporting, for discussing policy and devising implementation tactics; *ad hoc* task forces for initiating new developments and ideas; problem-solving meetings for dealing with grievances, crises, conflicts and difficulties between individuals and groups. Large amounts of paperwork were a further feature of the role: reading and analysing, preparing and writing reports, articles, speeches, committee papers and other administrative material. Ceremonial and social activities were also important, from the hosting of degree ceremonies, inaugural lectures and the opening of conferences to the attending of a variety of social events as host or guest. Many of these formal and informal activities necessarily involved time spent in travelling.

The pace, intensity and range of activities involved in the role of Vice Chancellor are comparable to strategic leadership in other contexts (Harvey-Jones, 1988). In common with other sectors, the task is both internal and external and has both a short-term and a long-term perspective. In terms of leadership, the role also has both an instrumental and a symbolic dimension in that the Vice Chancellor must actively engage in certain aspects of institutional life (for example, the chairing of professorial appointments committees or planning and resources committee meetings) and must be seen to engage in others (for example, the opening of a new building or the hosting of a reception for the mayor). The instrumental aspects of the role may be expected to have a direct impact on institutional functioning while the symbolic aspects have a less direct, but no less important, impact in demonstrating that the university is working in ways that are expected of it both by internal and external constituencies. The actions of the Vice Chancellor symbolize these expectations and positively or negatively reflect their fulfilment. We can see these different dimensions in more detail by exploring Vice Chancellors' own interpretations of their role.

Personal interpretations

Vice Chancellors drew attention to their priorities and personal aims, to the balance between internal and external activities, to their own success criteria and to the ways in which they exercised their role. For the majority of Vice Chancellors in our sample, priorities and success criteria were seen in terms of academic achievements and institutional positioning, the development of internal morale, and the maintenance of financial viability. In the words of one Vice Chancellor: 'The most important things I do are to position the University for 1995, to see that the finances are OK and to appoint the right professors because they stand for their subject.' This theme is echoed by another: 'I see my principal role as being to enhance the academic excellence of the university consistent with financial probity. I seek to attract the best students, the best staff, research money, to establish good relationships with the community and to make the books balance.' A third comment highlighted both action and style, while also exhibiting interpretive features of the role: 'I see my role as being to give clear direction to the university, to move forward by consensus where possible and to take maximum advantage of external opportunities when they arise, to find out exactly what is going on, what the words mean, who will decide and what is likely to happen.'

The declared aims and objectives of individual Vice Chancellors varied between the highly specific – changing the top structure, lightening the committee load, creating an Institute of Technology or Short Course Centre – to the general – giving confidence to staff and students, laying emphasis on the institution as a place of creative scholarship, establishing contacts to attract funds, 'trying to get the creativity and responsiveness right'. In judging the success of these aims, Vice Chancellors looked to internal and external indicators, of a hard (numerical) or soft (qualitative) kind. For example, hard indicators included increased research activity and external research ratings, while soft indicators included positioning the institution or encouraging creativity and innovation, demonstrated through external image, new developments, reputation and level of public interest in the institution.

In Birnbaum's study of the American college presidency, very similar findings were reported (Birnbaum, 1990). The author identified two major types of indicator by which presidents assessed their effectiveness: institutional performance and constituent satisfaction. In both cases presidents collected or received information from a variety of sources in order to judge their own performance, but relied in the main on personal interpretations of what they saw and heard rather than on other more formal or structured evaluations.

Following the pattern of Birnbaum's study, success (or lack of it), our Vice Chancellors felt, could only be judged some years ahead. Yet even at that point, assessments may be troublesome since the impact of individual Vice Chancellors on university achievements and outcomes is not only difficult to measure but is also difficult to interpret. As Birnbaum (1989a) suggests, successful outcomes may be attributed by campus constituents to effective

presidential leadership because of the visibility, prominence and expectations of 'the leader' rather than because of any significant acts on his or her
part. For Birnbaum, leadership may therefore be as much symbolic as real in
the university context – a point that we shall return to in a moment.

Variations in activities, style and areas of attention could be discerned
among the Vice Chancellors in our sample, owing to a number of factors,
such as: individual personality, personal choice and past experience; length
of time in office; size, culture and institutional circumstance; and balance of
interests and expertise among senior officers.

For some, external activities were the key to the Vice-Chancellorship
(often increasing with length of time in office). For others, greater emphasis
was placed on the internal roles of academic and administrative leader,
particularly at the start of their tenure when acquiring an understanding of
the university's staff, the range of internal constituency interests and the
variety of activities that were part of the university's remit was all-important.
Particular circumstances such as an industrial dispute or an unpopular political visitor also drew the Vice Chancellor's attention to internal matters.

Styles of decision-making and levels of interaction with individuals and
groups also varied, from predominantly directive and autocratic to cooperative and facilitative. Time and circumstance clearly produced variations
across a spectrum. In some cases the size of the institution made the Vice
Chancellor a more distant figure; in others, distance was maintained as a
feature of individual style. Although reports of these 'espoused' leadership
styles (cf. Argyris and Schon, 1974, 1978) are made here on the basis of Vice
Chancellors' own interpretations, the data collected from different categories of staff provide evidence of leadership styles 'in use'.

Where Vice Chancellors chose to elucidate upon their approaches to
institutional leadership, a number of points emerged. The nature of academic organizations was mentioned frequently as a consideration in Vice
Chancellors' leadership styles. The elements highlighted included: the variety of legitimate, but often conflicting, goals of universities; the variety of
internal and external constituencies; and the divided loyalties of academic
staff (to discipline and department rather than institution). The particular
characteristics of academic staff as a cultural group, conscious of their individuality, reputation and contribution to knowledge, were also noted. According to Vice Chancellors in our study, these features had implications for
leadership, acting as a constraint on the 'power to command' represented in
the title of Chief Executive and making the exercise of leadership a matter of
persuasion, negotiation and influence, achieved through the building of
trust and the development of consensus where possible, but also relying on
the political processes of barter, exchange and even threat. The following
comments demonstrate some of these influence strategies; they also point to
the importance of informal systems and networks within institutions:

> I believe that almost all information can be shared. This creates trust,
> therefore one can get away with things much more easily when necess-

ary . . . I tend to ignore the structures and go to individuals to get things done. This doesn't always work, it maintains internal cohesion but one can only push with the consensus. Here one cannot announce decisions, the process must be iterative; every academic development must be discussed, internal supporters must be identified . . . Achieving consensus is an important part of my style. I could achieve things faster by being more directive, but it is not worth it. I back off and wait if there is likely to be a storm.

(Vice Chancellor of a small university)

When the group of four senior staff have agreed that a course of action is in the best interests of the university and in line with the strategic plan – and if it is known that there are vested interests involved – the background explanation will be given to those who may be affected, in the form of an informal chat. It may be desirable to suggest that one could offset those who might be disadvantaged by one course of action by some compensating action on another matter . . . or it may be necessary to be more direct: without their support the taking of this course of action might be potentially harmful for them.

(Vice Chancellor of a medium-sized institution)

Birnbaum (1989a: 37–40) takes a more pessimistic view of the institutional leader's 'responsibility without authority', arguing that the presidency is an impossible job. Environmental constraints (state controls and directives, paucity of resources) limit the president's freedom of manoeuvre. Additionally, organizational factors (the dual academic and administrative structures) place incompatible demands and expectations on the president. And within institutions, the existence of conflicting goals, increasing fragmentation into interest groups, and the static nature of the personnel complement of the American university, impose still further constraints on presidential discretion. Because of these limitations (which have echoes in the current British context), Birnbaum argues that presidential leadership is more illusory than real, but that its symbolic features are crucial. In his words: 'It may be so vital, for symbolic reasons, for organizational members to believe that their leaders are important that both leaders and followers may cope with the reality of weak presidents' influence by constructing an illusion of power' (Birnbaum, 1989a: 51).

In the next section, we shall consider the perceptions of leadership expressed by members of institutions. The data support Birnbaum's contention that strong expectations of leadership exist within academic institutions, despite the real structural, political and economic constraints on the exercise of leadership. However, in contrast to Birnbaum, I would draw more optimistic conclusions about the prospects for leadership in universities. While fully acknowledging the importance of symbolic (and cultural) aspects of leadership within the role of the Vice Chancellor and senior management group, the current environment of change, with its 'quality, accountability and entrepreneurial' pressures, also requires substantive leadership at many levels of the institution. Furthermore, where there are strong expectations of leadership, which are subsequently met, the ground is laid for further action of a similar kind so that leaders and 'followers' expectations feed upon each other in a mutually self-reinforcing cycle. What is critical, of course, is the kind of leadership that is created through this process of mutual interaction and the extent to which it fits the culture, context and circumstances of the particular institution.

Expectations and perceptions of institutional leadership

External expectations of the Vice Chancellorship can be seen from reports, funding council memoranda, legislation and government White Papers. As head of a largely publicly funded institution, invested with important economic and social responsibilities, the Vice Chancellor is held accountable for the delivery of institutional efficiency and effectiveness. These external expectations have become increasingly strong in the second half of the twentieth century (Pollitt, 1990; Tapper and Salter, 1992).

Such external pressures are reflected in the appointment details sent to prospective candidates for the position of Vice Chancellor, at least in those cases where the desiderata were spelt out. The characteristics sought included the following: the ability to promote and develop the institution; a capacity to meet challenges; a proven record of effective management skills; the ability to build collaborative relationships with outside agencies and to represent the university externally; a creative vision and the ability to communicate it.

A number of skills were also mentioned: entrepreneurial and innovation skills, analytical and financial skills, policy making and strategic planning skills, public relations and negotiating skills. In these documents, leadership of an academic community also featured strongly, presented in terms of 'having an established academic reputation' or 'the ability to command the respect of academics'. Very few documents mentioned interpersonal skills (although these figure prominently in many conceptions of leadership and in the expectations of internal constituencies). Where interpersonal skills were mentioned, they referred to an ability to develop working relationships with Deans and Heads of Department, the capacities to lead and be part of a team and the Vice Chancellor's responsibility for acting as the main link between Senate, Council and the lay officers.

Formal expectations of institutional leadership thus present an amalgam of different conceptions of leadership, although trait, behavioural and power and influence approaches predominate. It is instructive to compare these with the expectations of internal constituencies.

Among senior staff, certain differences of view can be detected. Lay members of Council or Court placed most emphasis on the Vice Chancellor's responsibility for vision and direction, for positioning and accountability and for change and development of the institution. The importance of students and the quality of teaching were also of concern to this group.

Pro Vice Chancellors highlighted the Vice Chancellor's role as final arbiter, ultimate authority and decision-maker on behalf of the institution. They were also sensitive to the leader's responsibilities for strategy, direction and tone, as well as external liaison and fund-raising. Senior administrators echoed these views of leadership responsibilities, drawing attention to the need for hard decisions at a time of financial constraint and for the establishment of clear policies and direction for the institution. As a group, senior officers placed particular emphasis on team leadership (and the Vice Chancellor's role in its achievement), the interpretation and articulation of university values and interests and the motivation and encouragement of staff.

Some comments from Pro Vice Chancellors will serve to illustrate these dimensions and they also demonstrate that leadership is often seen as a collective rather than individual responsibility at institutional level. Embedded in these comments there are again different conceptions of leadership: in these instances, symbolic, transformational and political perspectives can be identified, as well as trait and behavioural assumptions.

Leadership involves openness, decisiveness, the ability to exercise judgement; the identification of university goals; setting a climate and operating style; interaction with people and direction through a team.

Leadership is a question of style. It involves instilling optimism. It includes representation and being a figurehead, visibility, gaining views and consulting, defining policy, interpreting and articulating collective goals and purposes. It is about the perception of needs, beliefs and aspirations, about creating climate, it is a political process.

Leadership is about getting others' ideas, enabling others to do things, motivating, directing, guiding. It involves an interest in people and an ability to release people's energies, an ability to encourage and support people and to be firm.

If we turn to other categories of staff, it is clear that at all levels and among all groups, expectations of the Vice Chancellor's leadership role exist, although detailed knowledge of specific tasks is not present at lower or more junior levels. There is a surprising degree of overlap in perceptions of leadership activities and responsibilities, although a variety of images – from hero to servant – can be seen:

The Vice Chancellor needs to be felt around the place and we need to know that we are being spoken for in the right places . . . he needs to be accessible . . . . Both internal and external roles are important, but the external one nowadays is the vital one. We need someone who is going to lead this university into the outside world, who is going to be our spokesman, our presenter, our safeguard and who is going to tell the outside world what we are wanting to do.

(Head of Department)

The Vice Chancellor's role is to define a corporate image and direction; he must get everyone to feel they share some common purpose. He must help the university to take advantage of new opportunities and must satisfy those within the institution. He must represent the interests of those within the institution and represent government's interests to those within; he must interact with other Vice Chancellors. He must be a figurehead and chairman of Senate, a chief executive, but not involved in detailed issues.

(Member of academic staff)

The Vice Chancellor's job is to decide where the university is heading and to ensure that his university gets sufficient funding and personnel and to make sure that the policy decisions that are made are carried out . . . The Vice Chancellor is also the main spokesperson for the entire university to the outside world . . . He is the PR man. He is like a president with his fingers in a lot of pies. He needs a group of advisers around him who will give him sound advice and on whom he can rely. But the buck stops at his desk.

(Chief Technician)

Leadership of the university involves overall responsibility for whatever goes on in the university; giving direction; following advice; being a human person (able to relate to the lowest or the highest), approachable through channels of communication.

(Member of clerical staff)

The Vice Chancellor's representative role as figurehead, ambassador and interpreter is evident here, as well as his or her role in establishing strategy, direction and climate. External liaison and fund-raising feature in expectations, as does academic leadership, both in relation to the institution as a whole (its academic direction and development) and to departments/ faculties (in terms of understanding their academic interests and activities, showing sympathy for their problems and offering appropriate guidance and support). There was recognition, especially from heads of department, of the difficulty of balancing internal and external roles, particularly as the latter increases in importance. To manage the many competing claims on Vice Chancellors, a number of different strategies were offered: skill in delegation, effective management systems and support; and strategic rather than tactical involvement by the Vice Chancellor in the detail of university operations, allowing faculties, departments and units to manage their own affairs with commensurate authority.

Views on the match between constituency expectations (and ideals) of leadership and the reality in each institution varied across the universities in our sample. Some Vice Chancellors were perceived as too much concerned with internal managerial detail, others were thought to have achieved an appropriate balance, while others still were reported as having yet to prove themselves as effective external spokesmen (or women).

Leadership profiles also differed, some Vice Chancellors clearly having a good reputation with internal constituents, others a more tarnished image. Where the profile was negative, it was associated (particularly by Heads of Department) with a sense of being isolated from the centre of power; of not being consulted by senior management in matters of concern to them; of being poorly supported from the centre and impotent to influence university strategy. Sometimes problems were associated with an absentee Vice Chancellor (preoccupied with the external role), with a 'meddlesome' internal stance or with interpersonal difficulties. Poor communication from the centre was a particular source of grievance (or lack of agreement with the content or style of communications from this source), together with a perceived lack of consultation over mission statements and strategic plans. Closely related to favourable images of institutional leadership was the sense of 'a corporate spirit' within the institution, whereas less favourable perceptions drew attention instead to divided territories and the prominence of sectional interests.

It is important to be cautious about these reported comments and perceptions since they are not balanced by evidence of university achievements (or failures) from the institutions surveyed. However, they do give us an insight into the criteria of successful leadership held by Vice Chancellors and also illustrate the strength and range of general expectations which are woven into the fabric of university leadership roles. The systematic collection of feedback from different categories of staff provides useful information for assessing the impact of leadership strategies on internal groups.

Vice Chancellors' leadership roles

The data collected from different sources and identified above suggest that the Vice Chancellor's role can be divided into five key elements, which we will explore in turn before going on to consider some of the other actors and their parts on the institutional stage. These five elements fall particularly into two areas of leadership, namely academic and administrative leadership, both of which are directly concerned with the running of the university. The third area that some Vice Chancellors were involved in, that of educational leadership, is a further dimension, but one that tends to be more directly associated with the personal position and reputation of the Vice Chancellor than with his or her role as head of the institution.

Clarifying and determining direction

Whether seen from an interpretive/symbolic perspective where members of the institution expect a leader to assist in making sense of an equivocal, turbulent world, or from a linear perspective, where the leader's vision is regarded as the blueprint for institutional direction and strategy, there exists a clear expectation that Vice Chancellors will develop a broad view of the university based on its current position, constraints and potential opportunities.

They are in an unique position to develop such a picture of the whole enterprise, which will then provide a basis for establishing institutional direction.

The 'vision' which may feature formally in mission statements and strategic plans, is usually developed through wide consultation, observation, analysis and review within and outside the university. It is not generally the Vice Chancellor's personal masterplan – and where it is perceived as such, collective ownership is unlikely to occur. Instead, the vision is usually an amalgam of goals and aspirations from all parts of the institution, formed with an eye to external circumstances and adjusted in the interests of the likely success of the whole. The Vice Chancellor is perceived to have a particular responsibility for enabling the vision to be created (and his or her personal stamp may clearly be upon it); for carrying the vision forward through a commitment of effort, ideas, resources and attention to strategic priorities; and for adjusting these priorities in the light of changing circumstances. In the words of one Vice Chancellor: 'Leadership is about vision. It is about persuading most of the people most of the time; it is about getting others to articulate their goals clearly, acquiring information and advising people about opportunities.'

Positioning the institution

A particular concern of lay members of Council as well as some Vice Chancellors, the 'positioning' element of the leadership role involves promoting the status of the university in the wider world and giving the institution a distinctive image or market niche. The financial viability and academic reputation of the institution are important ingredients in positioning it within the wider national (and international) university system. A range of strategies help to meet the challenge, including: the establishment or adjustment of internal systems (for resource allocation or quality assurance); the acquisition, monitoring and optimization of resources, financial, material and human; and the acquisition, synthesis and dissemination of relevant information to enable opportunities to be exploited. Appointing and supporting staff is a key element in 'positioning', as is the building of effective internal and external relationships. Positioning is closely linked to the creation of a vision and direction through the development of strategic priorities; it demonstrates the overlap between leadership and management action at institutional level. Targeting an appropriate position and building commitment to reaching – or surpassing – it requires leadership. Achieving and maintaining that position depends on effective management.

In common with many other aspects of leadership at institutional level, contributions to the activities involved in 'positioning' are made by many individuals and groups in the university. The Vice Chancellor's particular contribution lies in stimulating those activities and initiating some of them.

Improving the climate through communication

The development of a positive and creative ethos within the university is also seen as falling directly within the Vice Chancellor's ambit. The process was regarded as particularly important by senior staff, from both a psychological and a political perspective. They emphasized the need to maintain morale, to gain support for new initiatives, to reduce fear of change and to cushion the impact of cuts in staffing or activities. Informing, consulting, listening and persuading all form part of the creation of climate as well as being part of the political process associated with policy formulation and implementation. A comment from one Vice Chancellor gives a flavour of this aspect of leadership:

> Leadership involves setting a tone and a style, setting objectives and being involved in strategic thinking; identifying good ideas and relevant issues; it includes articulating and interpreting the university's purpose, its beliefs and values and setting a path to achieve the above.

Decision-taking and adjudication

The Vice Chancellor was frequently identified in our study as the ultimate arbiter and decision-taker, with authority to commit the university to a particular course of action on behalf of Senate and Council, or with the power to support or block particular initiatives, to set the institutional agenda or to define institutional priorities. These views reflect a managerial frame of reference, whereas the Vice Chancellor's task of mediation between conflicting territories and constituencies (administrators and academics, for example), which is another aspect of adjudication, constitutes a political imperative.

The Vice Chancellor must also maintain a balance between conflicting forces: preservation and innovation (in terms of disciplinary areas, activities or university values); equity and selectivity (in resource allocation terms or in relation to cuts in activities or personnel); centralization and decentralization (of managerial authority and control); and challenge and support (for individuals and groups facing changes in practice). Here decision-taking can be seen in a cybernetic perspective, as steering a path through rocky waters where manoeuvrability is limited and where adjustments in charting a course are important in arriving safely at one's destination.

Institutional representation

Institutional representation has two faces, which look, Janus-like, in different directions as the Vice Chancellor manages the boundary between two worlds. Public relations, lobbying and reporting serve to promote, explain and account for the university to external audiences. Internally, the Vice Chancellor is expected to describe and interpret the purpose, values and mission of the university within a system of higher education and in relation to the demands of the wider environment. These features of the role can be interpreted simultaneously as symbolic, in that the Vice Chancellor legitimates the activities of others and acts as figurehead and beacon for the university; and as bureaucratic, since the Vice Chancellor must report and account for the university's activities in legal and financial, as well as in promotional, terms.

As was mentioned earlier, the full exercise of institutional leadership is not only achieved through the actions of the Vice Chancellor. The expansion of expectations and pressures from internal, but predominantly external sources has made the notion of collective leadership more necessary and more obvious, not only at institutional level but throughout the university. For the present, the spotlight will be kept on the institutional level by examining the part played by Pro Vice Chancellors on the leadership stage.

Pro Vice Chancellors

Formal responsibilities

Unlike the Vice Chancellor's position, which is clearly recognizable to internal and external audiences, with similarities across universities as well as parallels in other organizations, the role of the Pro Vice Chancellor (PVC) is an ambiguous and unusual organizational role, subject to different interpretations in different universities.

According to traditional university statutes, the role is identified as the Vice Chancellor's understudy, with authority to assist the Vice Chancellor with 'whatever he or she delegates or entrusts to them'. Pro Vice Chancellors are usually senior members of academic staff, appointed on a temporary (and often part-time) basis for three to five years. Some universities have a full-time Senior PVC or Deputy VC, others operate a part-time, rotational senior and junior system between three or four deputies.

The Jarratt Report (1985: 3.63, 27) presented a clearer view of the role than can be obtained from university Statutes and Ordinances:

> Normally [the Pro Vice Chancellors] are senior professors who are given a reduced teaching load during their period of office. The Study Reports make it clear that they are not line managers. Much of their role depends on how the Vice Chancellor chooses to use them. Often they are given particular tasks in developing academic policy. At other times they are obviously valuable as trouble-shooters. But they are also a vital part of the mechanism for policy co-ordination in that they frequently have ex-officio membership of the key committees. They play an important part in the formal processes of policy development and co-ordination through regular meetings with the Vice Chancellor and the Registrar.

Personal interpretations

Pro Vice Chancellors described their own role in terms of their tasks and duties and the time spent in the role, their levels of discretion and success criteria. In addition, a number of issues were raised about the current position of the deputies in an old university.

Tasks and duties varied markedly across institutions, depending largely on the Vice Chancellor's disposition and the background and experience of individual Pro Vice Chancellors. In most cases, individuals carried portfolios covering university-wide activities such as information technology, continuing education or quality assurance; in other cases, portfolios were determined by committee responsibilities. For the most part, committees were chaired by the Pro Vice Chancellors, although in one university in the sample the PVCs were members of key committees, chairmanship being the prerogative of other senior academics or the Vice Chancellor. In this instance, the PVCs offered a central university perspective in some arenas and an academic and faculty perspective elsewhere, demonstrating very clearly the ambiguous nature of their role and the different organizational conceptions underlying it.

Beyond their committee responsibilities, some Pro Vice Chancellors had responsibility for particular faculties (science and technology, arts, humanities and social science) or for particular activities or groups (research, planning and resources, student affairs). They also set up or chaired task forces and working parties; provided support for the Vice Chancellor (in the Senior Management Group and informally); represented the university at formal gatherings; carried *ad hoc* responsibilities (managing the university's anniversary arrangements, setting up departmental reviews; establishing codes of practice; dealing with Funding Council requests for information); and dealt with problems and crises.

Although (often) officially part-time, varying between 50 and 75 per cent of a full load, most Pro Vice Chancellors regarded the role as virtually full-time in terms of energy and time commitment. In the remainder of the time available to them, they concentrated on keeping up with the academic activities to which they would return at the end of their tenure; in a few cases, they also carried managerial responsibilities as head of department.

The perceived levels of discretion available to individuals varied across institutions, related to a number of factors: to the background and experience of the Pro Vice Chancellors; to their formal status within the institution (full-time Senior PVCs often had considerable managerial discretion); to individual personalities; to the competence of the Registrar and senior officers; and to the position of Deans in the institution. In many universities, as another layer of management is added in the form of 'budget centre managers' (with financial responsibilities for collections of departments or schools), the position of Pro Vice Chancellors is likely to be affected. The leadership style of the Vice Chancellor also seemed a powerful determinant of levels of discretion, some Vice Chancellors having delegated extensive authority for specific areas to their deputies, others preferring to retain authority themselves, the Pro Vice Chancellors therefore operating in an advisory capacity. In all cases, the Vice Chancellor was viewed as the ultimate arbiter in university matters, particularly in sensitive areas (for example, in dealings with powerful or disaffected individuals in the university) or in areas with significant financial or political implications.

The responsibilities of Pro Vice Chancellors straddle the areas of policy formation and policy implementation; the individuals are linked both to the academic body and to central administration; they contribute to management and leadership of the institution at both formal and informal levels; and their roles are part-time and temporary. The role and scope for discretion of the PVC is often ill-defined. It is not surprising that 'success' in the role was defined in general rather than specific terms, with an emphasis on 'oiling the wheels' and creating internal constituency satisfaction, as these comments suggest:

> I judge my success by noting the response to initiatives . . . the willingness to do what should be done, the problems that people have in trying to do what should be done, feedback on faculty boards, 'noise' from the AUT, [Association of University Teachers] structural or personal difficulties in implementation.

> [Success involves] providing an environment in which to prosper – particularly in academic areas of study; efficient management; respect for the management team; that staff remain on board and that there is income there to support them; that an academic community is created.

> Judgement is easy . . . success involves making or keeping the university the sort of place I want to be an ordinary academic in, a university to go back to happily.

Expectations and issues associated with Pro Vice Chancellor roles

It is only at senior levels of the institution that staff appear well-informed about the nature of the Pro Vice Chancellor role. Even at the level of departmental head, knowledge of the number of deputies and the content of their portfolios was limited, unless there was direct personal contact with the PVCs in departments, on committees or as academic colleagues. Administrative staff were in general more knowledgeable than academic staff about the role, lending support to the view that the duties are becoming increasingly more managerial. As one academic commented, somewhat cynically:

> Pro Vice Chancellors define their jobs very clearly as representation of the academic voice in the government and management of the university. One has the feeling that the mission is stronger at the beginning of a four-year appointment than at the end of it. They gradually get absorbed into the administrative mould.

Registrars and their senior colleagues saw the Pro Vice Chancellor's role essentially as an adjunct to that of the Vice Chancellor, assisting in the fronting of change, the evolution and steerage of policy, and the development of institutional climate through the use of informal communication networks. In addition to these dimensions, Vice Chancellors saw their PVCs as consultants and advisers.

Pro Vice Chancellors made an important contribution in presenting an academic perspective within the 'Senior Management Group' or 'inner cabinet', and within the institution, in generating ideas and in acting as a sounding board for academic views and perspectives – 'for increasing the credibility of decision-making' as one Registrar put it. Some administrators also saw the Pro Vice Chancellor's role as providing a useful check on the power of the Vice Chancellor, although as their executive authority increases, concern was expressed that Pro Vice Chancellors might equally provide a threat to the Vice Chancellor's authority (or indeed to that of the senior administrators).

In some institutions, the present ambiguity of the Pro Vice Chancellor's role, partly associated with policy development, partly with its implementation, simultaneously managerial and representative, the expansion of its managerial elements and its position as a bridgehead between two different territories (the collegial/professional and the bureaucratic/managerial) clearly creates tensions between the Pro Vice Chancellors and senior administrators. Because of the lack of structural clarity over boundaries, the position relies on teamwork and good relationships, qualities which were constantly stressed by senior administrators (although not always in evidence to other constituencies within the institution). At present, the role reflects collegial, political or 'ambiguity' characteristics of the university, although as the position evolves further (perhaps towards models of permanent academic administrators as in the 'Deputy Director' roles of the new universities), bureaucratic or cybernetic features may predominate. A comment from one senior administrator draws attention to the role as 'leadership agent' for the Vice Chancellor; a role which could fit a number of different organizational perspectives:

> The roles [of Pro Vice Chancellors and administrators] should be complementary. Personalities are important. The Pro Vice Chancellors should be easy to work with. The Pro Vice Chancellors' role is to support the Vice Chancellor with managing the institution. Their involvement creates consistency of policy. Decision-making is going on all the time through the committees. The Vice Chancellor must trust the Pro Vice Chancellors to guide and influence the committees and the Heads of Departments and Deans. The same message must be pedalled in all the fora possible . . . A good Pro Vice Chancellor is the eyes and ears of the Vice Chancellor while the Vice Chancellor is out lobbying and representing the university. If trouble is brewing, or if opportunities are building, the Pro Vice Chancellors should bring these messages back to the Vice Chancellor.

Given the complexity and diversity of academic institutions, and in particular their dual (professional and bureaucratic) hierarchy, the Pro Vice

Chancellor role serves a useful organizational function in straddling the boundary of the two domains. The temporary tenure of the position may also be useful in allowing different disciplinary backgrounds to be represented at central level.

However, as the managerial element of the job grows, and the bureaucratic demands on the institution expand, the use of part-time, short-term 'amateur managers' with divided commitments is likely to be seen as inefficient. Such inefficiency will be compounded (at least temporarily) by any further blurring of the boundaries between academic and professional managers, a feature that is evident both at institutional and departmental levels, since tensions between the two groups will increase, not least because career and reward issues are at stake. For individual Pro Vice Chancellors, there is considerable strain involved in maintaining a high academic profile as well as a heavy management load; and at present, there is little reward beyond service to the institution, for undertaking a role which is still associated with a collegial sense of academic governance. A real tension exists between individual benefits and organizational benefits. In some cases, service to the institution might be better construed solely in academic terms. In small institutions, with fewer senior staff to choose from and under the pressures of research selectivity, assessment of teaching and increasing managerialism, such a choice (between academic or managerial service) is faced frequently by potential PVCs. The academic option may seem rather more attractive and as a result, filling the Pro Vice Chancellors' role from within the institution becomes increasingly difficult.

From all categories of respondent in our study, the message about the position of the Pro Vice Chancellors was clear: the role is usually ill-defined and often ill-understood; its proper exercise relies heavily on good relationships and teamwork; and its leadership and management responsibilities are increasing. This raises a number of structural and developmental issues for institutions. We might also add that the role is in transition, as academic institutions adapt their internal systems to meet the new demands of their external environment, including the challenge of an expanded and diversified system. As has happened over centuries, new organizational features are likely to be added, incrementally, to the traditional shape of universities in order to ensure the survival of the species.

Institutional leadership in theory and in practice

The first part of the 'play' presented above, with its focus upon the practice of institutional leadership, raises a number of issues for us in the audience. The range of perspectives on leadership presented in earlier chapters and their expression within different conceptions of the institution were clearly visible in our study. Such perceptions of a university – its constituencies, circumstances and modes of operation – are likely to act as powerful determinants of the approaches to leadership adopted. One issue here is whether the choice of approach to leadership involves a conscious, systematic and collective decision or an intuitive response based on past experience and individual preference. A second might be to consider which of these strategies is likely to be most effective.

Our data reveal a separation between individual (solo) leadership and collective leadership roles, which emerged in the formal and informal expectations of Vice Chancellors, as well as in perceptions of the Pro Vice Chancellors' roles. Collective leadership in practice is likely to require consistency in the messages presented from the centre and effectiveness in teamwork at the top. A third issue that emerges here is the extent to which leadership can any longer be an individual matter, given the complexity and scale of university operations and the expansion of the leadership and management task at institutional level. Fourth, if collective leadership is indeed the way forward, the full meaning and extent of the notion of *collective* leadership needs to be explored and its implications for practice highlighted.

Distinctions were apparent in our survey between formal expectations of leadership, associated in particular with the office of Vice Chancellor, and the exercise of leadership in practice. In some cases there appeared to be little congruence between the expectations of leadership held by constituents and the activities or signals received from senior staff. While differences in the styles expected of Vice Chancellors, at different times and according to the different interests and values of groups, are to be anticipated, problems arise in the case of stronger and more widespread disagreement between staff and senior managers about the way leadership is being enacted within (and perhaps outside) the institution. A fifth issue, then, concerns the extent to which, or ways in which, 'constituency satisfaction' is actively and systematically used as a measure of leadership effectiveness by those at the top of institutions.

It is clear from our data that internal systems and structures are being altered and individual roles are being redefined, largely in response to external changes and pressures. We noted these shifts in relation to the Vice Chancellor's position, where, for example, the external and financial elements of the role have greatly increased, bringing consequent changes in power and power relationships within the institution. The Pro Vice Chancellors' role is also in transition, from representative and collegial to more directly managerial, although ambiguities are still evident, and its ultimate shape remains unclear.

Changes in structures, systems and roles have also had an impact on the internal climate of institutions. Adaptation to the pressures of the external environment has created tensions of various kinds: between the territories of 'academic' and 'administrative' managers; between collegial/professional and bureaucratic/managerial values; between the old ambiguous, fluid and implicit order and the new structured, explicit and transparent regime. The changes and tensions have implications for senior staff in that internal and external constituents demonstrate strong expectations of leadership, of both a rational and an emotional kind. Institutional heads are expected to present a strategic direction and to develop strategic priorities for the institution; a difficult task given the uncertain planning horizons for universities. Institutional leaders are also expected to interpret the impact of change and to defend institutional values and interests. This is again a difficult task since there exists a lack of consensus, particularly between internal and external constituencies, as to which values and interests are most worthy of protection.

Most of the internal restructuring that has occurred in universities is likely to have been developed through analysis, consultation and conscious action at several levels of the institution. However, other less tangible consequences of change may not have received such systematic attention; for example, shifts in the balance of power, in the pre-eminence of particular values, in the attitudes and behaviour of individuals and groups to one another, in the habits, working practices and motivations of staff at lower levels of the institution. Change – at structural and affective levels – raises further issues for leadership since both internal and external constituencies judge the effectiveness of leadership in large part by the way in which the university responds to change. Paying closer attention to the stylistic and symbolic, as well as the substantive, aspects of leadership may provide a means to satisfy these expectations.

6

Institutional Leadership: Group Dimensions

Introduction

In our study we identified three kinds of leadership that Vice Chancellors typically exercise: educational, academic and administrative. Within these three arenas, Vice Chancellors perform a number of important roles, as we saw in the last chapter. The first arena, that of educational leadership, has an external focus and takes place largely on an external stage. It is concerned with leadership in the realm of ideas and involves contributions to national and international policy debate on issues of broad educational concern: for example, the relationship between industry and education; the purpose of higher education; or, perhaps, the role of education in the protection of the environment. Although many academics at other levels of the institution are actively engaged in educational leadership (as their media performances demonstrate), the status and position of Vice Chancellor raises expectations of such leadership and offers opportunities for its expression, whether exercised individually or collectively through bodies like the Committee of Vice Chancellors and Principals (CVCP).

The second area, academic leadership, is concerned with establishing and promoting the academic direction and enhancing the academic performance of the institution. This involves, for example, maintaining or changing the balance of disciplines and of academic activities across the institution; choosing professors; communicating and consulting on academic matters; taking decisions about major academic developments (the opening of a science park, academic collaboration or merger with other institutions, the establishment of inter-disciplinary research centres, or restructuring the curriculum into a modular pattern).

The third function, administrative leadership, is more directly concerned with the well-being, coordination and regulation of the whole institution: its diverse staff; its range of activities and resources, particularly finance; its extensive plant and equipment. As with the other areas of leadership, it includes active and symbolic elements: encouragement and communication with staff; the creation of an appropriate working climate; the balance and integration of institutional activities into a meaningful whole; interpretation of the external environment; external representation and fund-raising.

In Chapter 5, these three elements of institutional leadership, which in practice merge into each other, were examined in relation to the individual roles of designated academic 'leaders', the Vice Chancellor and Pro Vice Chancellors. Now our focus shifts to the contributions of non-academics to the institutional leadership domain (the senior administrators and lay officers) and particularly to the interactions and relationships *between* roles at institutional level. The part played by formal and informal groups will also be considered in terms of both structure and process (Becher and Kogan, 1992). We can go further with Becher and Kogan's model, by illustrating that both the structures and the processes can be viewed from normative and operational dimensions, that is either with a primary focus on 'the monitoring and maintenance of values' or with a focus on 'the business of carrying out practical tasks' (Becher and Kogan, 1992: 10). At the same time, different images of leadership and of organizations will again emerge.

Institutional leadership: the contributions of senior administrators and lay officers

Senior administrators

The senior administrator in a university is normally the Registrar (sometimes called the Secretary or Registrar and Secretary). In some universities, responsibility is divided between two senior administrators – a Registrar and a Bursar. We have been impressed by the range of tasks undertaken by the central administrations of the universities. They include servicing of the governing bodies and the committee system; academic administration which includes course regulations, student records, awards and welfare services; supporting the strategic planning process; financial administration; personnel work; and the maintenance of university property.

(Jarratt Report, 1985: 3.64, 29)

The Report commented further upon the complexity of administrative tasks, which extend across such diverse areas as the university's plant and equipment, range of academic disciplines, employment of different categories of staff, and external relations at local, national and international levels. Beyond these formal responsibilities, the officers also make important informal contributions to internal policy formation, to supporting the Vice Chancellor and to 'facilitating the main purposes of the institution' (Jarratt Report, 1985: 3.75, 29). Our data broadly support the Report's depiction of the senior administrators' role, but add some contours and colour to this outline.

Beyond the obvious structural distinctions between a unitary or bicameral administration, other differences were evident, for example in reporting lines:

individual unit heads (including the Registrar, Finance Officer, Personnel Officer, etc.) might report directly to the Vice Chancellor, while in other cases, the Registrar alone reported formally to the Vice Chancellor on behalf of other administrative areas. Sometimes dual reporting systems existed, for example where the Finance Officer reported to the Registrar and lay Treasurer of Council or the Registrar to the Vice Chancellor and to the lay Chairman of Council (although less frequently to the latter). Institutional history, individual past experience, personal preferences, and relative status and background of members of the senior management group were all reported as contributory factors in relation to differences across universities.

The role of the Registrar involves various strands, some of which can be categorized as leadership functions, others as management and administration. In terms of leadership, the role can be divided into leadership related to position, that is, as head of 'the administration' or sub-unit; and leadership related to a variety of internal fora as well as the boundaries of the institution and its environment. Both leadership and management functions can be illustrated with reference to the Registrar's tasks, duties and range of contacts.

Responsibilities of the Registrar's role include policy execution; advice and guidance to the Vice Chancellor on the development of institutional policy, strategy and tactics; interpretation and delivery of internal and external intelligence to the Vice Chancellor and Senior Management Group (an activity shared, of course, with others); income generation; the preparation of reports and papers as secretary to a number of statutory university committees; and the development, monitoring and coordination of systems and procedures. To use Becher and Kogan's terminology (1992: 13–15), the 'operational' elements include forward planning, maintenance of the institution and implementation of policy, while the 'normative' elements include providing evidence (particularly to external agencies) that the university is functioning as its sponsors conceive it should. A fuller description of the responsibilities of the whole administrative apparatus at institutional level is supplied by Lockwood and Davies:

> The primary role at the institutional level, whether it be in academic matters (curricular principles, degree structure, teaching methods, research strategy), resource allocation (budgeting, space allocation, etc.) and so on, is to lay down the general framework, to transmit and integrate the external signals, and to evaluate and judge the performance of the parts.
>
> (Lockwood and Davies, 1985: 104)

Both bureaucratic and political perspectives can be seen in the responsibilities outlined above and in the informal contacts associated with the job. These contacts begin to illustrate the collective nature of institutional leadership and management since it is not the Registrar alone who lays down that 'general framework' described by Lockwood and Davies. Registrars usually had daily contact with the Vice Chancellor; frequent contact with other senior officers, including those drawn from the academic body such as the Pro Vice Chancellors; held regular briefings before committee meetings; and had contacts with Heads of Department, Deans and committee chairmen (for exchange of information or influence, for 'leverage and steerage'). External contacts included discussions and meetings with registrar colleagues across the system (an important information and 'helpline' network) and liaison and representation with system officials and others (for example, local officials, business contacts, contractors, solicitors and international visitors). The different organizational perspectives are represented in Registrars' comments about their role; once again, functionalist and interpretive dimensions vie with each other:

> I am the Vice Chancellor's Chief of Staff and Policy Adviser. I am the executor of policy, either from the Vice Chancellor or from the committees. I provide leadership to the Administration – this is a two-way process.

> My role is to provide support for the Vice Chancellor by delivery of an efficient administrative service across a broad front, by the delivery of internal and external intelligence to him and by promoting teamwork in the university, that is, by assembling task forces according to need. This helps career development and the development of the university.

> My role is to advise, encourage and warn the Vice Chancellor and Pro Vice Chancellors. . .to ginger the Administration up and to relate it to the academic side of the university.

Descriptions of tasks, duties and relationships present one image of the senior officers' contribution to institutional leadership and management, but it is essentially a static and partial one. In reflecting on the exercise of the role, Registrars and other respondents brought out both the variety and the dynamic and changing nature of the role.

In commenting on organizational change, Registrars in our survey saw the impact of the external environment as critical. Financial stringency, the need to generate income from new sources, the growth of self-financing or commercial units and activities, the development of a cost centre approach at unit level, and the pressures for financial control, efficiency and accountability all had greatly increased the managerial and bureaucratic burdens within senior administrative roles. In other areas, socio-political as well as economic pressures were visible in requirements to implement new legislation or government initiatives (Health and Safety, Equal Opportunities, Quality Assurance); to expand areas of public relations, alumni relations, student recruitment; and to change personnel practices through merit award schemes, appraisal, staff development and formal changes in employment contracts. In order to effect changes, systems and structures were altered, for example in resource allocation, in performance review or, more broadly, in adapting and reconstituting the committee system.

All these structural and operational changes have in many cases affected the scope of administrative roles, expanding traditional administrative territories into policy and management arenas. The style in which administrative roles were traditionally carried out is also changing. We can expect these operational shifts to have an impact on the normative domain, challenging traditional beliefs and values about the role and purpose of management in academic institutions and the relationship between academic and administrative domains. In consequence, traditional cultural images of the university are likely to shift once again.

Respondents in our sample observed that the changes outlined above were reflected in the different individuals being appointed to Registrarial posts (in terms of their qualifications, background and experience), the status of senior officers, particularly within institutional management groups, and Registrars' conceptions of the role – although the picture was not uniform across institutions. Some comments illustrate the point:

> My view of administration is not the old view of 'administrators being seen and not heard'; senior administrators have a proper role to play in policy making, they are often the only ones with the relevant experience. Much of university policy making is not academic, it is tied up with finance, investments and industrial relations. Their [senior administrators'] role should be recognized – it has become more open since 1981. The notion of the 'eminence grise' is dishonest.

The shift in relationships between academic and administrative areas (and conceptions) of the university is further brought out in the following comment:

> Professional administrators have moved from being servators to facilitators and in some cases line managers. They no longer act like Civil Servants and the ideal is for administrators and academic managers to work in partnership. The change to greater managerial responsibility for administrators has brought an increase in personal satisfaction in the job.

However, for many academics in universities, these subtle but palpable shifts represent an invasion of the academic sphere by the bureaucratic sphere. A pervasive managerialist ideology, pushed by government and with roots in fundamentally different organizational settings, is blamed for this invasion.

An alternative view, which offers an adaptive and evolutionary perspective rather than a revolutionary one, is revealed in another observation. In this case, the 'onion-like' nature of the university as an organization is highlighted as it accommodates and adapts to a changing environment, adding new layers without fundamentally altering those lying beneath.

> There appear to have been three stages in the development of university management: first a self-governing body of academics. A Civil Service model was then grafted on to this self-governing body and a

managerial model was then brought in. All of this was achieved without changing the original structures. The three types of roles don't *necessarily* conflict, but it needs imagination, creative thinking and sensitivity to work. You can satisfactorily harmonise participation with good quality management.

While creativity and imagination are undoubtedly important when change is afoot, in our study we noted more evidence of tension than of harmony between academic and administrative domains, particularly between the centre and the academic units (departments, faculties, colleges). Some of these frictions are long-standing, some have emerged out of current circumstances. One frank comment from a senior administrator, whose bruises are evident, notes these tensions:

> The Administration is the natural kicking horse. People understand privately that administrators are making policy but it mustn't be admitted publicly . . . if the folklore is 'some bureaucrat dreamed up this scheme' then it changes the flavour of how it is received in departments and how it is implemented. Policy must come from the Vice Chancellor.

Different universities reacted in different ways to the changing pattern of institutional management and it was apparent that much could be done to mitigate the negative effects of change through sensitive leadership. For example, a Chairman of Council commented on the Vice Chancellor's role in 'managing the balance between the academic team and the administrators' and on the Chairman's own role in monitoring the process. An Administrative Secretary pointed to the management of relationships with academic staff as the essence of good administration, since 'the quality of trust and confidence they have in you is critical'. And Pro Vice Chancellors noted the importance of informing staff and consulting with them over proposed changes. An understanding of the range of interest groups within the university and an ability to see the institution from different organizational perspectives is likely to assist in developing the kind of leadership required.

Lay officers

We shall turn now to consider another group who contribute symbolically and actively to the success of institutional leadership, the lay members of the governing body: the Council in England, Wales and Northern Ireland; the Court in Scotland. Strictly speaking, the lay role is concerned with governance of the institution, that is, with 'the structure and process of decision-taking concerning the running of the institution' (Lockwood and Davies, 1985: 107). Legal and financial decisions which maintain the institution as a sound entity are of paramount importance. Councillors are not directly concerned with management, 'which includes governance but also the administration of activities, the implementation of decisions' (Lockwood and Davies, 1985: 107) or with those aspects of leadership which involve articulating values and developing commitment and cohesion within the institution. However, these distinctions are fine ones and the boundaries of governance, leadership and management necessarily overlap. As members of the governing body, lay members contribute to the creation of institutional strategy and direction and at a time of change and transition, greater lay involvement is noticeable in some areas of institutional management.

University Charters and Statutes define the Council as the institution's executive body, having responsibility for 'the government and control of the finances . . . the management and administration of the revenue and property . . . and the conduct of all the affairs of the University . . .'. Council is the university's employing body and through its committees (as well as the joint committees of Senate and Council) management is enacted and the authority of Council exercised.

The governing bodies contain lay and academic members, and the former (usually in the majority) may include both representative and co-opted members. Lay members are drawn from many spheres: local government, other sectors of education, the diplomatic service, industry and commerce, the media and elsewhere. These lay members link the institution to its local or regional context and also symbolically represent the voice of the wider society in the affairs of the university. Their contributions to the institution are not uniform: key officials such as the Chairman of Council or University Treasurer play a more active part than others, although contributions also varied depending on 'background, personality, willingness and ability' according to one Senior Officer, and of course on their availability, if employed elsewhere. As one Registrar tartly remarked, 'Some lay members decorate the committees, others play an active part.'

Lay members make both formal and informal contributions to the institution. The senior lay officers chair key committees such as Council itself or committees which report to Council, such as Buildings and Estates, Finance and General Purposes Committees (while senior academics chair committees which report to Senate). Through these chairmanship positions lay officers contribute to institutional direction and steerage. They may also chair or be members of other committees, for example the Safety Committee, Appeals, Joint-negotiating Committees (industrial relations), Commercial Policy, Student Residences and Honorary Degrees. *Ad hoc* working parties, such as those relating to internal restructuring or to fund-raising initiatives, will also seek contributions from lay members with relevant experience of the issues.

The formal activities of lay officers extend from ceremonial duties to the important responsibility of selecting and appointing the Vice Chancellor and Registrar and deciding their levels of remuneration. These responsibilities and duties were seen by lay members in our study as part of their duty (within Council) to monitor and oversee the affairs of the university. Through the committees, lay members perceived they were playing a part in policy formation as well as policy implementation. Their particular contributions were described in terms of bringing outside perspectives into the university, providing 'business experience and hard management knowledge', offering 'realistic' input to policy formation and generally ensuring 'that the university is run as well as possible academically and commercially'.

The assumptions that underpin such perceptions are revealing: that business experience is of relevance and value to the university and that commercial/industrial management practices are appropriate and useful in university contexts. Within the universities in our sample there was no consensus that these assumptions were valid (even if the commercial record of some sectors of British industry did not itself raise doubts about management and leadership practices in business contexts). These differences of view about operational practices and their normative dimensions – which touch important questions of values and purposes – continue to cause tensions between academics and managers/governors in some institutions.

We have considered the formal activities of lay members, but they also play informal roles, which were observed to be increasing in significance both by lay members themselves and by senior university staff in our study. For example, guidance, advice and support were offered both internally and externally for public relations and lobbying purposes. Senior lay members of Council (as members, or as friends of the university within the upper chamber) played an important part in representing the interests of the universities in the House of Lords during the passage of the Education Reform Bill in 1988, and no doubt assisted again in 1991.

Within the university, senior lay members often demonstrate a particular concern for students, being present at gatherings for overseas students and being involved in student welfare committees. Where university research is seen as a specialist academic matter, teaching is seen to be of broader and more direct concern to lay members as representatives of local communities, employers, or 'society'; many also have a personal interest as parents of university students. Lay members are in a position to provide some informal pressure to improve the quality of university teaching; they may also do so formally in the future under the banner of quality assurance at institutional level. For the most part, however, lay involvement is on the non-academic side of the university. In one institution in our sample, the Chairman of Council decided to redress this balance by introducing a system in which lay members 'adopted a department'. Through increased familiarity with departmental life and priorities, achieved by visits and contacts with staff, policy debates in Council could be better informed, particularly in cases where departmental interests were likely to be directly affected.

Lay members described their role as 'helping to manage the process of change' or as 'helping insiders to believe in themselves and to see themselves through the eyes of external constituencies'. Comments such as these recognize the impact of external pressures both on the morale of university staff and on the nature of university activities. Lay members also felt that their presence in the university illustrated regional commitment to the university and commitment by the university to the local community. Once again in these examples, symbolic and interpretive perspectives feature strongly.

Some lay members also saw the role as a political one, their presence helping 'to prevent the Vice Chancellor and Registrar running the university by themselves'. They were thus concerned to monitor the balance between the bureaucratic/managerial and collegial sides of the university, as well as the balance between financial viability and academic development. Taking this view, the lay members can be seen to provide a further layer of checks and balances on the exercise of power and authority in the university, a role that may serve the organization well even though, as in some universities, lay involvement was not seen by senior officers (academic and administrative) as useful, but as 'interventionist and obstructive'. The style of individual lay members, particularly those in senior positions, as well as their understanding and implicit assumptions about the university as an organization, were reported as critical factors in the way their contributions were received.

Where positive internal views of lay contributions were reported, lay members' own perceptions were confirmed. They were identified as 'a useful restraint', as 'watchdogs' and as providers of valuable external perspectives, external contacts and professional expertise (for example, in banking, law, architecture, personnel management, politics, the diplomatic service or the media). Lay members assisted with the routines of university business as well as being involved in sensitive areas such as moves towards managerial devolution or changes in the planning and resource allocation systems.

Chairmen of Council saw a close relationship with the Vice Chancellor as particularly important. Contact was both informal, via telephone conversations, *ad hoc* meetings and informal lunches, and more formal, in briefing meetings and executive committees. A satisfactory relationship could act as safety valve and support for institutional leaders, as both Chairmen and Vice Chancellors testified.

The Chairmen's responsibilities also extended to appraisal of the Vice Chancellor, in most cases informally, but in some universities formally. Judgements were reached in a number of ways: through observation and analysis of Vice Chancellors' reports to Council; observation of relationships among the senior management groups; attendance at social gatherings hosted by the Vice Chancellor; and internal contacts with Heads of Department, Deans and academic staff, in addition to contacts with administrative staff. External feedback was monitored (from local employers, businessmen, councillors, parents and the media) and comparative university statistics were a further source of data. As we can see from these disparate methods, sources and kinds of data, evaluation of the Vice Chancellor's performance is largely subjective, continuous and dependent on the perspective taken; it is also difficult to distinguish from performance of the institution as a whole. It will be interesting to watch, in the present enthusiastic climate for the measurement of performance and 'value-added', whether more formal evaluations will come into play, or whether this particular territory will remain sacrosanct.

In an examination of the responsibilities and functions of senior administrators and lay officers, it is clear that the exercise of institutional leadership and management is dependent on the activities and interactions of a
number of individuals, contributing to the whole on the basis of their own
conceptions of the university and their role and expertise within it (or
outside it), mediated by relationships and mutual expectations (Graen,
1976; Smith and Peterson, 1988). We have so far been considering individual sets of relationships, but we must turn next to look at the contribution of
groups to this complex tapestry. Two kinds of groups will be considered:
those that have a formal, constitutional existence within institutional structures and that are a familiar part of traditional university self-governance,
namely the committees; and those that are not (in the main) part of the
formal structure, but instead occupy a somewhat shadowy position beside
the committees in the old universities. We shall first consider the latter type.

Institutional leadership: group perspectives

'Senior management groups'

One of the most noticeable features of changing styles of management in
universities is the emergence of what can be loosely described as 'senior
management groups', which operate both apart from and in tandem with
the formal committees. Across the institutions in our study, the numbers,
sizes, titles, membership and purpose of the 'senior management groups'
varied considerably. In some universities, one group was clearly recognizable, in others up to four different constellations were defined as 'senior
management groups', with membership ranging from four (Vice Chancellor
and Pro Vice Chancellors) to twenty, where all heads of administrative units
were included or where the group in question involved the Vice Chancellor,
his or her immediate senior colleagues and the Budget Centre Heads.

The titles of the groups to some extent proclaim their degree of formality
or informality, that is, respectively, their structural relationship to the committees (and so to Senate and Council), or their freedom from direct accountability but with influence on action and decisions: the Strategy Group,
the Principal's Advisory Group, the Senior Management Team, the Vice
Chancellor's Monday Morning Meeting. Not all universities (or, more accu-
rately, their Vice Chancellors) had set up a group of this kind, some preferring a still more informal arrangement of *ad hoc* meetings with Pro Vice
Chancellors, senior officers or others. In larger institutions, more regulated
and formalized structures were the norm. Differences in the style of these
arrangements can be seen from the following comments from Vice
Chancellors:

> On Monday morning I meet with the Pro Vice Chancellors . . . this is
> both formal and informal [the nature of the business being divided

accordingly], on Monday evening with all the Chairmen and Deans . . . this causes me to decide things one way or another – again it is not a formal meeting. On Tuesday morning I meet with all the senior officers. On each occasion there is an open agenda, the Vice Chancellor raises issues and then goes round the table to enquire whether there is any-thing else that people wish to raise. There are two lay members of Council who are very involved because they are kept informed.

I set up a management group when I came. It consists of the Registrar, the Bursar and the four Pro Vice Chancellors. My predecessor had seen the Pro Vice Chancellors, the Deans, the Registrar and the Bursar sepa-rately. This didn't suit me so I set up a management group and gave each of the individuals specific responsibilities . . . the management group is an executive group which advises the Vice Chancellor. Each of the members has full delegated powers . . . the management group is now working to implement the University Plan.

A variety of purposes are served by these semi-formal groups. They act as a forum to discuss managerial issues associated with individual functional areas (Registry, Personnel) or portfolios (research, student recruitment, ex-ternal relations); to articulate policy options or to evaluate policy and imple-mentation processes; to discuss tactics and consultation strategies; and to brief and support members of the group. Within the context of the senior management group or groups, advice is sought, sensitive papers are checked, ideas are tested, reports are made, information is shared, and policy is shaped and evaluated. Bensimon's (1989) classification of the func-tions of senior management groups in the US context is helpful here. She identifies three domains of activity: the utilitarian (e.g. administrative/managerial functions), the expressive (e.g. supportiveness/counselling func-tions) and the cognitive (e.g. problem-solving/analytic functions).

The group(s) were reported as being useful in several ways: for day-to-day steerage and long-term policy development; for discussion of controversial issues and the political process of effecting decisions; for consultation and analysis of a range of matters. All 'large' decisions (i.e. with university-wide or financial implications, or with political repercussions) pass through the central management group(s) for debate, and will then be routed through the committee system. Business will also pass from the committees to the group(s).

Beyond the operational purposes of the groups, normative functions are also served. Through the ways in which business is conducted and in the choices of what is attended to as relevant business, the values of the institu-tion are upheld and reinforced, or tested and challenged. The nature of group processes will also bear directly on both normative and operational domains in that problem-solving, analysis and learning (as Neumann, 1990, has argued in the context of US presidential teams) will either be assisted or hindered by the ways in which the group or groups work together. The Vice Chancellor's leadership role as chairman and facilitator is critical.

The nature of the business dealt with by the senior management group(s) is as varied as the operations of the university as a whole. It might include proposals to build new student residences; frank discussion of the universities strengths and weaknesses; reports of research contracts and overheads received; discussion of special Funding Council initiatives; reports of storm damage; the implications of electricity privatization; the filling of a vacancy in the Registry; discussion of the university's strategy towards AIDS; development of part-time degrees; what students are thinking; which staff are likely to be troublesome; and a range of other matters. We are reminded of the comparisons made earlier with the pace and scope of executive business in other organizations, which is mirrored both in individual duties and in collective roles at the centre of institutions (Mintzberg, 1973; Stewart, 1976, 1982). In practice, the domain of 'administrative leadership' has many similarities now to strategic management in business settings.

A consideration of the operations of the senior management group(s) raises the issue of teamwork and its role in institutional leadership and management. It is an area that has received much attention outside universities (Belbin, 1981, 1992; Kakabadse *et al.*, 1992) and recently, within them (Bensimon, 1989; Neumann, 1990). Current management literature drawn from external contexts extols the virtues of teamwork, arguing that a team-centred managerial approach enhances the capacity of organizations to learn, particularly in a complex, changing and information-rich environment (Kanter, 1983). The evidence from within higher education is more equivocal (Bensimon, 1989: 49), suggesting that the independent actions of key players may be as fruitful as collective action in different kinds and sizes of institution.

Our study did not investigate teamwork in detail; the data collected only relate to individuals' perceptions of the issue. On the basis of these perceptions, it is clear that teamwork within institutional leadership and management arenas was regarded as important and necessary, though not always present.

Among senior staff, most welcomed the establishment of one or more management groups, seeing them as reflecting collective responsibility for policy formation and management (albeit a more restricted collectivity than represented by the committees). The group, particularly where only one existed, was likened to 'Cabinet Government' or to a company's 'Board of Directors'. There was a recognition among those senior staff who supported collective government, of the need for teamwork between individuals in the group and for the image of a team to be preserved, disagreements being kept private and a united front being presented in public. The Vice Chancellor was seen as the 'ringmaster' within the team, responsible for maintaining open relationships and productive group processes.

Where senior staff often saw the development of the senior management groups as an opportunity for quicker, more flexible decision-making than had been possible through the reportedly more cumbersome committee system, academic and administrative staff at lower levels were not always so convinced. Some were concerned about the legitimacy of the group(s) in relation to the committees; others with the small numbers of staff involved; and others still, with the potential for decisions to be made too quickly on the basis of 'undigested material'. In some cases, the group(s) were treated with considerable suspicion, as one Head of Department reveals: 'I'm not sure who runs the university. There is some inner body – one goes from one committee to the next – and I never seem to get to *the* body who runs it'. We might ask whether such a view reflects an 'organized anarchy' or a 'bureaucratic conspiracy'.

Some Vice Chancellors and Pro Vice Chancellors were aware of these tensions, as these comments demonstrate:

> I don't call my group of senior colleagues a management group as this would frighten some academics . . . the business goes on in my name rather than that of the whole group.
>
> (Vice Chancellor)

> Most things are debated in the Monday afternoon meeting; the Pro Vice Chancellors are seen as a management team and this is not approved of in the university. There is a feeling that too few people are involved in the management team.
>
> (Pro Vice Chancellor)

There is a suggestion in these comments that the position of Vice Chancellor has been granted the status of leader (with a different interpretation from the traditional *primus inter pares* role) and thus carries certain rights as well as obligations, as exchange theory would imply (Blau, 1964; Hollander, 1987). However, a broadening of the leadership role to incorporate other actors (particularly professional administrators) has perhaps not yet been accepted by many academic staff. Where the position of the group had been ratified by Senate or where decision-making authority and influence was more widely diffused in the university (among Heads of Department, the Professors' Group, strong trades unions, the Academic Assembly), the senior management group(s) did not appear to arouse as much concern.

The senior management groups present a micro-perspective on the enactment of leadership and management at institutional level. They demonstrate some of the ways in which 'cohesion, articulation, style and direction' are achieved. However, without looking also at the committee system, the picture will be only partial, with bureaucratic or political rather than collegial or cybernetic perspectives dominating.

The committee system

The main central policy committees, although having different names, generally had similar functions across the universities in our sample: Council or Court as the governing body; Senate or Senatus as the academic voice at institutional level; and a 'Planning and Resources Committee' (a joint committee of Senate and Council) representing an integration of academic, financial and physical planning at the centre. Beyond this fairly common configuration, structures differed, as did perceptions of the need for a committee system, the relationship of different groups to the committees and the distribution of power and authority within the central structures.

In most traditional universities, the committee system has slimmed considerably in the past fifteen years, in response to an external environment which has required faster and more flexible decision-making arrangements and much greater attention to financial control, efficiency and income generation. As well as committee systems being overhauled, individual committees have been reviewed, their terms of reference and compositions modified. The most significant changes in terms of internal norms and operations have been in the role and status of Senate, in the emergence of a central strategic planning committee and in the relationships between the official system and the 'unofficial' (or at least not yet formalized) management groups described above.

The changing external context, as well as the internal restructuring that has been proceeding in universities, has given cause for reflection about the role of committees in institutional governance and management. At one end of the spectrum of opinion evident from our data (i.e. from among the senior academic and administrative staff in our sample) were those who regarded committees as a necessary part of academic autonomy and self-governance, while at the other end were those who no longer saw committees as an appropriate mechanism. Comments from two Pro Vice Chancellors are representative of these divergent views; they demonstrate the continuing tensions between managerial and collegial perspectives of the institution:

> Committees are necessary for processing business, for consulting widely and as an aspect of good management – there is a chance to express views, for people to have their say and for people to be involved.

> Universities today need an executive structure, rather than the inertia brought on by management through committees. A committee structure can work very well in an expanding university system but in a static or contracting situation they are simply not able to make the necessary cuts and take hard decisions . . . At college level, committees have a genuine role to play in disseminating information and gaining ideas; but they should not play a key role in decision-making.

A position between these two extremes is represented by the suggestion that, in the absence of committees, other forms of meeting for consultation and ratification of decisions would emerge as a necessary aspect of management (as the emergence of the senior management groups suggest). There was also a sense that the constitutional position of committees acted as a constraint on highly centralized decision-making. The committees, in common with many other aspects of institutional governance, were part of a system of checks and balances, allowing different constituencies a voice and preventing dictatorship. However, it was also felt that this diffusion of authority might be more apparent than real, since committees could be steered:

> You must have committees to forestall a backlash. In some cases they make a useful contribution. You don't get massive debates about policy; the testing and formulation of policy has already been done elsewhere. For example, nowadays a letter from the Funding Council would not go to Resources and Planning Committee first. Instead, they would see a structured paper presenting various possibilities. We are operating more managerially by giving a lead to committees.
>
> (Senior Assistant Registrar)

Where views about the committee system as a whole aroused different degrees of passion, individual committees were seen as more or less useful depending on the need for consultation or endorsement of decisions. For example, consultation over services (the Library and Computing committees) and over resource allocation decisions (the Administrative Services or Estates committees) and consultation as part of change and development (the Academic Planning or Access committees) were seen as necessary and useful by academics and administrators alike. The more controversial issues related to the links between the formal committees and the senior management group(s) and to the role of administrators within the committee system.

The senior management group(s) may be regarded as 'informal' in organizational terms since they lacked constitutional status and their deliberations were usually not minuted. However, these groups were hardly free-wheeling since they usually acted as a conduit for business to and from the committees. Coordination between the two systems was ensured (in theory, if not always in practice) through an overlap in membership within the key committees and the senior management group(s) in the persons of the Pro Vice Chancellors and the committee secretaries (senior administrators). 'Coordination' of this kind was viewed by some as a sinister means of restricting debate, enabling Pro Vice Chancellors to push the management line in committees, but others saw the issue as a necessary aspect of increasing the speed of decision taking and of improving the overall responsiveness of the university. Links between the two systems can be seen in these comments:

> The Senior Management Team has no formal existence; it keeps its own notes; executive things that it does appear within committees, or appear from committees for executive action . . . the managerial consequences of doing something come first to the Senior Management Team and then go to the committees via the Pro Vice Chancellors.
>
> (Vice Chancellor)

Controversial decisions having been discussed informally among the senior staff are often taken to the Boards and committees . . . the committee structure is a method of consulting with a wider group as to whether the decisions being taken are the right ones.

(Pro Vice Chancellor)

The pressures of time on decision-making as well as the quantity of business requiring resolution were the main reason for the use of less formal structures – the senior management group(s) and short life task forces or working parties. These pressures have also affected the workings of the committees themselves in that committee chairmen were often empowered to take 'Chairman's action' when time pressures precluded opportunities for full consultation. Both Vice Chancellors and Pro Vice Chancellors commented upon the need to build trust among the academics in order that action of this kind could be taken, a point that is relevant to leadership style and was mentioned in relation to the leadership practices of individual Vice Chancellors.

In many universities, as a result of external pressures and the internal managerial changes which have been put in train, the bureaucratic perspective has gained ascendancy over the collegial, causing tensions and unease in many quarters (as well as satisfaction in others). Some individuals clearly feared that the 'managerialist party line' would reduce meaningful debate within the committees while others saw the streamlining of both the structure and the operations of committees as a positive contribution to efficiency and to the overall responsiveness of the university. Administrators were commonly in favour of the changing internal ethos since their contribution was more openly recognized, as this comment suggests: 'Because its position [i.e. the Senior Management Team] has been formalized, the administrators no longer have to talk in a guarded way to the academics; we also don't have to pretend that the senior management team doesn't exist and has no effect' (Director of Administrative Services).

The discussion above about the operations of the formal and 'informal' systems, and the differing perceptions of the two, illustrates the tensions that have always been present in universities between administrative and professional authority, but that are more pronounced at this time of considerable change. Birnbaum (1988: 4) argues that both forms of authority are a necessary part of institutional functioning, for 'without faculty participation in governance the institution is likely to be sterile; without administrative involvement, the institution can soon become unresponsive and ineffective. Both perspectives are necessary to guide a mature university.' It is the task of leadership (at various levels within the institution) to mediate between the different authority arenas and to utilize the strengths of the different systems for the benefit of the institution. As one Senior Pro Vice Chancellor put it, 'In practice the committees strain after equity while the Vice Chancellor and Pro Vice Chancellors strain after innovation and difference.'

To these efforts might be added the administrators' contributions to institutional coordination and regulation (as well as enterprise) and the lay officers' offerings in the form of critical questions, alternative perspectives and external influence on university objectives. All are required for effective functioning and for the survival of the institution in a competitive, complex and clamorous environment.

Institutional leadership: a complex drama

Many of the themes that were identified in Chapter 5 are evident again, but with a different gloss, in our discussion above. We can see, for example, that different assumptions and values influence views of how the university should be structured, organized and run, particularly in relation to a changing environment. It is clear that external pressures have greatly increased the importance of financial management and the burdens of accountability, both of which were keenly felt in the roles of senior administrators. Similar pressures have, in many cases, extended the contributions of senior lay officers to university management and governance. Measures to increase efficiency, such as a streamlining of the committee system, a growth in short-life task forces and other less formal groups, an increase in managerial discretion, and a tightening of financial and quality control systems across the institution, are further responses to external requirements and pressures. Our data show some of the structural changes made and also highlight the tensions that these have exposed between different 'territories': academic and administrative or lay and professional.

A second theme to emerge is the expansion of business at institutional level, fuelled by external interest and demands upon the university. 'Boundary management' has become as necessary in universities as in other public and private sector organizations. We have noted the consequences of this expansion of business in individual and collective roles and in the development of the senior management team(s); it has also strengthened the influence and importance of the institutional level as a whole. This shift in the balance of power (particularly between the centre and the academic units) is likely to be experienced most strongly in the roles of departmental heads, as we shall see in the next chapter.

A third theme, which we can now see in sharper relief, is the distinction made earlier between the power and influence of individual leaders and the image of leadership as a collective process. In the latter case, as our data reveal, leadership is expressed through the combined activities of informal and formal groups and in the relationships of individuals within, and to these groups. A third approach might take a 'both/and' rather than 'either/or' perspective, where leadership is enacted through the actions of individuals *and* the collaborative actions of teams at different levels of the institution. The presence of the committees and the traditions of the collegial ethic in universities also suggest a third possibility which extends beyond individuals or teams. This image is of collective leadership across the whole institution. In this case, leadership will be enacted through the relationships and interactions of groups and individuals, as many different staff contribute to and share responsibility for the shaping of institutional purpose and outcomes.

While leadership may be exercised by individuals, teams or a larger collectivity, it can also be exercised directly or indirectly. For example, a direct approach may be evident (at the individual level) through the chairmanship of Senate, when the Vice Chancellor exercises a right of veto, or when he or she provides the casting vote in a dispute over promotions or appointments. Leadership is manifested indirectly through the management of events that are routed through the senior management team, or when policy is legitimized by the Vice Chancellor's signature. Similarly, meetings between the senior management group and Heads of Department involve leadership that is direct, while indirect forms of (team or collective) leadership are enacted when policy is developed and implemented, as individuals and groups engage in 'reciprocal influencing' through the processes of consultation and negotiation.

Leadership will also be exercised in different ways at different phases of an event, for example at the stage of developing policy and at the implementation stage. Different actors are likely to be involved at these different stages. The various levels of leadership described above, and their enactment at different phases in the cycle of events, should not operate in isolation from each other, if consistency is to be established. When a new initiative is formed, such as the launching of a staff appraisal scheme, it is likely to be discussed in the senior management group(s), debated within relevant committees, negotiated informally with influential groups or individuals, announced in newsletters and promoted in staff meetings. As appropriate, systems and procedures, incentives and controls, will also be established to ensure that the innovation becomes part of institutional practice.

Yet the leadership drama is still more complex than this. At each level of leadership, whether direct or indirect, individual or collective, and at each phase of an event, the different layers of action, style and meaning will be invoked. I referred to these in Chapter 5 as the 'substantive, stylistic and symbolic elements of leadership'. If we take the Vice Chancellor's chairing of Senate as an example, the different layers will come into focus.

The action of chairing Senate overtly involves the processing of a business agenda. However, the time given to each item, the tone adopted (which may be conducive or not to discussion) and the individuals who are encouraged or not to speak are all aspects of style that will affect both how efficiently business is conducted and how effectively decisions are made. At the level of meaning, interpretations will be made about power and influence, depending on which interests were given a voice, whose feelings were aired and what responses were engendered. Individual participants at the meeting will have different perceptions of the level of understanding and appreciation of academic issues and perspectives that is demonstrated by the Vice Chancellor and any other senior officers present. Interpretations will also be made about the quality of the Vice Chancellor's judgement, depending on whether the outcomes of Senate were satisfactory or not to different individuals and their interests. Each layer – of action, style and meaning – will affect overall perceptions of leadership. Nor can this particular example be seen in isolation, since previous events and experience, as well as more deeply rooted traditions and values, will influence what is seen, done or understood as 'leadership'.

7

Leading Departments

Introduction

In earlier chapters we have noted the diffusion of power and authority in universities and the considerable degree of autonomy exercised at 'basic unit' and 'individual' levels (Becher and Kogan, 1992). These characteristics also provide scope for the exercise of leadership at these levels. In this chapter, therefore, the focus of attention moves from leadership at the institutional level to leadership elsewhere in the university, in particular to leadership as part of departmental headship. While exploring this dimension of leadership in its own right, the similarities, contrasts and links between leadership here and at institutional level will be identified.

On structures

Becher and Kogan (1992) use the term 'basic unit' to refer to internal academic functions that are organized and administered at a level other than that of the institution. Within the term, a number of different entities are included: the subject department; the more broadly constituted school of study; the faculty; the course or research team.

The main focus here is on the department as the basic unit and on the role of the departmental head in particular. However, within departments there are other levels of leadership in addition to that exercised by the designated head. And beyond the department, leadership may be exercised at faculty level by a Dean responsible for coordinating and presenting the collective activities of a group of cognate departments. In recent years, with increased devolution of managerial and budgetary responsibilities, some universities have strengthened this intermediate level of government, at the expense of individual departmental autonomy. In these cases, much of what is said about leadership at departmental level may also apply to the new roles of 'budget centre managers' (or to Deans whose functions have been extended to include responsibilities for finance and personnel).

A further point should be made about the nature of 'headship' in traditional universities. Although there is common ground in the scope of the role across universities in the UK and elsewhere (Tucker, 1984; Middlehurst, 1989; Moses and Roe, 1990), there is also considerable variety in its interpretation in practice given the range of structures and cultures of departments and disciplines and the range of personalities who become heads (Bennett, 1982). In particular, a distinction can be made between the role embodied in the title 'Chair' of department and that encapsulated in the title 'Head' of department (although the former is used generally in the United States). The distinction may reflect different selection patterns, for example, appointment by the Vice Chancellor (for headship) or election by the academic staff of the department (as the Chair) and may also represent different organizational images and their underlying values: collegial/professional or political/bureaucratic. In each case, the sources of authority which underpin the role are different and the ways in which leadership is exercised are also likely to be different. For the purposes of this chapter, the term 'head' will be used throughout, but its nuances should be borne in mind.

Leadership comparisons

If we compare leadership at institutional and basic unit levels, a number of points emerge. First, the relationship of leadership to management activity is likely to differ. At the institutional level, the leadership and management functions are often sharply delineated while at the departmental level, the two functions are typically closely integrated. The main reason for the difference is the existence and work of the university's administration, which, in providing the managerial framework to support institutional leadership, gives freedom for leadership to be exercised in its own right.

A separate and professional administrative network is not usually present in departments, administrative work being undertaken by academic and clerical staff, and in larger departments (particularly science and technology-based) also by technical staff. The majority of the administrative load as it relates to the department as a whole and the burden of responsibility for management has rested solely with the departmental head. However, recent trends towards devolved managerial responsibility have increased the numbers of departmental administrators so that a dual structure can also be seen at departmental (or faculty/school) levels. Accordingly, the way is open for a clearer and higher profile for leadership within the department.

The position of the Vice Chancellor, at the apex of the institution and with the authority to act as representative of the whole university, provides a further condition which assists the potential for leadership. In contrast, departmental headship is often perceived as a 'middle-management' position, having to respond to and implement initiatives originating elsewhere, particularly at institutional level, but also from individuals and groups within the department. Thus the room for manoeuvre for departmental leadership may be considered to be heavily circumscribed. As one Head of Department put it (Middlehurst, 1989: 175): 'the problem is that people who are running universities may not be looking for leadership within departments. Centralisation of authority may reduce the scope for leadership.' In the present climate of increased governmental pressure on universities there may be some Vice Chancellors who would echo these sentiments in respect of the constraints on institutional leadership.

On the other hand, there has traditionally been considerable autonomy at departmental level for developing the discipline and deciding the direction of teaching and research within the department. Devolution of managerial responsibility and an extension of entrepreneurial opportunities are likely to extend rather than diminish the scope (and expectations) of departmental leadership. The involvement of Heads of Department as important actors in the running of the university consolidates this position. The traditions of autonomy, the importance of basic units as key contributors to the university's educational mission, the role of heads in institutional self-governance and the opportunities for income generation all make the departmental headship role not directly comparable to middle management positions in private sector organizations.

A further reason for the greater weight of leadership over management at institutional level lies in the degree of 'leadership expectation' which is embedded in the role of the Vice Chancellor. These expectations come from external as well as internal sources and reflect beliefs in the omnipotence of the position as defender of the academic faith, initiator of institutional direction, symbol of university purpose and mission. While leadership expectations exist at departmental level, they are diluted by expectations of individual and group autonomy in academic areas and are balanced by strong expectations of management.

A second contrast between leadership at institutional and departmental levels is a distinction of scale and complexity. Although some departments and faculties are very large (i.e. with more than 100 staff, on several sites and with budgets in excess of a million pounds), for the most part the scale of operations is not comparable. A single department will usually possess a unified structure, even where several disciplines are encompassed within it. At institutional level no such unity of structure exists. While the internal complexity of departments is increasing as their range of activities and interests develop, it still does not match the complexity and diversity of institutional activities, services and personnel, which extend from the library to the sports hall, from academics to telephonists, from technology transfer to the management of the university's theatre or museum.

A third contrast is one of function and orientation. The departments are the 'production units' of the university, the place in which the main purposes of the university are fulfilled. The chief tasks at institutional level, on the other hand, are to create (or maintain) the framework and conditions in which productivity can be achieved and enhanced at other levels. An important symbolic function is also enacted at institutional level when the purposes and meaning of institutional activities as a whole is articulated. The focus of institutional and departmental activities is also different. In both its internal and its external orientations, the university's focus is a broad one (i.e. a range of internal activities and external 'markets', which include government, industry or society). The focus of unit level activity can be more narrowly targeted, towards the academic world (as the market for academic reputation) and the external world (as the market for academic resources and products).

If one takes the university to be an open system, then the leadership role at institutional level is to operate on the boundaries of one system (the university) where they abut on to other systems. By contrast, the department as a system can be more closed than open, although with the pressures of the market and the entrepreneurial spirit, less so than ten years ago. (Openness here refers to the relationship and influence of external constituencies upon the activities within the department/institution). However, there are – as always when discussing universities – caveats to be made. Some subject departments will need to be more open than others, if one contrasts medicine or law with classics or philosophy, for example.

The leadership role at institutional level is thus more obviously concerned with intercepting and interpreting external expectations of the university. In a very real sense, the task involves negotiating the boundaries of 'the university' as they shift in response to the new higher education system (following the Further and Higher Education Act 1992) or in response to new understandings of the nature of 'higher' learning and 'higher' education. The basic unit has, on the whole, a greater degree of integrity and cohesion than the university (although modularization may change this) and is less directly buffeted by external pressures and demands, being inside the curtilage of the university. The institutional leader looks out to the wider world; the departmental leader looks in, to the internal life and academic operations of the department.

A final and important contrast between departmental and institutional leadership is that departmental leadership can usually be more direct since relevant constituencies can usually be influenced through face-to-face contact. At institutional level, direct contact is not always possible so influence is more diffuse and must be transmitted through a variety of media and through a range of individuals and groups. This adds to the complexity of the task and to the potential for misunderstanding or inaccurate signalling. However, this is not to say that the impact of leadership is necessarily any less powerful: 'distance' can often increase the symbolic impact of leadership, and influence over appointments and promotions, for example, provides important opportunities for leverage at institutional level. The point that I am making here is that the means and complexity of 'delivering' leadership are different at the two levels.

Although it is still possible to make distinctions between basic unit and institutional leadership, in many cases these distinctions are becoming finer. Scale, size and complexity will remain constant differences, but the impact of external changes is altering the way in which basic units are constituted, the range of activities that are undertaken within them, and their relationship with the institutional level as well as the outside world. The development of the university into a 'holding company' for a number of semi-independent satellite units is likely to alter leadership concepts and practices at unit level as well as having an impact on the institutional domain.

Running departments

Having considered some of the general distinctions and similarities between leadership at the two levels of institution and basic unit, we can now fill in some of the detail by considering the formal responsibilities of heads, the shape of their roles and the expectations upon them, as well as heads' own interpretations of their role. We shall also explore the links between institutional and basic unit levels of leadership in order to reach a fuller view of academic leadership as a whole.

Following the Jarratt Report (1985), which promoted a tighter organizational structure for (the old) universities and a more managerialist role for departmental heads, many institutions developed new 'job descriptions' for the heads and also changed the procedures leading to the appointment of heads from permanent, to fixed-term and rotational arrangements, and often from a purely departmental election system to an appointment approved by Vice Chancellor and Council (Middlehurst, 1989: 164). In some institutions, these changes preceded the Report's publication and were independent responses to a changing environment. The evidence below is taken from the 'job descriptions' acquired in the course of our enquiry into departmental leadership and its development.

Across universities, the formal responsibilities of departmental heads are broadly similar, although the size, subject-base, traditions and culture of the basic units are likely to produce different interpretations of how these responsibilities should be implemented. For example, large science or engineering departments with a number of team projects in train, will organize themselves differently from the small department of Indonesian, whose research and teaching depends on the contribution of individual specialists. In the USA, researchers have found that the role of the departmental chairperson differs considerably across disciplines (Tucker, 1984: 59–60).

The duties and tasks of heads include: the setting and maintenance of academic standards and the monitoring of academic quality across the department; the organization of teaching and research; the acquisition and management of resources (finance, space, personnel, equipment); the implementation of university policy; internal liaison and representation; external liaison, public relations, marketing and representation; student and staff welfare, relations and development.

The range of formal responsibilities of departmental heads in the UK are comparable to those held in other countries, for example Australia or the

USA (Tucker, 1984; Bennett and Figuli, 1990; Moses and Roe, 1990). One recent classification from the many available is offered here (Green and McDade, 1991). Of course, the balance of activities undertaken by heads across the range below, and the extent to which the head shares these responsibilities or carries the major burden alone, vary across departments and universities.

Governing the department
- conducting departmental meetings;
- establishing departmental committees;
- establishing and implementing departmental plans and goals in collaboration with staff;
- preparing the department for internal and external evaluation;
- serving as an advocate for the department to central administration.

Managing teaching
- timetabling and assigning of teaching;
- managing of off-campus programmes;
- supervising and scheduling examinations;
- managing space and teaching budgets;
- ensuring that departmental curricula are vigorous and up-to-date.

Managing personnel
- selecting and recruiting staff (with central university administration);
- assigning responsibilities to staff;
- initiating and managing staff development activities;
- evaluating staff performance;
- supervising promotion procedures;
- dealing with unsatisfactory performance;
- participating in grievance hearings;
- making merit recommendations;
- informing and consulting with staff over departmental and university matters;
- preventing and resolving conflicts;
- promoting equal opportunities;
- ensuring compliance with legislation (e.g. Health and Safety).

Promoting departmental development and creativity
- fostering good teaching;
- assisting in the formulation of professional development plans;
- stimulating research and publication and maintaining a research ethos;
- encouraging staff participation in professional activities;
- representing the department at professional meetings;
- encouraging collaborative links within and between departments.

Working with students and student issues
- recruiting, selecting, advising, counselling and assessing students;
- encouraging student participation in departmental activities;
- monitoring student evaluations of teaching and pastoral care;

- liaison with student representatives;
- liaison with parents and employers of students;
- managing appeals.

Representing the department to the institution
- interpreting the discipline to the institution;
- representing departmental interests and requirements to central administration;
- building and maintaining departmental reputation.

Serving as link to external groups
- coordinating external activities;
- ceremonial functions;
- attending meetings of external groups (community, employers, funding agencies);
- processing departmental correspondence and requests for information;
- completing forms and surveys.

Managing the budget and resources
- preparing, proposing and managing departmental budgets;
- seeking external funding;
- promoting entrepreneurial activities among staff;
- encouraging grant proposals;
- setting priorities for conference and travel funds;
- monitoring consultancy activities among staff;
- preparing annual reports.

Using the broader concept of role, rather than the narrower aspects of functional tasks and duties, a recent Australian study of headship identified six major roles for departmental heads in universities: the head as academic leader; as personnel manager; as source and distributor of resources; as administrator; as advocate and politician within the institution; and as ambassador, lobbyist and negotiator outside the institution (Moses and Roe, 1990). Elsewhere, other studies have sought to identify the skills associated with headship or the leadership capacities required.

The picture that emerges from all these studies is of a wide range of activities, involving different constituency interests and requiring both leadership and management competence. The tasks facing Heads of Departments combine routine maintenance, long-term planning and performance review, with encouragement for departmental growth, development and collaboration. Some of the activities or functions may be in conflict with each other: short-term consultancy work and long-range undergraduate or graduate programmes; maintenance and control of traditional standards and innovation in programmes, in student clientele or in assessment methods. Others may be difficult to achieve despite formal expectations: maintaining a significant personal research effort while also managing a large and diverse department or school; or developing course teams in a department of individual specialists more used to competition than collaboration. Many of these conflicts and tensions arise from changes in the external environment, which are currently affecting the internal patterns of academic life.

As with institutional roles, headship responsibilities are unlikely to be fulfilled by one individual (except in small departments), so they will require some organization and delegation in order to spread the load. It is largely in the choice of personal priority areas in the activities of the head that a leadership (or management) orientation can be discerned. The choice is likely to be influenced by the traditions and culture of the department, by the preferences and experience of the head, as well as the expectations of staff.

Staff expectations

In Britain, an early, small-scale study of four departments in a provincial university found the following eight areas of activity to be of concern to staff: teaching, research, administration, departmental decision-making, general relationships between the head and other staff, appointments, promotions, and the relationship between the department and the university (Startup, 1976: 239–41). The study also demonstrated differences in the priorities attached to these activities by the staff in different kinds of departments. For example, in the two empirical science subjects, the head's research role (in gaining access to funds and facilities and in the stimulation of research) was regarded as most important while the classicists and mathematicians rated the head's teaching role more highly (that is, in the maintenance of teaching standards through personal example, being receptive to feedback from staff and students and being diligent in dealing with unsatisfactory performance). All groups were concerned about the head's role in relation to appointments since this was likely to have a direct impact on departmental staff relations.

In a more recent study in nine Australian universities (Moses and Roe, 1990), in the eyes of academic staff the head's most important functions (in rank order) were 'serving as an advocate of the department', 'to consider staff views', and 'developing long-range plans'. In this study, comparatively little importance was attached to the head's role in selecting staff and evaluating staff performance, both of which were regarded as important by Heads themselves.

Two American studies, one informal (presenting questionnaire responses obtained in staff development workshops: Hammons, 1984) and another formal survey of approximately 300 academic staff in one state university (Falk, 1979), provide further insights. Hammons reports that staff valued chairpersons who encouraged them to change, who facilitated their efforts, who recognized and rewarded effort, and who were knowledgeable about curriculum and instructional matters.

Falk's data reveal that staff are keen to work with heads who are engaged in both teaching and research (particularly the former); who consult with staff and listen to their grievances; who are involved in the selection of staff and in the setting of standards; who are successful in resource acquisition and in internal advocacy for the department; and who prepare and manage the departmental budget and are able to resolve departmental conflicts.

Although these data are difficult to compare, since the survey methodologies, scale and timing of the enquiries were different, some common threads do emerge. First, the head is expected to play a major role in departmental productivity by engaging in teaching and in promoting high standards in teaching, and by supporting research activity and assisting in the acquisition of funds. Second, it is anticipated that the head will be involved in staff selection and appraisal, in planning and in managing resources. Third, the head will be engaged in political activities, both externally and internally on behalf of the department, in order to maintain and enhance its reputation and that of its staff. Finally, the head is expected to consult with staff, to manage conflict, to support and recognize effort and generally to facilitate the creation of a climate conducive to academic productivity.

Both the formal, institutional expectations of Heads of Department and the expectations of staff highlight the management and administrative tasks that are associated with the position. However, there are also clear leadership responsibilities and expectations, ranging from mapping a direction for the department to creating an environment in which academic quality can be achieved. The importance of the head's role 'in the pursuit of excellence' and the ways in which leadership can be exercised to encourage and stimulate high quality teaching and research are reported in another study by Moses (1985: 346–7) in Australia. It was based in large part on academic staff perceptions of the headship role.

Moses found that research can be promoted by the head in at least four areas: (a) funding (by liaison with fund-granting bodies, by assisting staff with proposals and by good advocacy within the university concerning departmental needs); (b) distribution of funds (for example, by distributing funds in order to encourage new projects or new staff or as recognition for productivity, or by establishing a research committee to consider internal applications for funds); (c) facilities (by ensuring adequate facilities for research); (d) encouragement (by establishing regular research seminars, through monitoring and developing research skills via training or joint projects, by regular communication with staff over research and publications, by establishing an internal refereeing system for projects and publications, through celebrating effort and success in attracting grants, publishing and making progress in research).

Excellence in teaching, which is receiving considerable attention in British universities at national and local levels, is still not encouraged or rewarded appropriately by comparison with research (Boud and de Rome, 1983; Elton and Partington, 1991). Despite this handicap, Moses reports that there are a number of actions that can be initiated and supported by the head, which are likely to contribute to a climate of excellence in teaching.

These include: regular discussions of teaching and of the curriculum; regular evaluation of teaching and programmes; departmental resources allocated to teaching; peer review and team teaching; recognition of teaching through praise and in promotion recommendations; support for innovation and development in teaching practice; and encouragement of interdisciplinary teaching.

Interpretations of headship roles

We move now from staff expectations to heads' own perceptions of their role. Several studies have taken this perspective as their focus, investigating perceptions through interviews and questionnaires to heads (Startup, 1976; Tucker, 1984; Middlehurst, 1989; Moses and Roe, 1990). Each study sheds light upon different aspects of the role: its ambiguity and problems, the nature of activities undertaken; the knowledge and skills base required; the leadership opportunities afforded; or the developmental needs of new incumbents.

As we saw above, the task of headship involves a combination of day-to-day administrative routine with longer-term planning; a balance of leadership and management responsibilities and an internal as well as external orientation. Startup (1976: 238) categorizes heads' activities into three groups: *structural* aspects, which flow directly from the formal requirements of the role (such as writing promotion or appraisal reports, attending faculty boards and Senate); *conventional* aspects, which were not obligatory but were related to widely held staff expectations (for example, the initiation of a research programme, efforts to improve the quality of teaching); and *discretionary* aspects, where an element of choice was available to the head (these might include setting up a staff–student committee, delegating administrative tasks and special liaison with the Registry).

Startup points to differences in the *values* of heads in explaining variations in their activities, as well as to differences in their *knowledge-base*. He suggests that effective policy formation is dependent on at least three areas of knowledge: events outside the university; the workings of the university; and the characteristics of the department and the staff. The values he draws attention to include the relative importance of teaching and research, the democratic instincts of the head, and the extent to which the head acknowledges and recognizes individual autonomy and discretion in academic activities. Other researchers have highlighted the *skills* requirements of heads and chairs (Davies, 1989; Middlehurst 1989; Green and McDade 1991), which include creating vision, managing resources, leading people and communicating effectively, as well as an understanding of the headship role. Most of these are likely to incorporate Startup's knowledge bases.

Taking a different perspective, Moses and Roe (1990) identified the functions of headship that role incumbents ranked as most important, including selecting staff members, maintaining morale and developing long-range plans. The first and last of these were comparable with Falk's findings (1979: 82–5), while the other two of Falk's top four items might be considered as contributing to departmental morale, i.e. 'reporting departmental accomplishments to the dean' and 'involving faculty members in the decision-making process of the department'. Some personal interpretations of leadership by heads add colour to these findings:

> Leadership is the development of a vision which dictates the framework within which one seeks to move. Without vision you can't continue. A leader has to motivate people, making sure that they're all going in the same direction. A leader has to maintain momentum and keep morale high. This involves getting people together, talking to them and listening to their views. A leader also has to see possibilities.

> Leadership in a chemistry department means academic leadership. It means not only being a good researcher oneself but also having a high profile among other chemistry departments nationally and internationally. It means having the authority and status to impose one's views on the department and know that the department accepts you as a leader because you are who you are.

The findings reported above may give the impression that the headship role is relatively straightforward and that leadership is essentially unidirectional, from leader to led. Yet most studies also point to the ambiguities, problems and pressures of headship and to the reciprocity of influence between head and staff in particular. The ambiguity arises from the nature of the position, which carries a dual identity, as academic colleague and as manager/leader (reinforced in the case of fixed-term and rotating headships). Ambiguity also lies in the potentially conflicting expectations of students, the personal and professional hopes of staff and the requirements and priorities generated at faculty and institutional levels. The potential for role conflict has greatly increased as heads find themselves simultaneously expected to act as agents of institutional management, required to deliver according to institutional objectives, and to act as first among equals in a unit where all are engaged in a collective enterprise. As best they can, departmental leaders must balance the needs of both constituencies. Yet many heads express concern about the power and authority at their disposal and the difficulties of managing academics:

> Many academics do not see themselves as belonging to a structure that has to be managed at all.

> The problem is in managing academics; they're highly individualistic with no strong sense of corporate identity either to the department or the university.

> Heads of department in universities have no effective managerial power and operate by inspiring or engineering consent.

Although the power to command is limited in the university context, the influence and authority (and even power) available to heads comes from several sources: their formal position and statutory obligations (for example as a pathway to rewards and sanctions, as a conduit of information, as a champion of departmental interests); their professional expertise; and their personal style and characteristics: credibility, fairness and accessibility being among the qualities valued by staff (Middlehurst *et al.*, 1992).

Beyond the difficulties of headship which arise from within the department, there are others, according to heads, which emerge from without: lack of support, feedback and communication from central administration; poor management information systems; external pressures for income generation, for efficiency and for accountability in all aspects of departmental activity (Middlehurst, 1989). The role is challenging but essential since, in important respects, the basic unit *is* the university (Moodie and Eustace, 1976) and the departmental head is responsible for the effective delivery of its academic services. In the words of Bennett (1988: 57):

> the quality of the core academic success of the institution depends on the quality of the chairpersons – their dependability, their resourcefulness, their appreciation of academic values and their insight into the abilities and weaknesses of their colleagues; in short, their ability to manage and lead.

Leadership at institutional and basic unit levels: the links explored

Much of the recent literature on organizations, particularly that which has focused on managing change and transformational leadership (Peters and Austin, 1985; Oakland, 1989), has promoted the building of a corporate culture with shared values and common systems throughout the organization (as in total quality management). For the most part, responsibility for initiating such developments is expected to rest with top management, while middle-management levels must first buy into the philosophy (through briefings, training sessions etc.) and then cascade it down through the organization.

While there are universities in the UK (for example, Aston and South Bank Universities) that are embracing the TQM philosophy and its methodology, for the most part a purely top-down, hierarchical leadership approach is likely to encounter structural and cultural resistance within institutions, particularly in the academic domain. As has been discussed earlier, the notion of corporateness sits uneasily in an organization which is so diverse, which contains many conflicting goals, which engages in a wide variety of activities for the benefit of highly divergent client groups, and whose primary purposes are dependent on the productivity of sub-units, teams and individuals with considerable (necessary) autonomy. Weick (1976) described the structural relationship between institution and basic units as 'loosely coupled' since one level does not necessarily exhibit tight correspondence with the needs and requirements of the other.

The present environment of universities, with its strong managerial and accountability requirements combined with its competitive and entrepreneurial pressures (for marketing, corporate image, consistency of service), has prompted a tighter coupling between institutional and unit levels. However, both the myth and the reality of relative independence between unit and institutional levels remain in many universities for a number of reasons.

First, the expertise in teaching and research exists at basic unit level and therefore discretion in the organization and development of these activities must reside (in large part) at this level. Second, the drive to examine critically contemporary knowledge and to develop new understandings rests ultimately on the efforts of individuals and groups at basic unit level. For its fullest creative expression, this drive must remain as unfettered as possible (which is not to say that some chanelling may not be appropriate). Third, the speed, number and complexity of decisions that must be made – in a competitive, entrepreneurial context – demand a large degree of discretion and flexibility of response at departmental level. Fourth, there is general consensus that those who 'own' their decisions (that is, who have been involved in their making) are more likely to engage fully in their execution; this argument can be extended to other areas of university life. Fifth, academics may be described broadly as 'professionals' who, having been successful at apprenticeship and initiation phases, are permitted to practice academically, subject only to professional ethics, regulations and reviews.

On the other hand, the university is a social institution, which is largely publicly funded and which is hedged around by legal, political and economic constraints. It will also have community and international links, a history, an identity and a varied staff complement. The university, seen in this way, has a range of accountabilities, attributes and networks that are different from those of the units, although there is obviously considerable overlap.

In essence, the institutional level carries an ongoing, general responsibility for regulation, facilitation and external monitoring (which is mirrored at departmental level in the role of Head of Department). In some areas, for example in selective resource allocations, in the initiation of collective quality procedures, in the implementation of employment law, and in certain circumstances (crises, academic decline, financial survival) stronger institutional-level initiative is called for. Otherwise, the task within this domain is to create frameworks for productive activity, in terms of policy, systems and procedures as well as climate. In other areas, particularly where change and innovation are concerned, strong channels of communication and habits of negotiation need to exist between unit and institutional level (and also within and across departments) so that a joint interpretation and commitment can be developed towards the new directions proposed (whether initiated at institutional or basic unit levels).

Birnbaum's (1988, 1989c, 1989d) cybernetic model of the institution takes account of the particular organizational features of universities and describes the system of feedback loops which exist to ensure both adequate flexibility and consistency between centre and units. In many cases, no doubt, the reality is less tidy and less effective than the ideal model, as some of the Academic Audit Unit Reports (DQA) on universities' quality assurance mechanisms imply (Williams *et al.*, 1992). What seems clear from Birnbaum's studies, as well as others, including our own, is that successful operation of the cybernetic system relies not only on free-flowing information (which is greatly assisted by information technology), clear policies, systems and procedures, but also on some key values, practices, interests and interpretations of the external and internal worlds that are shared at institutional and departmental levels. The creation of this kind of internal climate is dependent on leadership that can accommodate difference as well as build consent – if not full consensus – and that is essentially concerned with maintaining a balance between a range of countervailing forces.

The means to create the links between departmental and institutional levels rely on a variety of arenas and sources of influence. The formal arenas include the committees, briefing meetings, seminars, visits to departments or to central offices where senior staff (administrators, Deans, Pro Vice Chancellors, Heads of Department and professors) can exchange information, negotiate priorities, progress business and exert influence upon each other's understandings of the university and its environment. Informal arenas include social gatherings, away days, staff common rooms, conferences and inaugural lectures as well as chance encounters. Many of these arenas of influence involve direct contact between senior staff and departmental heads and rely on discussions as well as written material. Indirect contacts include telephone and electronic communications between the centre and departments, written communications and 'documentary' communication in the form of policies and procedures. As writers on culture suggest, messages are also transmitted through traditions, symbols, rituals, sagas, legends and physical features of the environment.

The free flow of information, as well as the leadership effort to build a level of agreement about the direction and organization of department and university, should not stop at the position of departmental head. A danger arising from the increasingly pressured time of academics – because of larger numbers of students, more research and scholarship, more entrepreneurial initiatives – is that decreasing numbers of staff have access to the information and to the arenas in which priorities (and understandings) are developed. The onus for communicating with staff on a regular basis rests largely with departmental heads, although institutional responsibilities exist here too. In order to improve the information flow, committee representation will need to be shared among departmental staff, and the involvement of individual or group interests at faculty and central levels monitored. It may also be necessary in some cases to change the traditional constituencies from which committee memberships are drawn in order that participation (and thus communication) is spread more widely.

The sources of influence, beyond the media chosen, which are open to leaders at institutional and departmental levels have been described in more detail earlier, but include physical, financial or psychological resources (for example, the right to negotiate salary, the ability to assign departmental space, to select Heads of Department or members of staff), academic expertise and reputation, personality and political credibility. These sources of influence can be deployed in a number of ways, from coercive to supportive or challenging. They may involve barter and exchange, the withholding or withdrawing of resources or, more positively, the free expression of thanks, the giving of praise, moral support and encouragement. The strategies can be exercised skilfully or ineptly, deliberately or unconsciously. In large measure, they rely for success on understandings of reciprocity and on attitudes of respect, trust and confidence, and on a willingness to take the initiative as well as to listen, negotiate and learn – at both levels.

In order to maintain a degree of equilibrium between institutional and departmental levels and between internal and external priorities, the university has over time developed complex systems of checks and balances. These have ensured its survival and protected its core activities. A major problem at present is that this equilibrium is being disrupted. Changes are taking place in the relationship between internally and externally driven priorities and, in consequence, in the power relations between institution and basic units. These shifts and the resulting imbalances raise questions about the appropriateness, or degree of subordination, that academic and departmental purposes should have to the corporate interests of the university. The questions expose very real fears among academic staff that the dominance and expansion of operations at institutional level, driven by financial and accountability considerations, will gradually undermine departmental autonomy and thus damage the vitality and productivity of the basic units.

While the fears may be justified, such a pessimistic conclusion is not inevitable. However, the development of a new state of equilibrium between the different levels and interests that contribute to the university's survival depends on skilful management *and* leadership at departmental and institutional levels. Effective management is needed to satisfy legitimate financial and accountability demands and to identify the least intrusive means to their achievement. Effective leadership is required to negotiate the level of 'demand' that the university can and should accommodate, to interpret the nature of the external demands and to develop creative responses which are not incompatible with academic integrity and purpose. As we have seen, leadership also involves interpreting and powerfully representing the university's (or department's) productivity and value to external audiences. It is part of the argument of this book that knowledge of leadership (and management, although that is not our primary focus) and of the university in its past and present, general and specific configurations, is important to success. Important, too, is a large measure of *simpatico* for the purposes and values of academe and for (all) those who contribute to their fulfilment.

8

Individuals and Leadership

Introduction

The history of Western civilizations over the past three centuries demonstrates a continued striving towards the ideals of personal liberty and equality of opportunity for all citizens, trends that have fostered the growth of individualism and magnified tensions between the individual, the collectivity and authority. The dominance of an individualist culture in North America, Britain and other European countries (in contrast to the collectivist cultures of Eastern societies) is attested to by studies undertaken by Hofstede (1980) and Smith and Peterson (1988), who have investigated cultural differences in approaches to leadership. In professional organizations and in universities in particular, individualism is clearly represented within the ideals of professional autonomy and academic freedom, although it should not be forgotten that these ideals are also tempered by collective values of consensus and community. The importance of the 'individual domain' in universities requires us to consider its particular implications for leadership.

Earlier chapters have considered various aspects of leadership and individuals: leadership models which take account of individual needs (Chapter 2); the problems of leadership in an organizational culture which places a premium on individual autonomy (Chapter 4); the individual roles of Vice Chancellors or Heads of Department (Chapters 5 and 7). However, there are two further dimensions that need to be explored. The first is concerned with examining the opportunities for individuals to exercise leadership; the second draws attention to those elements which are associated with the exercise of individual leadership. These two matters are linked by a common concern to illuminate the conditions that foster leadership. The discussion is divided into four sections: conceptions of leadership at the individual level; individual characteristics and leadership; academic roles and the place of leadership; and context and opportunity for individual leadership in universities.

Conceptions of leadership at the individual level

As Bryman (1986) and others (Etzioni, 1965; Kochan *et al.*, 1975) have pointed out, the study of leadership has long been bedevilled by conceptual ambiguities and confusions. Some of these have been referred to in Chapter 2 in the discussions of leadership as distinct from other forms of social influence (namely the close associations between leadership and power, leadership and motivation, leadership and headship and leadership and management). In this section, I will focus on two issues: the relationship between leadership and headship and the question of the direction of leadership influence.

Formal and informal leadership

In many research studies, leadership is not kept separate from the occupancy of a position, or from formal status in an organization to which power and authority are attached. Accordingly, researchers have examined the behaviour of formal leaders in positions of authority as a way of exploring leadership. Although in practice it is necessary to consider leadership in relation to power and authority, since these two sources of influence form an integral part of the conditions and resources for leadership, it is not always useful to focus solely upon formal roles. When considering the exercise of leadership at the individual level, a further notion of leadership is implied, which goes beyond the constraints and opportunities of status and position. This kind of leadership, as Blau (1956) has suggested, is relatively idiosyncratic and may not always be directed towards organizational goals. It may also be exhibited in many contexts outside formal organizations, for example in sport, within teams of explorers or in the championship of moral causes.

Within the literature, distinctions are made between the concepts of 'formal', 'informal' and 'emergent' leadership. The first of these has been our chief focus until now. The last type tends to be used in relation to 'leaderless' contexts (such as Whyte's (1943) study of an American street corner gang or Nelson's (1964) study of emergent leadership in Antarctic scientific field stations), while the second category refers to leadership exercised within organizations, beyond the boundaries of formally designated positions. Informal leadership is closely associated with the informal organization (Selznick, 1943), that is, with the cluster of unofficial practices and structures, the patterns of social influence, relationships and interactions which are distinct from the official, public operations and structure of the organization.

Some of the distinctions between formal and informal leadership are visible in differing perceptions of appointed and elected leaders. These suggest that the two authority-bases permit different amounts and kinds of influence to be exerted. Hollander (1987: 13), taking up this theme, suggests that 'there is a good deal of evidence for the proposition that election creates in followers more sense of responsibility and higher expectations for the leader's success'. The perception of different sources and levels of influence associated with different selection strategies can also be seen within studies of departmental leadership in universities (Bennett, 1988; Middlehurst, 1989; Moses and Roe, 1990).

Here, my main concern is the notion of 'informal' leadership as exercized at any level within the institution, but especially among academic staff. However, two points need to be remembered. First, the ideas of both informal and emergent leadership may be usefully applied to students as well as to other categories of staff. The second point creates a link between formal and informal leadership. As John Adair argues in his leadership seminars: 'You may be appointed a leader, but you are not a leader until your appointment is ratified in the hearts and minds of those you lead.'

Whether elected or appointed, leaders need to build a relationship of trust with those whom they hope to lead. Formal appointment into a senior position within the organization, or to the headship of a group, carries with it certain role expectations of which leadership is one (see Mintzberg, 1973). However, in order to be perceived to be exercising leadership, certain conditions need to be met. Often these are unspecified; they are also likely to be subjective varying between contexts and constituencies. In earlier chapters we have looked at some of these conditions in terms of task requirements, academic culture, external pressures and different constituency perceptions of leadership roles. In this chapter, attention will be given to individual personality characteristics that contribute to perceptions of leadership. However, before this, there is one further conceptual matter to be raised.

Leadership: the direction of influence

Much leadership research in the context of formal organizations concentrates upon the unilateral downward influence of leader upon subordinates. The studies of Whyte and of Hollander cited above instead draw attention to the two-way influence between leaders and their followers. These studies suggest that leaders acquire power (or are assigned authority, in the case of formal leadership) on the basis of their perceived competence in relation to the group's primary task or area of interest, and their conformity to group norms and affirmation of collective values.

Hollander (1987) and his colleagues (Hollander and Julian, 1969) in their 'idiosyncracy credit (IC) model' elaborate on this image of leadership as a social exchange between leader and led. In simple terms, their model is a sophisticated version of 'brownie points': the leader, through displaying competence and conformity early in his or her leadership term, is able to build up credits which can be encashed later when making changes or introducing innovations. This kind of trust-building can be seen in our research into institutional level leadership (see Chapter 5). Credits may also be built up as a result of seniority, reputation, high socio-economic status, consultation or the demonstration of ideas and strengths relevant to group (or individual) needs at a particular time. The nature and balance of credits is likely to vary across an organization, reflecting differing interests and priorities.

Further dimensions of the IC model and social exchange theory draw attention to the nature of the leadership transaction which involves the leader giving followers benefits (whether economic, social or psychological) such as a sense of direction, recognition of needs, achievements and efforts, a sense of security and of self-worth, while followers in return provide leaders with responsiveness to influence, greater status and esteem. A fair exchange is implied, associated with mutual responsibilities, expectations and regard, since in the words of Homans (1961: 286): 'Influence over others is purchased at the price of allowing oneself to be influenced by others.'

Social exchange theory shares some features with Adair's (1983: 85) image of the written or unwritten 'political constitution' in an organization which can either liberate or constrain decision-making. Handy's (1985) 'psychological contract' is still closer to the idea of social exchange; here, individual performance is related to the fulfilment of expectations and obligations by the employing organization. The legitimacy of the leader, which is manifested in his or her right to lead as seen by the group, is not a fixed but a dynamic attribute. It is dependent upon the perceptions of others and their degree of responsiveness towards the exercise of leadership as much as to the leader's deliberate exercise of power and authority.

Yet reciprocity of influence is not only vertical; it may also be lateral, upward or external, as leaders engage in different relationships and play different roles. The picture of leadership that then emerges is one of a dynamic system of interconnected relationships which involve a balance of give and take and push and pull from different directions. Although the position of formal leader allows a considerable degree of leverage to be exerted on these relationships, influence can also be exerted by those outside formal positions. Kerr and Jermier (1978) remind us that in some organizations aspects of their culture, norms or structures can produce similar effects to the actions of a leader (in terms of guidance or support, for example) and in this way may substitute for leadership. When looking at leadership from these perspectives, the limitations of simplistic views of leaders directing and followers responding can clearly be seen. The value of adopting a systemic approach to leadership then becomes apparent, where 'leadership' is expressed through the organization's framework and ethos as much as through the actions and interactions of individuals and groups. It is important to keep these perspectives in mind as we turn to consider individual traits and leadership since such traits are only a part of the fuller leadership story.

Individual characteristics and leadership

A recent comprehensive survey of leadership research is offered by Hunt in his book *Leadership: a New Synthesis* (1992). Within his 'multiorganizational level leadership model' we are presented with a full range of elements and influences which impinge on the exercise of leadership (for example, critical tasks, knowledge, the external environment and societal forces, organizational culture and climate). We are concerned here with one element of Hunt's model, that of individual capability. Hunt examines this dimension in terms of personal background factors and preference aspects, cognitive complexity and social cognition, transactional and transformational leadership skills. I shall follow Hunt's lead in the discussion below.

Personal background factors

Many studies have given attention to the circumstances of individual backgrounds in connection with leadership capacities (McCall, *et al.*, 1988; Bennis, 1989; Kotter, 1990). The kinds of background factors which impinge on individual capabilities include: family and childhood experiences; educational experiences; previous and current career experiences, which are likely to have a strong influence on occupational and professional socialization; age and cohort history.

Within the world of higher education, detailed investigation into the relationship between background characteristics and leadership has not yet been undertaken (beyond career paths and professional experience). There is no reason to suppose, however, that personal background factors are any less important for leadership in academe than in other contexts.

Elements of personality

Understanding individual personality and its connection to leadership brings us back to 'trait theories', which had waned in importance after many studies earlier in the century had produced inconclusive or conflicting findings. The main difference in recent studies is that traits are now conceived in a more sophisticated form and in close association with other variables.

Hunt draws attention to a number of 'predispositions or preferences' which can be measured as traits. The first of these is the will to exercise leadership (similar to McClelland's (1985) need for power, Kotter's (1990) internal drive to achieve and succeed, or Bennis's (1989) combination of passion, curiosity and daring). This trait or group of traits is generally considered to be innate or to be developed in early childhood.

Close to the desire to exercise leadership is a sense that 'it can be done'. This feeling entails a belief and confidence in one's own abilities and competence to lead, a sense of 'self-efficacy' as described by Hunt. When linked with the opportunity to exercise leadership – as formal, informal or emergent leader – these 'preferences' act as a springboard for leadership. However, to continue this analogy, certain other predispositions are needed before an individual is enabled to jump: intellectual predispositions in terms of the ways in which an individual collects, processes and assesses information, and certain value preferences.

The intellectual predispositions are described by Hunt as 'cognitive style' and by others in terms of decision-making or problem-solving styles. They refer to ways in which information is gathered and evaluated by individuals and can be assessed using measurement instruments such as the Myers–Briggs type indicator (MBTI; Myers and McCaulley, 1985). Using the MBTI, an individual demonstrates a preference for one trait out of each pair below:

Extraversion (E) or Introversion (I)
Sensing (S) or Intuitive (N) perception
Thinking (T) or Feeling (F)
Judgement (J) or Perception (P)

Using the MBTI produces a detailed portrait of individual cognitive style preferences which have been related to decision-making strategies, career choices, organizational designs and developmental inclinations over time (see Hunt 1992: 112–17), different individuals exhibiting markedly different preferences and patterns. For example, individuals with an ST preference (sensing-thinking) tend to focus on facts, to stress impersonal analysis, to value technical skills and to emphasize practicality. Others with an NF (intuition-feeling) preference tend to focus on possibilities, to stress personal warmth, insight and enthusiasm, and to emphasize understanding and communication.

When linking features of individual personality to leadership, three main arguments are put forward. First, these cognitive preferences are likely to influence the emergence of leadership; second, particular cognitive styles are likely to be more or less appropriate to different kinds of leadership contexts; third, such individual preferences need to be matched with leadership requirements at different levels of the organization. In some cases the argument is taken further still in that complementarity is sought between the cognitive styles of individuals within teams, particularly at senior level, in order to enhance creative strategic decision making over time (Hurst *et al.*, 1989). For the most part, these hypotheses are still tentative and require testing, particularly within higher education. However, in some areas preliminary findings have implications for leadership. For example, there appear to be a higher proportion of NT types (intuition-thinking) at senior levels of organizations than NF (intuition-feeling) or SF (sensing-feeling) types (Barber, 1990; McCaulley, 1990). An NT preference tends to focus on possibilities, to stress personal analysis, logic, ingenuity and theoretical and technical development.

The Myers–Briggs type indicator has been linked to other features of the individual in addition to cognitive style, such as creativity, risk, stress and burnout, change and organizational environments (McCaulley, 1990), all of which have a bearing on leadership. However, I will not discuss these here since my intention is merely to map the range of influences upon leadership at the individual level.

The fourth area mentioned by Hunt (1992: 108) in his 'preference network of leaders' is that of values. Here values are related to the individual, rather than to societal or organizational values (which will also have an impact on leadership, as was discussed in Chapter 4). These individual values create particular 'preferences for actions and outcomes', which are likely to shape the way an individual approaches a leadership role. Two particular frameworks are seen by Hunt as having potential relevance for leadership. The first, formulated by Hambrick and Brandon (1988), includes five dimensions:

Collectivism – to value the wholeness of humankind and of social systems; regard and respect for all people.
Duty – to value the integrity of reciprocal relationships; obligation and loyalty.
Rationality – to value fact-based, emotion-free decisions and actions.
Novelty – to value change, the new, the different.
Power – to value control of situations and people.

The second framework, which arises from the research of Meglino and his colleagues (Meglino *et al.*, 1989, 1990), has been developed out of empirical work and includes four dimensions.

Achievement – getting things done and working hard to accomplish difficult goals in life.
Helping and concern for others – being concerned for other people and helping others.
Honesty – telling the truth and doing what one feels is right.
Fairness – being impartial and doing what is fair for all concerned.

The 'achievement' and 'helping' dimensions in this framework carry echoes of the dimensions of leadership style identified in the Ohio and Michigan studies of the 1940s and 1950s: task-centred and relationship-oriented behaviour (see Chapter 1).

It is not yet clear precisely how such value frameworks operate (for example, which values lead to effective leadership? Which values are most relevant to particular contexts and cultures?) None the less, the frameworks offer some preliminary conceptions of the range of values which may be important for leadership. In the academic world, for example, I have already pointed to values that have been given a high priority in universities – and that have influenced leadership styles in the past – for example, 'collectivism' in the form of collegiality and 'rationality' in the form of reasoned argument. Some support for Meglino's framework can also be found in our investigation of staff expectations of university leadership, although here values are related to the preferences of followers rather than to the preferences of leaders. The characteristics that were mentioned most frequently in relation to desirable leadership styles included decisiveness, sensitivity to others, willingness to listen, ability to command respect and honesty (Middlehurst *et al.*, 1992: 126).

Five potential linkages between leadership and values at the individual level are suggested by Hunt. First, values may have a direct effect on action so that a leader makes a particular decision based on his or her preferences. It is easy to conceive of a Vice Chancellor, for example, who places a high value on power, taking a series of actions which support this preference: chairing all key meetings, selecting senior staff who can be directed or manipulated, allocating resources selectively, subtly altering structures and procedures to support central initiatives and perhaps playing up the perception of external threat to the institution as a justification for these actions.

Alternatively, values may have an indirect effect, whereby they influence a leader's perceptions of stimuli and these perceptions influence action. A third possibility is that values have moderated effects where, for example, the leader's degree of discretion can moderate between values and perceptions and between perceptions and actions (stronger associations being predicted where leaders have greater discretion). Fourth, the effects may be reciprocal so that values influence action and in turn are influenced by actions. We might envisage here a new Head of Department who initially acts on the basis of professional values in encouraging self-assessment of teaching, but who is subsequently obliged to conform to the values of others by setting up procedures for assessing teaching in more bureaucratic ways.

Fifth, congruence in values may, or may not, correspond between leaders at the same and different levels, and between leaders and their subordinates, as well as in different leadership situations (formal, informal or emergent). Again, this last linkage is not difficult to envisage in some universities where there is concern about the divergence of values between management and staff, for example over such issues as who controls the curriculum. The literature suggests that for organizational change to occur and for the changes to become embedded in practice, values need to be congruent between organizational levels. Achieving this difficult task is part of transformational leadership, an approach that is being encouraged in universities as a response to their present environment.

Connections between leadership and values are widely recognized by practitioners and researchers alike; for example, the shaping of collective and transcendental values is a key part of strategic leadership while the leadership responsibility for 'creating climate' at other levels of the organization is also linked to individual and collective values. However, the precise linkages between leadership and values in leader–follower relations are not yet well understood.

Cognitive complexity and social cognition

The resurgence of interest in trait theory mentioned above, arising largely out of recent work in psychology, has focused attention on other cognitive aspects that are associated with ideas about leadership. Two that have particular relevance are cognitive complexity and social cognition (how people make sense of themselves and others).

Cognitive complexity is a construct which is interpreted differently by different authors. Jacques (1989) describes it as a combination of mental power (which enables a person to sustain increasingly complex thought and decision processes) within a time-span; the longer the time-span, the greater the person's need for cognitive power or complexity. Those involved at the systems leadership level, for example, are expected to be involved in critical tasks with a time-frame for their completion of twenty years or more. They will therefore require a level of cognitive complexity that enables them both to operate within these time dimensions and to cope with the complexity of the tasks and decisions facing them.

Another interpretation of cognitive complexity is to be found in the work of Streufert and his associates (Streufert and Streufert, 1978; Streufert and Swezey, 1986; Streufert and Nogami, 1989). They argue that the way in which a person processes information is at the heart of cognitive complexity and emphasize the dimensions of differentiation (defined as 'the number of dimensions that are relevant to an information-processing effort') and integration ('the relationships among these dimensions') (quoted in Hunt, 1992: 122). Cognitively complex individuals are able both to differentiate and to integrate more elements than are less complex persons; a case of being able to see both the forest and the trees, as other authors put it (Senge, 1990). Both Jacques and Streufert *et al.*, suggest a match between organizational requirements and an individual's cognitive complexity.

As we saw in Chapter 2, Bensimon and her colleagues have related cognitive complexity to the academic environment. The complex realities of academic organizations, these researchers argue (in terms of cultural groups, range of activities and diversity of goals), require leaders with the capacity to use 'multiple lenses'. The ability to interpret events through the framework of different organizational realities, Bensimon suggests, will enable more flexible and more wide-ranging behavioural repertoires to be developed (1989: 72). The emphasis of this research is on strategic leadership, but cognitive complexity of this kind is likely to be exhibited in other areas, for example in managerial decision-making, or academic analysis. Perhaps in years to come an assessment of the ability to handle cognitive complexity will form part of more systematic selection procedures for leaders.

Both the notion of cognitive complexity and that of social cognition fall into the area of 'cognitive theories' of leadership outlined in Chapter 2. The second of these, social cognition, has three elements which are important for an understanding of leadership: cognitive schemata, attributions and implicit theories.

Cognitive schemata are a means of describing the way in which knowledge is organised which then influences what is perceived and remembered by individuals. These schemata explain how individuals create meaning and how they make sense of new situations. 'Attribution theory', which builds on the notion of cognitive schemata, is a set of ideas that suggest that individual perceptual bias acts as a filter on the interpretation of events and outcomes.

Pfeffer (1978: 31) explains this process in relation to leadership which he sees as:

> the outcome of an attribution process in which observers – in order to achieve a feeling of control over their environment – tend to attribute outcomes to persons rather than to context, and the identification of individuals with leadership positions facilitates this attribution process.

In other words, leadership is in the eyes of the beholder, rather than in the hands of the leader.

However, the same process (of perceptual bias and attribution) can be related to leaders themselves, causing them to make errors of judgement or to overestimate their impact on events. Again, this concept may be usefully applied in the academic context, where the level of ambiguity, conflict and variety of constituency interests makes simple cause–effect relationships difficult to sustain conceptually or to identify in practice. While senior staff may claim that their leadership has produced particular innovations, these achievements may instead owe more to the industry and ingenuity of other people, working to produce an innovation through a network of activities and interactions.

Closely related to attributions is the notion of 'implicit theories', Hunt's third element within the area of social cognition. These implicit theories enable individuals 'to give meaning to events, to attribute causes to phenomena, and to see patterns and regularity in the world around them' (Hunt, 1992: 135). In terms of leadership or organizational effectiveness, such implicit theories may influence what is believed to be successful or good in any particular context as the individual follower compares a leader's behaviour against a mental 'prototype'. It is not difficult to extend this concept from the individual to the group level, where particular cultures may develop strong 'myths' about ideal leaders or strong beliefs about appropriate forms of leadership, which will then be hard to change; for example, the notion of 'first among equals' in academic cultures. These implicit theories will also be carried by leaders themselves and so will influence their own conceptions of leadership.

Birnbaum (1989b) has examined the concept of implicit theories in relation to American college and university presidents. He found that the majority of presidents held an implicit theory which identified leadership as a process of influence directed towards the achievement of goals. They also viewed leadership essentially as the manifestation of an individual's (the president's) behaviour. A smaller group saw the concept differently. In this case, the role of the institutional leader was not to direct the group but to facilitate the emergence of leadership latent within it (p. 9). These implicit theories of leadership influenced presidential approaches to the practice of leadership in their institutions.

Birnbaum argues that some implicit theories may be at odds with university realities (for example, those which foster command-and-control approaches) and questions why such traditional and directive views of leadership should predominate among the presidents in his study. In keeping with the discussion of cognitive processes above, he suggests either that the behaviour of directive persons is attractive to presidential search committees (who are also operating on the basis of certain implicit theories of leadership) or that directive-style behaviours are developed once in office because of pressures to 'act like a leader' (p. 11). In the latter case, it is the assumptions (or implicit theories) of external groups that influence the approach to leadership.

There are obvious parallels between Birnbaum's work and the British higher education context, where, for example, the Jarratt Report (1985) made explicit the desirability of more directive leadership in universities. These expectations are now often incorporated within the 'person-specifications' designed by universities when they select new Vice Chancellors (as presented in Chapter 5). When these implicit theories of directive leadership are made explicit within the university, the consequences for 'constituent satisfaction' are not always positive.

This section, in essence a revisiting of trait theories, has concentrated on some of the cognitive and intellectual elements that are associated with the emergence and practice of leadership. In the next section, behavioural and social power approaches to leadership will be revisited in order to highlight another important feature of leadership capabilities at the individual level: the skills of leadership and the ways in which these are deployed.

Leadership skills and styles

There have been, until recently, three main trends in research on managerial or leadership behaviour. In the early part of the century, the focus was upon classifications of managerial *functions* and their operation in practice (for example, planning, organizing, controlling, decision-making). A second theme emphasized managerial *outcomes* (performance, goal achievement, employee satisfaction) and heralded the beginnings of serious study into leadership. A third theme has emphasized the *realities* of managerial work and the nature of organizational life. A well-known example of this last theme is Mintzberg's (1973) three-fold classification of managerial behaviour into interpersonal roles, informational and decisional roles, each of which is then broken down into more specific roles.

Within these broad themes, different typologies of skills and roles have been developed, at different levels of abstraction, for example, the micro-skills approach of Alban-Metcalf (1984) and Wright and Taylor (1984) or the macro-skills approach. A common distinction is made between different types of skills required for leadership: technical skills (methods, processes, procedures and techniques for conducting a specialized activity); human relations or interpersonal skills (the ability to establish cooperative and effective relationships, the ability to communicate clearly and effectively, knowledge about human behaviour and interpersonal processes); and conceptual skills (general analytical and problem-solving ability, conceptual-ization of complex and ambiguous relationships, creative idea generation, inductive and deductive reasoning) (Hunt, 1992: 158). Political skills are a further addition.

A third means of classification can be seen in Yukl's (1989) typology, which identifies four behavioural dimensions linked to a number of specific skills:

Influencing people – motivating, recognizing and rewarding.
Building relationships – supporting, networking, managing conflict and team- building.
Giving/seeking information – informing, clarifying, monitoring.
Making decisions – problem-solving, planning and organizing, consulting and delegating.

The variety of classifications makes the behavioural area confusing. This is not helped by the difficulty of identifying key skills for different levels of leadership; by the problem of determining proficiency in the use of particu-lar behaviours; or through the masking of actual behaviours by 'implicit theories' where descriptions of leaders' behaviour may be based as much on implicit theories of leadership characteristics as on actual behaviour. Recent studies have attempted to clarify and integrate findings so that a more coherent picture can be obtained. A number of points emerge.

First, technical skills are particularly required at lower organizational lev-els, while at higher levels a premium is placed on conceptual skills. For example, technical skills in engineering are required to build a central heating system, but are insufficient by themselves to run a company which designs, builds and sells central heating systems. Technical skills may be a necessary but not sufficient condition for leadership. In the academic world, most universities seek institutional and departmental leaders who have (at least) a credible academic reputation but who also exhibit managerial and enrepreneurial competence.

The second point is that skills or behaviours do not usually operate in isolation but are to be found in what Boyatzis (1982) terms 'competency clusters', which combine motives/traits, self-image/social role and skills lev-els. An ability to give a successful public lecture, for example, depends on knowledge and enthusiasm for the subject matter of the lecture, sensitivity to the interests of the audience, self-confidence and skill in presentation tech-niques. The reputation and position of the speaker is also likely to affect the overall impact of the lecture. Other writers, such as Quinn (1988), draw attention to a different cluster of elements: values, roles and competencies. Both authors raise the important point that 'skills' cannot be separated from affective or cognitive elements since these latter two elements influence the behavioural expression of the skills in question.

A third feature of recent studies is the attempt to distinguish between transactionally oriented skills and transformationally oriented skills, a dif-ferentiation which also reflects conceptions of management in contrast to leadership. Hunt (1992: 154–5) provides a summary of *transactional leadership* skills, which integrates the findings from a number of earlier studies, spanning research over four decades. His typology includes the following behaviours: supporting; consulting and delegating; recognizing and rewarding; motivating; harmonizing; developing; clarifying. Other behaviours cited by Hunt are similar to Adair's (1983) leadership functions and reflect early studies of managerial functions as well as contemporary views of managerial competences: problem-solving, informing, monitoring, representing, interfacing.

Transformational leadership is associated with both organizational and individual transformation and has strong links with charismatic or visionary leadership. Different behaviours are emphasized by different writers, but broadly they encompass aspects of vision and culture-building, such as: producing a vision; focusing attention on the vision; articulating and communicating the vision; aligning the organization and individuals with the vision; emphasizing and interpreting organizational values; interpreting the external environment; demonstrating charisma; taking risks; challenging the status quo; inspiring and stimulating followers (Conger, 1989; Sashkin and Burke, 1990). In most cases, transformational leadership is linked to strategic or institutional leadership rather than to middle-management or supervisory levels, although such a clear-cut distinction does not always follow in practice. The separation is not wholly appropriate in the academic context, where there is scope for transformational leadership at several levels.

Leadership writers commonly make connections between leaders' personal characteristics, particular organizational settings and their dynamics, and specific actions that are taken by leaders. It is the convergence of these factors that encourages transformational leadership. The personal characteristics mentioned are those highlighted above, such as self-belief (self-efficacy), social power and cognitive complexity, while the organizational dynamics can be encapsulated in Tichy and Devanna's (1986) five phases: a trigger event (which calls for movement beyond the status quo); a perceived need for change (this may be obvious, or part of the leader's task to create, particularly among key actors); creation of a vision (communication of a desired future state); mobilization of commitment (among a critical mass of organizational members); and the institutionalization of change (in which a new culture is developed to reinforce the vision).

It is worth reminding ourselves once again of the direction of influence. Most studies of transformational leadership are essentially leader-centred, but the discussion of 'implicit leadership theories' above highlights the importance of followers' expectations. In reality, there is likely to be a degree of reciprocity between leader and follower behaviour. Remembering the distinction made between formal and informal leadership, the stimulus for change, and the excitement and energy which can be generated in the process of change, may originate outside the formal structure. High status (and even low status) 'opinion formers' can create this sense of arousal, which is then spread among the social network of the organization, to be capitalized upon (perhaps) by formal leaders. This 'social contagion' (Meindl, 1990) is likely to have greater relevance within the fluid organizational structures of universities than in the direct leader-centred approach that is assumed in many versions of transformational leadership, unless extreme circumstances create an acknowledged need for strong, directive leadership either in departments or in the university as a whole.

Within academic organizations, there are many factors that militate against the exercise of transformational leadership where it is initiated solely from the top and where it is aimed at changing the whole organization, as the ideas of total quality management, for example, envisage. In the words of Bensimon *et al.* (1989: 74): 'Under normal circumstances, the exercise of transformational leadership in colleges and universities would be extremely difficult, and in many cases it could have disastrous consequences for those who dare to attempt it.' The authors go on to argue (p. 75) that:

> it would appear that it is good transactional leadership that affects the life of most colleges most of the time. To the extent that failure of a college can be attributed to a failure of leadership, it is usually not the result of a lack of charisma but to lack of basic organizational competence.

Bensimon and her colleagues seem to have three images in mind here. The first involves transformational leadership, which, as we have seen, emphasizes vision, charisma, risk-taking and challenge to the status quo. The second is transactional leadership, which implies a reciprocity between leaders and followers and which relies on leader actions such as consulting, delegating, informing, negotiating and representing. The third image, expressed as 'organizational competence', we can interpret as a combination of management and governance functions (for example, coordination, regulation, monitoring and reporting, financial and quality control, evaluation and review), which are then complemented by 'good transactional leadership'. The authors suggest that transformational leadership has little place in universities because they are decentralized institutions, with strong traditions of faculty autonomy and few common interests or goals that are shared across the institution. Universities also require internal stability to provide the right conditions for the pursuit of research, scholarship and teaching, conditions which are unlikely to prevail where risk-taking and challenges to the organizational status quo are constantly being promoted.

While organizational competence (i.e. management and governance) is clearly necessary for the running of a complex institution like a modern university, it is not enough in the present British environment. A combination of transactional *and* transformational approaches to leadership is likely to be important in universities, in response to external pressures, but also to challenge internal beliefs, patterns of organization and operational practices. While I recognize some of the constraints on transformational leadership raised by Bensimon *et al.*, this combination of leadership approaches is none the less likely to be a necessary aspect of university leadership (at least for the foreseeable future) for several reasons.

First, the pace of change is accelerating, both within disciplines and in the world outside the university. Second, there are a range of legitimate but competing interests associated with universities, so that consultation and negotiation over priorities will be required. Third, resource issues and questions of quality and standards are unlikely to disappear. They will need to be addressed in ways that satisfy both efficiency and effectiveness criteria and therefore will rely on management and leadership action. Fourth, the nature and consequences of change need to be debated and interpreted practically and symbolically in the light of university values. Finally, lest bureaucratic and managerial imperatives are perceived to be the sole driving force of change, individuals and groups within the university need vision and inspiration to lift their horizons above the instrumental and mundane towards a new conception of university purpose.

In our study of institutional leadership, some of these points were recognized implicitly by respondents in the distinctions they made between leadership and management and in their analyses of the changing environment of universities. Respondents associated leadership with creating institutional strategy and direction, and with institutional change and development. Other aspects of leadership included the articulation and representation of institutional goals and values and the generation of institutional commitment, confidence and cohesion. Particular competences or characteristics were associated with leadership in our study, for example vision (strategic imagination), policy formation (agenda setting) and the development of climate. The characteristics of leadership identified by our respondents combine both transactional and transformational elements.

Management was associated with policy coordination and execution; resource deployment and optimization; procedural and regulatory frameworks; planning and control systems. It was linked to particular competences: in planning, systems design, measurement, coordination and organization. Both management and leadership were seen as necessary to ensure institutional survival as well as development, particularly by senior staff. Where tensions and disagreements were evident was in the appropriate balance between the two and the appropriate style of each.

Hunt raises the issue of balance and linkages. He argues that leadership behaviours should not be examined in isolation but in terms of clusters and configurations that are in a temporary state of balance with each other while at the same time being in a state of tension with other 'Gestalts'. An example of this from within higher education (at the level of institutional leadership) is the Vice Chancellor's role in balancing such conflicting forces as preservation and innovation, equity and selectivity, centralization and decentralization within the university, where it is necessary both to think through and actively to support different scenarios in close proximity to each other. The balance between one emphasis and another will change, perhaps subtly, perhaps dramatically, in response to new circumstances (such as receipt of the funding council's decision on the amount of institutional grant).

This theme of balance, linkages, tensions and dilemmas is echoed in the writings of many authors. Kotter (1990) argues for leadership and management to be viewed as two complementary systems of action (as we saw in Chapter 2); Badaracco and Ellsworth (1989) suggest that certain guiding prejudices, underpinned by a particular philosophy of leadership, help to steer a path through the dilemmas of managerial life; Pascale and Athos (1982) highlight the conflicts between advocates of the 'cold triangle' of structure, systems and strategy and the 'warm square' of shared values, staff, skills and style. These perspectives on leadership are clearly cybernetic, carrying an image of leadership as 'helmsmanship', which involves charting a course, being aware of deviations and making appropriate corrections to the course being steered (Hampden-Turner, 1990b).

It is interesting to reflect that the perspectives outlined above have emerged primarily from empirical work in private sector organizations but demonstrate strong parallels with studies in academic organizations (Birnbaum, 1988). A convergence between approaches to leadership and management in the two sectors is underway, such that university models should have wider relevance than in the past. Influential writers such as Peters (1991) and Drucker (1988) have already predicted the value of looking toward universities as prototypes for organizations of the future. It is ironic that, at the same time, reports such as Jarratt (1985) urged universities to look to (outdated) business models for *their* organizational prototypes.

Academic roles and individual leadership

We turn now to a closer consideration of the scope for leadership in the roles of individual academics. Several authors have delineated these roles. Clark (1987) and Becher and Kogan (1992), for example, list the roles of the academic as teacher, researcher and scholar, academic manager or administrator, and as entrepreneur or service-giver. Those roles can be further subdivided: teacher into preceptor, facilitator, counsellor, supervisor, assessor; or entrepreneur into negotiator, initiator, risk-taker, business developer. A simpler and more generic classification might combine certain roles. For example, teacher, researcher or scholar can be subsumed under the heading of 'expert' or 'professional'; academic manager and administrator can be reclassified as 'manager'.

At least two points emerge from whichever classification is adopted. The first concerns the language used and the value associations that are attached to any of the labels. The associations not only reflect expectations of the nature of the activities which will be undertaken as part of the roles – *and* the way in which the roles will be undertaken – they also reflect certain cultural assumptions about the organization as a whole. In this way, teacher as expert implies a different kind of relationship with the learner from that of teacher as facilitator; and academic as administrator implies a different kind and source of authority from that of academic as manager. These distinctions of language and classification are as relevant to conceptions of leadership as they are to an understanding of roles. Changes in language can be linked to changes in meaning and ultimately to changes in behaviour.

The second point is the variety of roles expected of the ordinary academic, although as Becher and Kogan (1992) argue, expectations differ across disciplines and according to personal and departmental circumstance, so that where an individual chooses to place his or her main emphasis and effort will vary. Within each of these academic roles, there is a considerable expectation of autonomy since individual freedom of choice, inculcated as part of a general academic apprenticeship and associated particularly with the primary academic activities, is psychologically extended into all areas of academic life (that is, from teaching and research to management and governance).

This expectation of the ability and the opportunity to exercise independent judgement and discretion, to be able to shape and direct one's own work is also a necessary part of the conditions for leadership. As a feature of leadership, this kind of drive and motivation is described in several ways by different writers: as 'challenging the process' and 'modeling the way' by Kouzes and Posner (1987); as 'self-efficacy' (Hunt, 1992); as 'taking charge' (Bennis and Nanus, 1985). The common denominator in these examples is a feeling of confidence, which enables the individual to exercise initiative and to step outside his or her personal comfort zone. In analyses of innovation, change and transformational leadership, this capacity is described in stronger terms as risk-taking, non-conformity and the will to challenge the status quo (Kanter, 1983; Tichy and Devanna, 1986; Conger, 1989). Of course, for many academics, the exercise of initiative will not extend beyond their own areas of academic work; but for others it may be manifested in the leadership of teams, departments or the institution.

The variety of roles available to the academic provide an opportunity to deploy different skills and behaviours and to develop different characteristics and attitudes in several contexts, many of which are also important for leadership. For example, in relation to teaching, presentational skills, diagnostic skills, skills of organization, synthesis and judgement will be called upon as well as enthusiasm, concern and sensitivity. In research, skills of critical reflection, analysis and interpretation will be required alongside patience, commitment, creativity and intellectual honesty. In the entrepreneurial domain (when selling academic services), negotiation, interpersonal and political skills, initiative and imagination may be called for, while management will require skills in planning, problem-solving, monitoring, decision-taking and information-processing.

There will of course be overlap in the skills required in different activities; and the degree of skill congruence between different activities will also vary (teaching and management, for example, have certain similarities in skills terms). Individuals are likely to develop strengths in different areas and will be more or less effective in their different roles. The point is that the variety of activities open to academics enables individuals to develop strengths in one or more areas and to exploit a range of skills. Academics are also expected to build internal and external networks in respect of their professional activities. If we link the development of academic competence, the establishment of contacts, the building of relationships and the exercise of initiative, a basis for the exercise of leadership by individual academics can begin to be established. The foundation for this association can be found in our earlier discussion of the ways in which leadership is shaped – at least in part – by individual characteristics and interpersonal capacities.

The argument above has been used to illustrate the potential for leadership in *academic* roles. Where similar conditions exist and similar opportunities are exploited within other functional areas and among other categories of staff, leadership potential will again be present, as examples from the catering department, the conference office, research teams or the students' union can testify. Whether the potential for leadership is exploited will depend on a range of circumstances, an important one being the degree to which leadership is sought and recognized within the institution. This condition is discussed below to round off our exploration of leadership at the individual level.

Context and opportunity for individual leadership

There are a number of different contextual factors that can impinge on leadership. The first of these is the external environment, with its mixture of cultural and social values, political and economic pressures. The nature of this environment has been described more fully in Chapter 4, but some points can be re-emphasized since they offer scope for leadership at the individual level as well as elsewhere in the institution.

Many of the changes currently affecting universities have important consequences for the day-to-day practices of individual staff. In many cases, action can be initiated at the individual level, which will produce positive rather than negative consequences for individuals and groups. For example, how to generate income and whom should be targeted are decisions that will need to be taken by individuals as well as by departments and institutions. Ideas as to how to market programmes, to develop new courses or to attract research contracts also rely on individual initiative. Strategies for teaching more and different kinds of students, for improving the quality of academic activities or for developing interdisciplinary research can be developed by individual academics and will need to be implemented (and owned) by individuals. Influencing the adoption of ideas relating to research, the curriculum or the structuring and prioritizing of activities involves opportunities for exercising leadership at the individual level.

If we turn to the internal environment of institutions, then other contextual factors emerge. The nature of academic organizations has been discussed in Chapter 3 and elsewhere in this book and I have argued at various points that the special characteristics of universities have implications for leadership. These implications are often paradoxical. For example, the fluid reporting structures and sometimes ambiguous decision-making systems in universities can inhibit formal leadership, but may facilitate informal leadership within the individual domain. It is possible, for example, for a course team (perhaps stimulated by the actions of the course leader or the ideas of members of the team) to develop curricular innovations – such as compacts between academic staff and students, learning activities that foster student independence and creativity, or systems of peer-review for teaching – without needing to be directed to do so from above. Achieving these outcomes within a single programme calls for leadership; and leadership will also be required to disseminate such practice from one programme to others in a department or elsewhere in the institution. Finding and using these individual 'champions of change' is a key task for departmental or institutional leaders.

Another aspect of the academic environment that is also paradoxical in relation to leadership is the issue of expertise and reputation. Expertise in a field can be developed young and will be demonstrated by junior as well as senior academics. External reputation and status may well be higher than an individual's internal position or rank would suggest. Such professional expertise is needed for teaching and research and must often be managed by those with less (or different) expertise. On the one hand, these high status individuals may pose problems for leaders since they can be difficult to persuade or direct; on the other hand these academics can use their own expertise as a source of influence upwards or laterally to achieve desired outcomes. In this way, leadership can be exercised by both formal and informal leaders (in the individual domain and at other levels) and is likely to be widely dispersed in institutions. Its exercise will also vary within individual roles since in one situation an individual may act as leader, while in another he or she may act as subordinate or colleague.

The features of the academic environment described above relate to universities in general and will be latent within all institutions. Whether or not these elements are activated positively will depend on at least two other dimensions that will vary between institutions. The first of these dimensions involves the 'hard systems' of the institution. These systems are aspects of the organization's infrastructure and include reward structures, selection procedures, resources and their allocation, reporting and decision-taking structures, evaluation systems, management information systems, and the pattern of day-to-day tasks and operations. The way in which the organization is designed, the shape of these 'hard systems', will have an impact on behaviour. These systems can operate to encourage or to discourage leadership, but do not work in isolation from the 'soft systems' of an organization.

The soft systems, which include values, norms, traditions, habits of thought, symbols and rituals, managerial styles and priorities, language and labels, complement the hard systems of an institution. Together the two systems create ethos, climate and, in the longer term, culture. Both symbolically and actively, these systems can generate virtuous or vicious cycles of behaviour, to use Hampden-Turner's phrase (1990b). The soft systems influence individual leadership by facilitating or inhibiting its development and its manifestation. The ability to see the interaction between hard and soft systems and to integrate the two so that they provide mutual reinforcement instead of internal conflict is an important aspect of leadership at senior levels. At the individual level, an understanding of the interactions between hard and soft systems will provide individuals with the potential to act more effectively as leaders.

This brief survey of the context and opportunities for leadership rounds off discussion of leadership at the individual level, while this chapter completes our exploration of leadership at different institutional levels. Throughout the discussion in this second part of the book, ideas about leadership outlined in Part 1 have been related to leadership practice in order to demonstrate the interplay between the two perspectives. The resulting picture is complex and dynamic, revealing leadership as a concept and a process that is affected by many elements. The convergence of these elements – individual characteristics, institutional systems and culture, external pressures, prevailing myths – may happen by luck or by design. If luck is described as the point at which vision and opportunity meet (Turrill, 1986) and design as the conscious creation of opportunities, then there is scope for the development of leadership within academe. It is to the subject of leadership development that I shall now turn.

Part 3

Developing Leadership

9

Leadership Learning

Introduction

One of the purposes of this book is to demonstrate that there is much to be learned about leadership. In Part 1, we considered the variety of ideas on the subject and then paid particular attention to the exercise of leadership in an organizational setting. In Part 2, the organizational setting became more specific, the focus moving to the practice of leadership in academic institutions. In Part 3, we turn to an exploration of issues related to the development of leadership, at both individual and institutional levels.

'Leadership learning' is an ambiguous notion; it points towards a number of propositions about leadership development. The first of these is that leadership – or aspects of it – can be learned. The second is that learning to lead and learning about leadership are linked. In other words, leadership development includes learning to know about and to understand the art of leadership, in addition to learning to act as and learning to be a leader – in the fullest sense. The process of learning is therefore active, involving engagement with leadership at intellectual, emotional and physical levels.

The third proposition is that learning for leadership takes place in a variety of ways and relies on a range of strategies and opportunities. The potential for leadership learning is created from the interaction between individual or group effort and the particular context in which the individual or group find themselves. Such interaction between person(s) and situation can be simultaneously planned and also random since it is never certain that the planned development opportunity, for example, will be so timely and so well crafted as to trigger the appropriate combination of motivation, competence and belief in the capacity to lead. Nor can one be sure, even where individual or collective capacities have been developed, that others will attribute the mantle of leadership to those individuals or that group. None the less, individual and institutional planning is likely to reduce the problems associated with randomness (such as lack of leadership or emergence of inappropriate leaders) while an element of randomness is essential to flexibility and creativity in leadership and its development.

The fourth proposition is that leadership and learning are closely related.

Without an open approach to learning, opportunities for understanding and mastering leadership will be lost. And without an open attitude to leadership that allows one to play with a variety of perspectives, opportunities for improving the capacity to learn will also be missed. Yet there are deeper implications in this relationship between leadership and learning.

Leadership development is a long-term process, beginning in early childhood and subject to a range of influences and experiences. The ability to capitalize on these life-events (in the interests of leadership, but also for a full realization of personal potential) relies on continuous, active learning to try to understand more fully the interconnections between the organization (or other setting), its purposes and environment, the behaviours and experiences of individuals, groups and self, and the different tasks of leadership – and then to test out these understandings through action and reflection. For this kind of realization to take place, individuals and institutions need to be conscious of the learning process. They need to identify and evaluate the nature of their learning, the means and circumstances by which it was achieved, and its applicability in different contexts. This fourth proposition, then, implies that learning for leadership depends on 'learning to learn'.

A final proposition – which is more of an aspiration than a proposition – is that universities will develop 'a learning leadership' at the top of institutions, which will serve as an example for other levels and which will promote and facilitate learning throughout the institution.

This chapter will pursue these propositions by examining what needs to be learned, how learning can take place and who is responsible for the learning needed for leadership.

Key ingredients

When leadership is set within the context of formal organizations, several dimensions are apparent. First, leadership development depends on both individual and organizational effort (Sadler, 1989; Conger, 1989). Second, development is a continuum that ranges from planned events to natural processes, each of which can take place within the organization or outside it (Burgoyne, 1988; Lombardo and McCall *et al.*, 1988). Third, the term 'leadership development' includes education, training and experience, some of which is approached on a short-term, some on a long-term basis (Hunt, 1992). Fourth, the elements that are associated with leadership learning encompass the full range of human capacities; for example, knowledge, beliefs, attitudes, values and competence in several domains. Finally, leadership learning is essentially a social process, involving self-analysis and reflection, but chiefly a continuing dialogue between the self and others. These interconnections are outlined in Figure 4 (adapted from Burgoyne, 1985). As Burgoyne says, 'the surface skills and immediate performance are the essential bridge between inner values and beliefs, and influence in the world' (p. 50).

Internal influences

External influences

Figure 4 The learning environment of leaders

Learning about oneself

As Figure 4 suggests, leadership development must involve – and perhaps begin with – knowledge and understanding of oneself. This starting point has prompted considerable investigation into the legacy of heredity and childhood experience. Kotter (1990) for example, identifies four attributes that have their origins in early life and that, he suggests, seem to define some minimum requirements for leadership (particularly in 'big jobs'): personal drive and energy level; intelligence and intellectual skills; mental and emotional health (which we might interpret as a sense of self-worth); and integrity. Later life brings experiences and opportunities which enable these foundations to be built upon.

Other writers have looked more closely at elements of suffering or crisis in childhood. Zaleznik (1977) has suggested that leaders can be divided into 'once-borns' and 'twice-borns'. The former have had a relatively smooth early path and have been shaped by their fortunate circumstances, while the latter have suffered, felt different or isolated. Through these experiences, 'twice borns' develop an elaborate inner life which, as they mature, enables them to rely on their own beliefs and ideas. These leaders become inner-directed, independent, self-assured and truly charismatic, according to Zaleznik.

Bennis (1989) also sees leadership learning as a process of self-development through the growth of self-awareness and the practice of self-expression. The leaders he studied, while differing in terms of background, experience and vocation, had in common: 'a passion for the promises of life and the ability to express themselves fully and freely' (p. 2). For Bennis, such full and free self-expression is the essence of leadership. It is acquired by 'mastering the context' (instead of surrendering to the habitual practices and modes of thought around one); through understanding the basic ingredients of leadership; by getting people on one's side and forging alliances; by seeking experience that will stimulate and challenge and so yield new perspectives and insights; by learning to cope with ambiguity and change while paying attention to present realities; by seeking and listening to feedback. Bennis's basic ingredients of leadership are:

- a guiding vision – knowing where you are going and why, personally and professionally;
- passion, enthusiasm, optimism;
- integrity, which involves self-knowledge, openness, candour (described as a fundamental 'soundness and wholeness') and maturity;
- trust (which must be earned);
- curiosity and daring, which encompasses a deep desire to learn and a willingness to take risks.

Bennis's emphases have much in common with Cunningham's (1992) work, in which he attempts to find links between the concrete 'doing' level and the less tangible 'being' level of leadership. To make this link, Cunningham uses the concepts of 'centredness' and 'groundedness'. The former (derived originally from Eastern thought) refers to an integration of physical, emotional, spiritual and cognitive domains. Cunningham describes it as 'harmonizing and focusing energy' so that congruence is achieved between theory and practice, word and deed. He suggests that centred leaders meet the challenge posed by Argyris and Schon (1974) to bring together espoused theory and theory-in-use; they 'walk the talk' as Tom Peters would say. 'Groundedness', on the other hand, arises from being rooted in or connected to something: a profession, a sense of history, a set of values, stable personal relationships. These two dimensions form part of an individual's impact on others, creating an impression of substance, integrity, confidence, presence; and for the individuals themselves, achieving 'centredness and groundedness' make possible an alignment between 'being and doing' which is likely to lead to greater happiness and contentment (Handy, 1991). Those who carry an aura of inner certainty and who act with integrity are often identified as leaders.

The theme of self-knowledge and self-development is echoed by other writers, albeit in more prosaic terms. Adair (1988) defines the process in terms of assessing personal strengths and weaknesses, wanting to be a leader, seeking opportunities for learning about leadership (through leading, reading, formal programmes, observation and discussion with others), accepting challenging opportunities and learning from successes and failures. Kouzes and Posner (1987) highlight three ingredients that contribute to leadership learning: trial and error; interactions, relationships and feedback from people; and formal education and training. Like Bennis and Adair, they emphasize experiential learning which involves challenge combined with the ability to analyse and reflect on successes and failures, for 'embedded in experience [we find] the grains of truth about ourselves, others, our organizations and life itself' (Kouzes and Posner, 1987: 286).

In Britain, outdoor leadership training is particularly noted for its emphasis on self-development and self-awareness. Usually through the medium of a range of physical tasks, undertaken in teams, participants are stretched physically, emotionally and intellectually. Their experience and performance, the interaction of the team and the group leader's role are then discussed and evaluated in order to identify personal strengths and weaknesses, aspects of leadership and leadership potential. Through these events, participants are expected to reveal and discover more about themselves, particularly their reactions to stressful or new situations, and to gain confidence in their abilities and potential (Charlton, 1992).

Learning about others

While understanding of self is a central feature of leadership learning, it is usually developed in relation to other people. Becoming aware of one's response to others, one's impact and influence upon others, is essential for leadership. The parallel perspective, of noting the influence and impact of others upon oneself, is also necessary. Both are assisted by having an interest and curiosity about human interactions and the variety of human life.

Since leadership depends in large part on relationships between people, leadership development will include interpersonal skills development and analysis of human interactions in a variety of settings. Continuing the theme of addressing understanding, being and doing in combination, the learning is likely to be achieved in part through observation, reflection and analysis and in part through practice and interaction in different contexts; for example, domestic or recreational settings, in departmental or institutional meetings, through managing projects, negotiating deals, or in the artificial 'goldfish bowls' created on training programmes.

Several authors point to the contributions of other people in leadership learning. Significant others (for example, colleagues, managers, mentors) may act as role models for appropriate behaviour and can highlight inappropriate behaviour. They can also offer inspiration, advice, feedback, instruction, counselling or sponsorship (Kouzes and Posner, 1987). Building and working through networks of different relationships, noting how power is created and deployed, what patterns of communication are effective and how to gather relevant information, being tolerant of difference, learning when to stand firm and when to bend, are all part of leadership development. This kind of learning will again take place in many contexts, inside and outside the workplace, through interactions with other people (Kotter, 1990).

The kinds of capacities that are required will include communication, negotiation, team-building and conflict management, as well as supervising, giving and receiving feedback, confronting performance problems, and approaches to motivating and encouraging performance. Building and managing relationships, dealing with political situations, lobbying, representing the institution, unit or group and negotiating with a variety of constituencies will form a major part of the challenge and the interest of leadership.

As with all aspects of leadership development, the key to *learning* rests on the individual's willingness and capacity to test and challenge assumptions, to try different strategies and their willingness to be vulnerable, to be open to new experiences, to listen and to hear the inner voice as well as the external voices – and to watch and reflect systematically on the whole process. In those who listen, absorb and learn through working with others and through reading their environment, a capacity for 'judgement' can be developed, that intangible element which is often linked to leadership. It involves knowing when to act and when to wait, discerning what is important and what is transitory.

Leadership and organizational know-how

Developing self-awareness and understanding of the behaviour of others are important capabilities for leadership. However, we have been discussing leadership that takes place in the setting of organizations, specifically academic institutions. There is much to be learned, therefore, about leadership and its application within different roles, functions and levels within the institutional context. The knowledge and skills required will include critical tasks (such as preparing a departmental or institutional plan, chairing meetings or appraising staff) as well as competence in professional areas such as teaching, research, accountancy or librarianship. Strong track records in professional areas provide credibility, which is an important resource for leadership, although by themselves strong professional records will not guarantee effective leadership.

In order to set and implement agendas at different levels of leadership and more generally to fulfil its associated responsibilities, formal leaders will need to understand the day-to-day operations of the organization (the timetable of committees, the sources of useful information, the relevant precedents, essential control mechanisms) as well as the points of leverage, the interests of key stakeholders and the purpose and consequences of their interventions. They will be assisted by developing an understanding of different approaches to leadership, through an appreciation of different models of organizational culture and design, and through knowledge of the nature and context of their business.

Accumulating knowledge and know-how of this kind takes time and effort and involves a variety of activities played out in different roles (for example, chairing meetings within professional associations; negotiating contracts and providing consultancy services; presenting papers at conferences; discussing managerial problems with counterparts in other sectors; keeping abreast of national and international developments in higher education; managing projects, teams and budgets; developing new products or processes; initiating and maintaining networks of contacts; dealing with crises, problems and conflicts). Learning through experience, particularly through challenging activities, will provide insight into the nature of responsibility and accountability, will expose personal and cultural values, and will highlight one's 'managerial temperament', that is, one's instinctive reactions to people and problems of different kinds. Each activity has the potential to contribute to the broadening and deepening of experience necessary for leadership.

There are two specific tasks required of academic leaders where an understanding of leadership and of the institutional context of leadership is particularly necessary: envisioning a future and shaping and interpreting values and culture (Green and McDade, 1991). In the former case, the task will include defining a mission, setting priorities, communicating a sense of direction and enabling others to take initiative, both in the development of mission and in its fulfilment. These responsibilities will require information-processing skills as well as imagination and the ability to communicate clearly and effectively. Green and McDade (1991: 28) argue that leaders who nurture their intellectual vitality (by maintaining an active interest in a range of subjects and activities outside their managerial responsibilities) can encourage their own and others' creativity, since 'a fertile and active mind, a finger on the pulse of the institution and the larger community, and the deliberate pursuit of new ideas and information are the underpinnings of vision'.

The task of interpreting and shaping values and culture is still more intangible than creating vision, since culture is created simultaneously while living it. In order to have an impact on culture, the rules, myths, rituals, history and symbols of the culture (or the several cultures of the institution) must be learned through watching, listening, asking questions, establishing a frame of reference, interpreting, soliciting feedback and encouraging dissonant views. These activities will help to develop the multiple lenses and cognitive complexity referred to in Chapter 8.

Management skills

While the emphasis of this book has been on examining leadership, the reality of leadership practice demonstrates a close association between leadership and management. Kotter offers a clear description of the intertwining of leadership and management – and power development, as a resource for both activities – in his study *The General Managers* (1982):

> They did not manage for fifteen minutes and then lead for half-an-hour. Instead, in the course of a single, five-minute conversation, they might try to see if some activity was proceeding as planned (a control aspect of

management), gather information that was relevant to their emerging vision (the direction-setting part of leadership), promise to do someone a favor (an aspect of power development), and agree on a series of steps for accomplishing some objective (the planning part of management).

(quoted in Kotter, 1990: 104)

The relationship between leadership and management is also recognized by other writers. For example, Green and McDade (1991: 29) suggest that 'the aggregate of management decisions and procedures also performs leadership functions, translating a vision into practical applications'. Formal leadership is practical as well as visionary and so will encompass: the setting of priorities; the establishment of plans, strategies and procedures; the development of policy; and the acquisition and allocation of resources.

In order to carry out the responsibilities associated with formal leadership in an institution, technical skills (such as budgeting, personnel management, fund-raising, an understanding of statistics, the uses of information technology) and general managerial skills, will be required. The latter include planning and organizing techniques, system and task design, decision-making and problem-solving abilities, time-management and delegation, diagnostic skills, appraisal and evaluation, as well as an understanding of the shapes that these functions take in the particular context of a university. Broad knowledge of how an institution, department or unit functions operationally will also be needed.

While the degree of knowledge and competence in technical and managerial areas will vary according to role, level and specialization, a basic knowledge is likely to be required by all formal leaders in institutions. This is for reasons of accountability, in the interests of creating a common language (for example, between centre and departments), and in order to develop an awareness of major functions, such as the management of resources. An understanding of management processes is also necessary in order to be able to challenge assumptions and habitual ways of approaching a problem by asking critical questions – within committees or working parties and in contacts with the administration. In the complex institutions of today, managerial capability is a necessary adjunct to leadership as well as a resource for leadership credibility.

Intangibles: ambiguity, dilemmas and balance

In his essay *The Postmodern Challenge* Scott (1991) points to a retreat from certainty, an increase in diversity and an emphasis on the anarchic and irrational at the expense of the rational in many areas of public life. (Such currents are evident in approaches to leadership and organizational behaviour and so have implications for leadership development.

Being able to cope with uncertainty (the implications of research selectivity or new funding methodologies), to live with ambiguity (the difficulties of identifying the locus of power in a university or of judging the success of leadership strategies) and to face dilemmas (educational priorities ranged against financial priorities) is part of leadership in a complex system. To an extent, preparation for managing this messy reality occurs in the course of academic life; for example, through learning to balance the different requirements of teaching, research and administration or the roles of counsellor and assessor of students. However, in formal leadership positions, the uncertainties are likely to be more threatening and the need to resolve apparently impossible dilemmas more pressing, particularly when leaders are viewed as 'problem-solvers in chief'.

The difficulties of achieving rationality – in strategy and decision-making – in a complex, turbulent and information-rich environment are widely recognized as a key problem in business management. Several authors point to the need to develop alternative mind-sets about the future (Morgan, 1988; Handy, 1989); to the importance of thinking creatively and laterally by using metaphors and mental-mapping techniques (McCaskey, 1982; de Bono, 1984; Morgan, 1991); to the ability to re-frame dilemmas (Hampden-Turner, 1990b); and to the need to think systemically and to exploit double-loop learning (Birnbaum, 1988; Senge, 1990; Lessem, 1991).

These ideas have also emerged within leadership development, where there is a growing interest in the use of intuition and judgement in learning (in addition to more traditional analytical or skills emphases). Developing these skills relies on techniques such as using guided imagery, looking for patterns where none are obvious, playing with ideas and scenarios, reading in fields unconnected with the problem area, listening to music, meditating, and surfacing dilemmas, conflicts and feelings. Systematic attempts to incorporate these techniques into leadership development programmes (to improve 'Janusian learning', that is, the ability to perceive and use several perspectives on organizations, or to work with different layers of meaning in the behaviour of individuals and groups) are being developed, for example, by Quinn and his colleagues (1990). They are also part of efforts to encourage new approaches to strategic planning (Hampden-Turner, 1990b). As with other aspects of leadership learning, the full potential of such approaches is only likely to be realised through the medium of an open mind – tinged, perhaps, with a degree of healthy scepticism – and a willingness to expose oneself to new perspectives.

Learning media

How do leaders learn?

The propositions outlined at the beginning of this chapter suggest that learning is both planned and random and that the settings and circumstances in which it occurs are many and varied. A motivation to learn has been stressed, alongside the holistic nature of the process (incorporating cognitive, affective and motor elements). The duration of the learning journey was also noted. To quote 'Attila':

> Those of you who are overly ambitious may attempt to acquire [leadership] qualities over a short period. As I, Attila, have found in my own life, these qualities . . . simply take time, learning and experience to develop. There are few shortcuts. There are simply rare opportunities to accelerate competence, and without paying the price, no matter how great or small, none will become prepared to lead others.
>
> (Roberts, 1987)

Bearing in mind these aspects of leadership development, we will concentrate on activities which are particularly associated with leadership in an organizational setting.

Mumford *et al.* (1987) and Mumford (1989) provide a model of three types of learning process based on the study *Developing Directors.* Type 1 is labelled 'informal managerial' or the accidental learning processes that occur naturally within managerial activities. Type 2, 'integrated managerial', describes the opportunistic processes where natural managerial activities are structured in such a way as to make use of the available learning opportunities, for example providing feedback to a colleague on the chairing of a meeting or videoing a presentation for subsequent analysis. Type 3 includes the planned processes that are part of 'formal management development', that is, those planned activities which take place away from normal managerial activities. These different types of learning opportunity are echoed in Green and McDade's handbook of leadership development in higher education (1991) and in our own study (Middlehurst *et al.*, 1992).

Informal learning processes will include observation, reading, films and videos, discussions with colleagues, friends, advisers, family and others. Bennis (1989: 42) stresses the importance of individual initiative in leadership development so that leaders 'invent themselves' – through interrelating their own perceptions of themselves with the perceptions of other people – taking full advantage of the rich variety of opportunities to learn about self, context and others. While many of these opportunities will occur spontaneously and randomly outside the institution, they can also occur internally in common rooms and corridors, in the students' union, during open days for public and parents, or around a dinner table.

Formal activities fall loosely into the categories of education and training and may be professional, managerial or general in scope. For example, university administrators attend professional gatherings (regional personnel meetings; national and international conferences for university administrators) and academics attend subject-based conferences or conventions where trends in the discipline are discussed and contacts are developed. Both groups attend 'issue-based' programmes (quality in higher education, the development of NVQs, fund-raising in universities) as well as courses aimed at particular roles: heads of department, admissions officers, student counsellors and external examiners. Other programmes may address skills or specific topics such as time management, international relations, computer skills or business strategy. General programmes will cover broad topics such as 'Universities in the twenty-first century' or 'Education for capability', attracting audiences from within and outside higher education. Retreats, sabbaticals and study visits may also be employed.

Programmes can be short (a half-day, up to three days) or longer (anything from a week to two years, on a part-time basis). The location may be in-house, overseas, in other institutions, in companies, at management centres, at prestigious places such as the Royal Society; or programmes may be undertaken by means of distance learning. Programmes may be designed by others (staff development personnel, training officers) or by oneself (for example, a sabbatical). Programmes are likely to include a range of activities from formal lectures to simulations, games, outdoor exercises, case studies and action-learning projects. Remembering the need to integrate understanding, doing and being, the most relevant and useful programmes are likely to be those that contain active elements, that emphasize self-managed learning (Cunningham, 1981), that are stimulating, challenging and fun.

Both within higher education (Middlehurst *et al.*, 1992) and outside it (McCall *et al.*, 1988) considerable value is placed on learning from experience, particularly that gained 'on-the-job'. Sometimes this kind of learning is structured, for example when shadowing a predecessor in your role, undertaking a developmental assignment or being coached, but generally the learning is less systematic, involving observation, discussion, trial and error.

The kinds of experience that have developmental potential include special projects, tasks or responsibilities with a broad scope, exposure to role models, conflicts with superiors/subordinates, and assignments which require re-structuring or re-designing systems or units. Green and McDade (1991) present a useful chapter about 'on-campus development' (pp. 213–34). Some examples from their handbook include new assignments, joining committees and task forces, job-rotation, switching between staff and line responsibilities. We can add inter-institutional projects, part-time secondment to national bodies, participating as tutors in internal management programmes and involvement in national initiatives (such as the Enterprise in Higher Education programme).

Green and McDade's 'inexpensive development ideas' are equally useful (pp. 235–43). They include several categories of activity: bringing people together inside the institution, particularly across levels or territories; expanding individual and collective experience by switching roles, visiting departments, explaining the institution or department and its activities to visitors; writing case studies of internal management problems; creating relationships, for example pairing new Heads of Department, academic staff or administrators; learning in the community and outside the institution, for example by encouraging staff representation on corporate boards, through staff involvement in local projects and by using outside consultants (such as lay governors) in self-evaluation exercises.

Much of the literature focuses upon the content or the activities that provide opportunities for learning about leadership. However, attention to the *process* is more important if learning is to become less haphazard. It is still likely to be highly idiosyncratic, individuals learning different things from the same experience and some learning more than others. However, the learning process can be helped through a variety of strategies. These include: increasing the amount and immediacy of feedback; designing experiences or activities that require learning; conducting self-assessments (via instruments such as the learning styles questionnaire; Honey and Mumford, 1992); analysing managerial processes in detail, for example process evaluation of teamwork; recording individual and collective responses to initiatives; and charting learning, for example, from novice stages through competence and proficiency, to expertise and mastery.

Purposes and benefits

The purposes of leadership development range from the systematic to the accidental, and from basic to sophisticated in terms of design and outcome. Some obvious purposes include induction and orientation to new roles, skills development, awareness raising, assessment of potential and enhancement of individual performance. Some that are less obvious or more intangible include team-building, reward and motivation, enrichment of ideas, culture and attitudinal change, establishing networks and contacts, developing more complex thinking, developing policy and strategy, and creating a common language.

The benefits of undertaking leadership development can be individual and institutional (Green and McDade, 1991), as well as collective, as I shall argue below. For the individual, many aspects of leadership development are relevant to continuing professional development in general; for example, planning or budgeting skills, and communication or team-building skills. Other aspects, which involve re-conceptualizing old problems or extending the range of one's vision, may also have general applicability. Several can be of personal value; for example, increased self-confidence, respite from pressure and routine, and intellectual and emotional stimulation. Contacts and networks can be established, and support, encouragement or challenge can be obtained through the broad range of activities that constitute leadership development.

For the institution, there are also multiple benefits. Investing in leadership development (as Green and McDade put it), ensures and improves competence, matches individual needs and strengths to the institutional agenda, assists in fostering shared goals and common understanding, promotes institutional renewal and encourages pluralism. Benefits that can accrue to any organization from leadership development include improved communication, the identification of new leaders, reduced turnover of staff, encouragement of equal opportunities and stimulus for changes in practice and outlook.

The achievement of these benefits and the realization of purpose depend upon commitment and effort at individual *and* institutional level, commodities that are sometimes in short supply. It is to the issue of different levels of responsibility and to the problems of commitment that we now turn.

Responsibility for leadership learning

Preliminary issues

Without an interest in leadership and in leading, combined with an individual and collective motivation to learn and develop, leadership will not flourish. This poses a particular difficulty in some parts of the academic community, where leadership and management are often under-valued. In these settings, management is often perceived either as 'mere' administration or as a threat to individual autonomy through the exercise of bureaucratic procedures and controls. Leadership also carries negative connotations where it is associated with commanding others (which does not fit with collegiality) or with charismatic inspiration (which arouses scepticism in a culture of rationality).

Similarly, the idea of wanting to lead is viewed with suspicion. It may be perceived as an exhibition of anti-democratic tendencies, as a sign of a wish for power, or even as a substitute for a declining record in teaching and research. While the existence and the need for leadership roles *is* recognized in universities, legitimacy is often conferred (in some of the 'traditional' universities, at least) by electing, rather than selecting people to these positions, by placing more emphasis on the 'invited applicant' than on the 'supplicant' who responds to job advertisements, and by rotating the role so that real power cannot be amassed. By maintaining managerial leadership either as faintly subversive or as a low status occupation for academics (except at the level of the Vice Chancellor), by regarding the role as secondary and often supplementary to academic roles, there is little incentive to reward the position, to value individual leadership contributions or to denote it as a legitimate career aspiration for those with talent for the task. Instead, the role is likely to be regarded simply as one of service to the institution, performed in the spirit of community and with no wish 'to rock the boat'. Given the increasing burdens of some of the formal leadership positions in universities (for example, the Pro Vice Chancellors or Heads of Department), service to the community may in practice result in a disservice to oneself since it may be difficult at the end of a three-year, five-year or longer term to return to academic work at the level that one had reached earlier. Service to one's colleagues, although a worthy motivation for management, is not by itself a guarantee of effectiveness or an adequate reward for the personal investment involved.

It is interesting that these connotations do not seem to be associated with academic leadership within a discipline, where seniority and expertise confer almost a 'natural' right to provide direction for research and teaching. Leadership in this context is not perceived as being in conflict either with individual autonomy or with democracy. The image of leadership that seems to prevail on the academic side is one in which guidance and steerage feature strongly and where the task is to create a framework, in collaboration with colleagues, within which individual and team performance can be maximized. What is perhaps forgotten is that successful academic leadership relies as much on certain specific leadership competences as it does on professional academic expertise (for example, vision, agenda-setting, prioritizing, interpersonal skills, representation internally and externally).

While some of these academic leaders may 'emerge' in the sense that they are acclaimed and offered the mantle of leadership by their colleagues independent of initiatives on their own part, most are likely to arrive at this point through deliberate efforts to enhance their professional practice and their influence on the development of their subject area. The process could be made less haphazard and more open to a larger pool of talent, if serious attention was given to the means of developing leadership. There is also no inherent reason why the same image of leadership and similar attention to development could not be used for managerial leadership in universities. The best of the collegial ethic could be maintained and any dysfunctional elements lost.

Unfortunately, there are also some difficulties with the notion of development, particularly where it involves 'training'. The idea of training – and leadership or management development in particular – clashes with several cults in academic life:

1. The cult of the gifted amateur (any intelligent, educated individual can undertake the task – in our case, leadership – without training).
2. The cult of heredity (those with natural talent will emerge since they are born to the task; leadership is an art and therefore unteachable).
3. The cult of deficiency (training is essentially remedial or for those who are personally ineffective; 'training is for the second eleven' as one PVC put it).
4. The cult of inadequacy (once qualified, loss of face is involved by admitting gaps in one's knowledge or competence).
5. The cult of the implicit (development takes place by gradual induction into the norms and operations of academe; learning by osmosis is the hallmark of success).
6. The cult of selection (the selection of good staff will ensure good performance and will obviate the need for – and the cost of – development).
7. The cult of the intellectual (there is no scientific basis to 'management', therefore it does not deserve to be taken seriously).

There is no easy or quick means to dissipate the force of these cults since some are engrained in the background and experience of our most senior academics, while others are part of traditional academic (and perhaps national) culture (Constable and McCormick, 1987; Handy, 1987). The growth of staff development in universities, fuelled partly by external politi-cal pressure and partly by rapidly changing circumstances and demands on universities, has made some inroads into these negative and complacent views. More positive perspectives will be achieved as institutions recognize the need to encourage the intellectual and personal growth of their staff; the need to develop new skills as markets change (disciplinary, research and teaching markets); the need to broaden their staffing profile; and as they recognize development as a means of maintaining competitive edge and of ensuring institutional survival. Recognition of the existence of negative views should also challenge providers of training and development for academics (and for all staff) to design services which are relevant and worthwhile.

Individual responsibilities

Motivation to develop, grow and change rests chiefly with the individual, although positive signals in the form of structures, incentives and climate are an institutional (and a collective) responsibility.

For individuals, maximum advantage will be gained from formal oppor-tunities in leadership development if these follow from a diagnosis of need and involve careful planning and preparation. For example, the learning needs of a novice research team leader are unlikely to be the same as those of a new Head of Department who has had experience of managing projects in industrial and commercial environments before joining the university. Learning will need to be integrated with past experience and opportunities for learning should be timely and relevant. The chance to test and use learning directly is likely to help its retention and refinement. Finally, review-ing and reflecting systematically upon the content and the process of learn-ing will also enhance potential outcomes.

Where the above responsibilities are general, there are certain respon-sibilities which are specific to different roles (Green and McDade, 1991; Middlehurst *et al.*, 1992). These are too numerous to report fully here, but some examples will provide a flavour. At the top of the institution, Chairmen and other lay members of Council can assist in developing a strategy for leadership development, while the institution can do much to ensure effec-tive lay contributions to institutional governance. Induction of new members of Council/Court, encouragement of debates with lay members about issues of importance to higher education, and identification of mechanisms whereby lay members can aquire a better insight into the operations and culture of the institution, are all developmental activities of potential bene-fit. These ideas are developed further in a recent publication from the Universities Staff Development Unit in the UK (Guildford, 1993).

Vice Chancellors can set a personal example which demonstrates the pri-ority and value attached to leadership development. They can take a particular interest in the professional development of senior colleagues and can create a climate and a strategy for development within the institution. This strategy can be activated by the efforts of other senior staff, for example, senior administrators, Deans and Heads of Departments, in identifying and encouraging talent, in promoting high standards of performance (and in noticing and challenging non-performers), in acting as mentors, coaches, advisers and appraisers, and by making available the financial, technological or human resources necessary for leadership development. Personnel officers or staff developers have a professional responsibility for ensuring that leadership development strategies are coordinated, purposeful and relevant in their implementation. Where the status and credibility of these staff is high, they will also be able to participate in the shaping of a strategy for leadership development which is of mutual benefit to the institution and to individuals.

Team leadership and its development

Building effective teams can be a difficult task in the academic world where individual achievement is often more highly prized than group collaboration. Yet management and leadership rely on achieving goals through (and together with) other people; effective teamwork can often be a key to success, so it is important to find ways of achieving it. Green and McDade (1991) offer several reasons why teams fail in universities and suggest some ways of building successful teams.

The causes of failure may include: lack of understanding and communication among specialists; over-emphasis on competition at the expense of collaboration; reward structures that give recognition only to individual performance (particularly since it is more difficult to evaluate team performance); factions and territorial disputes; tension between personal agendas and institutional or group interests. The authors suggest that time and effort need to be expended on building a shared sense of purpose, common interests and experiences among team members. This will involve both an initial team-building focus and a continuing awareness of how the team is working together to achieve a task. Social events, the assistance of consultants and participation in programmes focused on common areas of interest are useful methods for encouraging teamwork. An effective team at institutional level is likely both to encourage teamwork elsewhere in the institution and to have a positive effect on perceptions of leadership.

Institutional responsibilities

At the institutional level, leadership development in UK universities is either unrecognized as a central concern or uneven and marginal. There is a considerable distance to travel, for example, to Burgoyne's (1988) stage four of 'organizational maturity', where management development helps to implement corporate policy, or to stage five where management development is the focal point in policy creation. Burgoyne's model rests on the premise that promoting the professional development of managers will ensure their continuing creativity, and that management competence is itself necessary to the successful performance of other staff and the organization as a whole.

Although we may disagree with Burgoyne's emphasis on *management* development alone, we can go some way with his ideas. The notion that a mature organization places a premium on the development of its staff is important for universities (as a recent CVCP report: *Promoting People*, 1993, recognizes). A second point, that development is integral to effective policy implementation, is also relevant. And a third, that development (or more broadly, learning, about new trends and institutional responses to them) is a major focus in policy creation, is a worthy aspiration for universities which face a turbulent and changing environment.

In academic institutions, the fostering of creativity and initiative and the building of networks and understanding between 'tribes and their territories' (Becher, 1989) is important at all levels. There are several approaches that can assist towards these goals.

An evaluation of current institutional (or departmental/faculty) performance in leadership development, through an audit of existing practices, offers a starting point. Incorporating leadership development and staff or professional development more generally into institutional planning and decision-making is a second step. Promoting a search for, and actively using, informal learning opportunities (for example, encouraging self-assessment of chairing skills, encouraging staff to seek feedback from colleagues on project management, promoting initiatives in developing new approaches to teaching) offers a third opportunity for leadership learning. Further strategies include: developing a comprehensive institutional philosophy and plan for leadership development; visibly engaging in leadership development activities, particularly among senior staff, in order to legitimize the activity; demonstrating the benefits of development; and encouraging explicit target-setting in different areas of the institution. The process is unlikely to gain momentum without an allocation of resources, provision of incentives and support, and a recognition of achievement. Systematic evaluation will then reveal the ways in which the investment made was worthwhile and the ways in which it may be extended.

Collective responsibilities

A traditional aspect of university culture, expressed in the notion of collegiality, suggests a further level of responsibility for leadership learning. This level is subtly different from that of the individual, from the team (whether research team, course team, management team), from the group (department or faculty) or from the institutional level as I have described that above, and in Chapters 5 and 6. The level in question can be described as 'collective' and offers an image of shared responsibility both for leadership and for leadership learning.

The idea of collective responsibility emerges from certain features of university culture, such as the value placed on self-governance, and from particular aspects of leadership. At several points in this book, I have drawn attention to the transactional nature of leadership, particularly in the academic context, and to the opportunities (and need) for interactive leadership at many points in the institution. In this discussion of leadership development, I have also tried to emphasize how learning takes place through the interaction of people and events in different settings, and particularly in situations that offer challenge and provide direct feedback. The combination of challenge and feedback ensures that individuals and groups are made aware of their strengths, weaknesses and potential, and also alerts them to alternative perspectives and viewpoints.

The notion of collective leadership, and collective learning, can be developed still further. Within interactive arenas (from committee meetings to appraisals), learning could be a reciprocal process, although the individual outcomes of learning will be different. The idea of 'learning leadership' builds on this reciprocity of influence between leaders and colleagues by emphasizing mutual responsibilities. Nurturing such an ethos within a university depends on creating a continuing and open dialogue about the institution's purposes and outcomes, the means of achieving them and the contributions of individuals and groups to the whole; and in reverse, it depends on demonstrating the university's contribution to individual and group learning and creativity. Both aims can be achieved by actively welcoming and encouraging individual and team initiative and ideas in all areas of the institution, for example in approaches to the evaluation of teaching, in developing innovative practice in research training, in improving customer care or in resolving management problems.

While the development of an appropriate ethos – through dialogue and communication – is essential, it is the outcomes that grow out of this ethos that illustrate its worth. These outcomes, which include leadership development, improvement in collective morale and a sense of shared 'ownership' for the university, may be measured in the level of institutional health (Lysons, 1990; Lysons and Hatherley, 1991). They are only likely to be realized if the framework which is established at institutional level is then lived in the relationships and interactions of people at all levels. Developing an ethos of constructive challenge and self-critical dialogue is a key task for 'a learning leadership' in a collective culture where individual autonomy and professional responsibility are also highly prized.

10

Endings and Beginnings

Introduction

As psychotherapists, teachers and organization consultants recognize, it is often necessary to review and take stock of past knowledge and experience in order to understand the present and prepare for the future. In this chapter, a similar path will be followed by first considering the ideas visited in the course of this book and reflecting on current understandings of leadership in academic settings. We can then look towards the horizon to see in which directions universities may be heading – and with what consequences for leadership.

Popular views

In the first two chapters of this book, the question of what leadership is was explored in popular and in analytical terms. Popular conceptions cast leadership in different lights each one highlighting a separate facet of the subject. First, leadership is commonly associated with providing a vision and direction which others will subscribe to and follow. Second, leadership is often linked to the authority of position and to 'taking charge', which legitimates the exercise of influence over others, although with an expectation that the exercise of such influence is based on consent. Third, leadership encompasses 'initiative' both as a quality and as a responsibility for action, for example through initiating projects, ideas or developments. Leadership is also linked to achievement and to successful outcomes. These last two facets (of initiation and completion) are closely connected to the first two above, that is, to direction-setting and the exercise of authority. Together they provide a complete circle of responsibility and expectation: from origination to conclusion of a task, a vision, or some individual or collective purpose.

A fourth aspect of leadership is contained in the notions of 'difference' and 'distance' in the sense that leaders are set apart from others. There are several dimensions here: that leaders are exceptional individuals, that leadership provides an example for others and that leadership is linked to the idea of following. Pursuing this theme of difference, a fifth element which is commonly connected to leadership can be identified. This is an assumption that different styles and patterns of leadership will exist in different settings. Finally, leadership often carries strong moral and ethical connotations. These relate to symbolic aspects of leadership where the representation of individual or collective values, interests, aspirations or achievements are at stake. We can see such dimensions in the two quotations below, one from Egypt in the twenty-fourth century BC and one from Britain in the twentieth century AD:

> If you are a leader
> Governing the lives of the masses
> Seek out for yourself every good deed
> So that your actions shall be faultless.
> Great is truth, enduring is its power.
> (Egyptian historian recording the views of 'prime minister' Ptahhotep, ruler over the Land of the Nile, twenty-fourth century BC; quoted by
> D. Keys in *The Independent on Sunday*, 10 January 1993)

> Something conclusive could be done about the beggars and the homeless, mobilising us all, irrespective of party dogma. All that is needed are the right words. We should be told that it shames each and every one of us so long as a single teenager begs on the Tube, a single brazier burns under the Waterloo arches, or a single tattered body freezes near the glittering facade of The Savoy. All that's needed, in short, is something which seems to have vanished as a prerequisite of government. It's called leadership.
> (P. Norman, *Guardian Weekend*, 27 January 1993)

In summary, popular conceptions of leadership focus particularly on five 'Is' which are either explicit or implicit in discusions and expectations of leadership: integrity, initiative, influence, inspiration and imagination.

Scholarly views

The themes that are identified above are echoed in analytical conceptions. Beginning in Chapter 1, the links between leadership and personal qualities were considered before examining the perspectives on leadership that were revealed through studying the behaviour and styles of leaders. These two themes contained some enduring features: that certain characteristics appear to be common to successful leaders (such as confidence, creativity, persistence, integrity, persuasiveness) and that particular actions are linked to leadership (for example, supportive behaviour, an emphasis on achieving high quality outcomes, on facilitating group and individual tasks, as well as group relations and interactions). However, these areas of research ultimately proved inconclusive in identifying or predicting leadership.

With the development of contingency models, new perspectives on leadership were opened up, most of which have been sustained into the present. An important breakthrough associated with 'contingency' or 'situational' assumptions was that leadership is not unidimensional or static. The shape of leadership changes according to a number of factors: the culture and organizational setting in which leadership is located; the historical era in which leadership is exercised; and the prevailing economic, social or technological circumstances of that period. The nature and purposes of the tasks that leaders and followers are engaged with, the expectations, values and interests of the individuals and groups who participate in, or who are associated with the task, are also important variables. Contingency models highlight the complexity of leadership, a feature that remains evident in recent works.

Studies with a 'new leadership' focus draw attention to leadership as a process of social influence whereby a group (or groups) are steered towards a goal. Attempts to identify the sources of this influence have led researchers to consider the ways in which different kinds of power are exercised (for example, power based on expertise, position, tradition, relationships or personality) and the ways in which leadership is linked to values, beliefs and attitudes. In following these directions, further facets of leadership have been exposed.

Lines have been drawn between formal and informal (or emergent) leadership, the former being associated with appointment to a position of leadership, the latter with the spontaneous appearance of 'leadership' among a group. Distinctions have also been made between rational or objective views of leadership and interpretive or subjective views. Adopting an objective perspective, leadership is real, measurable and substantive; taking a subjective view, leadership is intuitive, intangible or symbolic. Within the former perspective, we can detect at least two underlying assumptions: (a) that leadership resides in the conscious or unconscious exercise of influence by leaders; and (b) that the influence of leaders makes a material difference to individual or group outcomes.

In the second case, looking at leadership through a subjective lens, the assumptions are different. First, leadership may reside elsewhere than in the actions of leaders, for example in the minds of the beholders or in the systems or norms of a group. Interpretive or subjective notions concentrate on the ways in which leadership is socially constructed by the mutual interactions and interpretations of leaders and their constituents. Writers in this tradition suggest that there are some prevailing myths about leadership which exist in the collective consciousness of groups (in external cultures and sub-cultures as well as those internal to the group or organization). Among subjectivists there is less certainty that leadership makes a material difference to group outcomes. Where agreement exists that leadership can or does make a difference, this is attributed to a need among people to believe that leadership matters or to a particular set of circumstances which create a perceived leadership imperative, such as a crisis or need for change.

Objective and subjective perspectives reveal further facets and complexities in 'leadership'. Recent studies have shed new light on earlier schools of thought, for example by seeking to discover how leaders construe their role, the intellectual power required for different kinds of leadership, the ways in which implicit models and myths influence the design of organizational structures and systems, or the motivational climate in which activities are performed. With a loosening of the conceptual ties between leadership and the actions of formal leaders, the potential locus of leadership has become more fluid and diverse. For example, the responsibility for exercising leadership may shift within a project team from one individual to another, depending on the expertise required at a particular moment; in this case, leadership may be described as a collective responsibility. Leadership can also be shared among a senior management group, so that the team as a whole presents a united front. Finally, it may be distributed widely within an organization, emerging at different levels, in different forms and in different circumstances.

Leadership in organizations

The focus in Chapter 3 moved from the idea of leadership itself to its exercise within an organizational setting. The intention here was to illustrate how different images of an organization (collegial, professional, political, bureaucratic, cybernetic or entrepreneurial) have particular values, practices or ideas attached to them. These properties help to shape the organization, its decision-making and control structures, its reward and financial allocation systems, the ways in which power and authority are distributed and the ways in which communication and information are channelled. Over time, these organizational images harden through the habitual activities, interactions and patterns of thought of individuals and groups within the organization, as well as some outside it who are concerned with the organization's survival and development.

Leadership was linked to this organizational milieu in various ways, illustrating both objective and subjective dimensions. The existence of certain policies and operations, particular habits and shared or competing understandings about the organization may constrain or support the exercise of leadership, or influence perceptions of leadership in positive or negative directions. Particular organizational features may determine the most appropriate style of leadership, or point to the kind of personality required in a position of leadership. The stage of development of the organization (newborn, middle-aged, declining), the period in which the organization was established (the thirteenth or twentieth century), the 'technology' of the organization (learning or banking, manufacturing or services), the purpose and activities of the organization and the people who choose to work – or find themselves – within its boundaries, will all impinge on leadership. All these factors create particular expectations of leadership and require certain actions and responsibilities from leaders.

Seen from an objective perspective, leaders can actively and directly influence or change the organization – its structures and systems as well as its activities and culture. Through a subjective lens, formal leaders may be only one element in the construction, maintenance or reconstruction of the meaning and life of the organization. Leaders' ability to influence events is often indirect (exerted through systems, ideas, other people or events). Leadership influence may operate at different levels, for example through language and communication (the choice of words, the medium of communication), in vertical or horizontal directions (system-level leadership or leadership among peers). It may also be contained within the boundaries of the organization or be mediated by external influences; and it may be sent or received through direct signals, such as specific policies on health and safety or equal opportunities, or in the 'noise' emanating from the measurement of performance or the sources and mechanisms of funding. We may see these different levels and media as tools for leaders or as substitutes and neutralizers for leadership. Whichever perspective is adopted, it is clear that adding an organizational dimension to leadership further enriches (and complicates) our picture.

Leadership and academic traditions

In Chapter 4, I turned from organizations in general to look specifically at the academic context. First, the traditions, methods of organization and cultural values of academe were explored. Some of the core features of academic institutions were identified: the operation of individual autonomy; the importance of individual expertise and reputation; the existence of a dual hierarchy of professional and administrative authority; the value placed on consensus, on reasoned argument, on self-governance and self-determination. Features which are common to other professional groups, such as loyalty to a subject area or discipline, were highlighted before pointing to the diversity of interests and purposes enacted within a university. These elements created an impression of organizational fluidity in universities; they were institutions that were held together by tacit assumptions, values and norms (shared by internal and also, to a large degree, by key external constituents), by the scope for individual achievement and self-realization, by loose rather than tight coordination and control systems, by a constant flow of adequate resources and a lack of competition for their monopoly of 'higher learning'.

I considered the implications of this kind of organizational environment for the exercise of leadership at different levels (institution and department) and within different territories (academic and administrative), providing evidence and examples in support of two opposing arguments:

(a) that leadership has always existed in academic institutions and *is* culturally appropriate; and (b) that leadership has never fitted the academic value system or the structure and operations of the university because there are too many 'normative' and 'operational' constraints which hinder its exercise.

Having gazed into the past and recognized its hold on current conceptions of the university, I turned to examine how and why these traditions were being challenged. The pressures for change in universities were traced to the macro-environment (particularly to technological, economic and socio-cultural influences) and to the emergence of certain political forces in late twentieth century Britain: the ideology of the New Right, the economic squeeze on the welfare state, and shifts in the dominance of particular industries and economic sectors. The dynamic of change has not operated in a direct, linear fashion since macro- and micro-environments have acted upon each other in mutually reinforcing or in reactive cycles. With their particular technology (knowledge creation, articulation, development, dissemination and critique) universities have been simultaneously shapers and subjects of change in their external and internal environments. At some levels, for example in research in biotechnology, the shaping of change may involve conscious action on the part of individuals and groups within universities. In other areas, such as the gradual and increasing economic interdependence of universities and the state, conscious, collective and timely awareness of change has sometimes been lacking.

Four major external currents have affected and continue to affect the internal life of universities: first, political demands for efficiency, accountability and value-for-money in the use of public funds; second, political pressure to reduce institutional dependence on public funds as the largest or sole source of revenue; third, a requirement to educate and train more people to higher levels in order to create an expanded and more highly skilled work force; fourth, pressure to tailor university activities and services more directly to the wealth-creation needs of 'UK plc'. These demands are couched in various ways and are underscored by different kinds of rationale, both economic – growth for the nation, jobs for individuals – and socio-political: more adaptable employees, more individual choice, more educational opportunities for more people, and the development and encouragement of better citizenship.

The changing university

Within universities, the external currents have been felt in both administrative and academic areas and have had an impact in a myriad of ways. For the most part, the internal adaptations have been gradual and incremental, so that the full impact and strategic longer-term consequences arising from these external currents may not always have been fully appreciated. On the administrative and managerial side, universities have: tightened their coordination and control systems (assisted by information technology); streamlined their decision-making processes; integrated their academic, financial and physical planning; improved their cost-control procedures; devolved many managerial functions from institutional to basic unit and individual levels; restructured operational units; created new functions and posts (public relations, marketing, a development office); developed new policies; and shifted from collective to individual managerial responsibility and accountability. Reporting, analysing, measuring, checking and evaluating have become a central concern at all levels and in all areas of the institution.

Many of these changes, of course, have consequences for the academic activities of the university. In the academic domain, structural changes have occurred in the planning and management of teaching and research, in the organization and development of consultancy activities and in the facilitation of technology transfer. Research parks, joint ventures, new companies, centres and units have mushroomed either within universities or on their boundaries. Closer links have been built with employers, local communities and industrial and commercial clients for the provision of initial and continuing professional development, for the creation of new programmes or the development of existing curricula. Teaching and learning strategies are changing as programmes move to a modular structure, under the impetus of new kinds and larger numbers of students, and against a background of change in other educational sectors (the National Curriculum and GCSE courses in schools, National Vocational Qualifications, access programmes in further education). Additional external factors, such as the methods of funding students, are also having important consequences for teaching, student choice and student/parent expectations of higher education.

In Chapters 5 to 8 some of the broad operational consequences of internal and externally driven change were considered as well as the impact of change at cultural, personal and emotional levels. A number of themes can be identified. First, at all levels of the university, there has been an increase in the prominence of management, whether management of research, management of the teaching function, management of student learning, management within administration, self-management or the management of others.

Second (and not unconnected to this phenomenon), there has been a steady increase in bureaucracy and a steady decrease in the amount of time available for core academic activities, particularly at senior levels. These factors may have reversed some of the earlier efficiency gains made in the 1980s; many university staff also believe they have reduced academic effectiveness.

Third, there is a greater differentiation between 'operational' and 'strategic' domains as the nature of the tasks at each level has expanded and changed. The prominence of the institutional level of the university has also grown as external liaison has become of critical importance, as priorities and choices have had to be made, as regulation has become central and as university activities have diversified and become more complex.

On the teaching side, the stability, continuity and relative simplicity offered by a focus on the single honours degree taught to 18 to 21-year-old undergraduates, resident for three or four years within the university, is disappearing quite rapidly in some institutions. In its place comes the diversity, fragmentation and complexity of teaching many different ages and kinds of students, with different educational backgrounds and diverse employment prospects, who create their own patchwork degrees and who study at their own pace in accord with their domestic and financial commitments. While the changes on the research side are not as stark, they have also served to increase the prominence of the institutional level of the university. Examples here would include the separation of teaching and research for costing and measurement purposes, an increasing emphasis on contract research, on consultancy, and on other research and development activities as sources of revenue as well as performance indicators.

For individuals and groups, the impact of change has also been widely felt. Roles have altered: for example, the head of department is now viewed (at least from an institutional perspective) as a manager of financial and human resources and individual academics are finding themselves being channelled, sometimes imperceptibly, sometimes overtly, in the direction of teaching *or* research, rather than both. The activities of clerical, technical and administrative staff are also changing, often to include more management responsibilities and sometimes more 'academic' responsibilities as the skills of these staff are more closely integrated with the teaching and learning effort.

Personal and emotional responses to these currents and shifts have varied between individuals and levels and across institutions, as power and status differentials have been touched, as access to resources has been restricted, as traditional territories have been invaded, or as role conflicts have emerged. The effort to codify, measure and evaluate university activities, to make explicit what was implicit, to reassess priorities, to learn new skills and to change old habits and practices has put many individuals and groups under pressure, not least because innovation and change have had to coexist with the maintenance and delivery of current activities.

We drew attention to the tensions that change has brought or has accentuated. Sometimes these tensions have erupted into open conflicts, at other times they have simmered under the surface, or have been evident in individual physical and emotional responses to change. Some clear fault-lines can be seen between, for example, academics and administrators, staff and 'management', researchers and teachers, notions of equity and selectivity, preservation and innovation in academic life, quality and excellence, collaboration and competition. The abilities of individuals and groups to cope with and adapt to change are also coloured by a number of widely held internal perceptions, for example that the work of academics is not publicly valued or that individual and collective autonomy and independence are being eroded. For some individuals, change has also produced a feeling of being deskilled, as traditional skills, knowledge or activities are no longer relevant and as new areas have not yet been mastered. Such uncertainty and personal discomfort is also accentuated by current emphases on performance measurement and by views of training which are often deficit-based.

Perceptions of change have by no means been universally negative. For many, the buzz of excitement generated by being involved in the shaping of change, at institutional or departmental level, is evident. This positive energy is also noticeable among those who are engaged in building new programmes, developing new avenues for research, attracting new clients or achieving success in entrepreneurial ventures. Many have welcomed more open management in universities and a decrease in collective decision-making processes. For some, new posts have offered alternative careers or have increased the importance and value of their professional contributions. And for others, who have escaped the challenges and stimulation associated with innovation or the management of change, there is also satisfaction to be found in successfully protecting traditional activities and values against managerial or market-driven encroachments. The kinds of changes that are being felt in universities are also being experienced across the public sector and in other professional organizations. Opportunities therefore exist for scholars to draw comparisons, to critique current trends and to make academic profit out of the present dynamic context.

On leadership, change and academe

At several points in this book, connections between leadership and change have been noted. Leaders may themselves initiate change as part of their role, while the impact of a turbulent and uncertain environment creates a felt need for leadership. There are several purposes for leadership during a period of change; many of them are also required in more stable or certain times.

At a physical and material level, leadership is required to initiate the development of new structures and systems, new posts and new activities. At a cognitive level, it is required for the development of ideas, interpretations, explanations and analyses, for scenario planning, policy-making and steerage. At an affective level, leadership is necessary for the articulation and representation of values, for the development of a productive working climate, for building and maintaining effective working relationships and for the reiteration or reshaping of informal codes of conduct. Leadership also plays a part in the emotional domain: by confronting fear, anger and loss, tension and conflict; by providing challenge, respect, enthusiasm or inspiration; and by creating and maintaining trust. At certain times, particularly within a secular society, leadership may also be looked to for spiritual or ethical guidance and support. Personal integrity and the articulation of higher, altruistic purposes for the organization or group are part of these moral dimensions.

As we have seen in Chapters 5 to 8, no individual has a monopoly on leadership in a university, although formal leaders at different levels of the institution carry particular leadership functions. The expectation and the potential for leadership are widely distributed. Initiatives (for new policies or new activities) may originate at lower or at higher levels, although endorsement for new developments will usually need to be acquired from formal leaders and their constituents. Formal leaders share a responsibility for the establishment of regulatory frameworks, for challenging existing practice, for confronting sensitive issues and for promoting innovation. There are strong expectations (particularly in a changing environment) that they will also give attention to the cognitive and affective domains described above, although in practice many individuals provide informal leadership in these areas.

Expectations and experiences of leadership, as well as the prevailing circumstances, colour both individual and collective perceptions and practices. For these reasons, different features of leadership are brought to the foreground, or seem most relevant, at different times. However, all the features are interconnected and should be in balance; none can be completely ignored without loss to the whole. For example, the development of an inspirational vision may be important at one point in the management of change, while the qualities of integrity, personal example and persistence may be necessary at another point. Yet without linking vision to example and persistence, as well as to the development of policies, systems and operations, there can be no certain match between 'practice and preaching'. In the areas of equal opportunities, marketing or quality assurance, for example, this missing link, or even mismatch, can undermine worthwhile policies and good intentions.

The idea of interconnections and balance helps to align theory and practice in leadership. The qualities of individual leaders are linked to their actions and to their interactions with others, to their conceptions of the university and their role within it, and to their interpretations of the external environment. Each of these factors will affect the leadership style adopted. The perceived value of leadership within a particular culture (in our case the academic one), within a particular frame of time and circumstance, also influences individual and group perceptions of leadership. Once again, these different aspects work upon each other in mutually reinforcing (or inhibiting) ways.

We can also bring objective and subjective perspectives of leadership together by building on the physical, cognitive and affective purposes outlined above. Both substantive and symbolic aspects of leadership are required in the management of change. The active and material dimensions of leadership (which fit the physical and cognitive purposes of leadership described above) call for the development of a strategic agenda, for the establishment of institutional and departmental priorities and for the creation of implementation frameworks and schedules. As we have seen, they involve leaders in policy-making and decision-taking, engage them in communication and information exchange, in developing networks of relationships, in resolving conflicts, in initiating projects and new developments, in acquiring and channelling resources. These aspects of leadership provide the bones of the framework in which academic work can be achieved.

The other less tangible sides of leadership, which put flesh on to these bones and which make the university a more or less stimulating and productive place, come into play through the ways in which the substantive aspects are presented and interpreted. These symbolic and interpretive aspects fit the affective purposes of leadership. Symbolic features can be identified in: the language and communication media used; the styles of interaction and degrees of listening between leaders and their constituents; the level of support, interest, encouragement and challenge offered by leaders; the 'messages' sent by policies and systems; the interpretations presented to internal constituents about the outside world as well as those presented to outsiders about the activities of the university.

These symbolic aspects are at the heart of the 'process of social influence' whereby leadership touches the emotions, values, self-image and perceptions of individuals and groups. They can contribute to feelings of self-worth (or the opposite), can help to motivate (or de-motivate) individuals and groups and can assist in confronting the pressures and consequences of change, channelling these in more (or less) positive directions. In complex environments, and in universities in particular, these symbolic aspects are of great importance, not least because other kinds of leverage on performance and morale, such as financial incentives or clear promotion prospects, are often absent. They are also important in bringing a degree of cohesion to a potentially disparate and fragmented enterprise; and in nurturing creativity, learning, autonomy and collegiality – the traditional hallmarks of a university – at a time when these characteristics are under some pressure.

In an academic environment, the five 'Is' mentioned earlier as part of popular conceptions of leadership can be augmented by two further elements: intellect and interaction. These two elements have formed a major part of my analysis of leadership in theory and in practice within an academic setting. The intellectual dimension is required in order to diagnose, interpret and reconcile competing demands upon the university and rival views of its traditions and its future, and to be able to communicate with and to influence different stakeholders. The interactive dimension is necessary in order to capitalize on the full range of ideas and expertise available within the university, to encourage participation from all quarters in the reassessment of the meaning, purpose and design of a university in the twenty-first century, and to build a sense of collective responsibility and commitment to the survival and development of the institution. Both intellectual and interactive elements are central to the successful integration of past values and present (or future) imperatives.

Leadership and learning

In Chapter 9, a number of connections between leadership and learning were outlined, suggesting that these two activities called upon similar capacities, that they were processes which contained similar elements and that, in combination, they offered a particular approach to the internal and external 'positioning' of the university, which seemed to offer potential benefits for institutions.

At one level, the link between leadership and learning was made in terms of training and continuing professional development. At another, it was associated with the testing of ideas, with the development and evaluation of alternative planning scenarios, with collective problem-solving and with active and self-critical reflection on performance. Listening, challenging and supporting, seeking feedback, tolerating mistakes, initiating opportunities for learning and developing a conscious awareness of the learning process (both individually and collectively) all featured as part of the development of a constructive institutional and departmental ethos. I argued that a continuing and open dialogue was necessary between different levels of the university, in order to inform and extend leadership, as well as to reduce the potential separation between strategic and operational concerns. The notion of a 'learning leadership' seemed to capture the reciprocity between the two concepts and to offer a view of an appropriate style of governance for the future.

New vistas

While it is always difficult to predict the future, it is a leadership responsibility to consider trends, to conjure with possible scenarios and to contribute to the shaping of ideas and events. The raw material for these activities exists in the present and will also have links with the past. From these starting points, we can identify a number of themes that are likely to continue to affect universities into the next century.

Underpinning these themes are some assumptions: first, that the financial climate in which higher education operates is unlikely to improve dramatically. Financial constraint, the acquisition and distribution of scarce resources, will continue to be a major preoccupation for leaders. Our second assumption is that the demand for higher education will remain buoyant, although the sources and nature of the demand will probably change (for example, from full-time to 'flexi-time' students, from a primary emphasis on undergraduate education to an increasing focus on postgraduate education and continuing professional development). A third assumption is that higher education, the state and the economic and social needs of society will remain closely connected (and may well tighten further). On the basis of these assumptions, it seems likely that institutions will continue to operate in a competitive environment in which the choice of priorities will be important to institutional success and perhaps to survival.

At least three themes seem likely to prevail into the future and to be of relevance for leadership in universities. The first, and perhaps most obvious, is the importance and impact of information technology. New techology will alter the management of teaching, learning and research, will provide new channels and means of communication, and will alter patterns of work. It will also change the boundaries and the idea of 'a university' as networks, franchises, out-stations and open learning centres proliferate, both nationally and internationally. Developments such as these are already altering core activities; they have consequences for individual roles, employment contracts, training and re-training, job and status definitions, and leadership. Direct contact between formal leaders and staff may be rare, so that some aspects of leadership will need to be built into the systems and norms of the institution, while others will be devolved to team leaders and to individuals themselves. A premium may once again be placed on professional autonomy and self-direction, particularly as external monitoring can now be streamlined.

A second theme is interdependence. It arises partly as a result of the possibilities of information technology and partly out of the resource environment. As institutions are obliged to become more selective in their activities, as they seek to fill gaps in the services that they offer, or as they try to develop new products, services and benefits, the degree of interdependence between institutions, sectors and groups is likely to grow. For example, some companies can offer a research environment that is as good as (or better than) that available in some universities. Joint projects and shared research training may be envisaged. Similarly, in the area of professional development, companies may seek validation for their own programmes or may look to develop joint learning packages with universities.

These kinds of connections are already in operation in some universities and are becoming common between different levels of education, for example in franchising arrangements. Regional and community needs will encourage such developments. They have implications in a number of areas, for example in exchanges of staff, in the provision of joint services (libraries/computing, personnel, marketing), for quality assurance and for the development of particular skills. They may also require a cultural shift from an emphasis on individual effort and attainment to collaborative effort and cooperation.

Several aspects of leadership are called upon to facilitate and guide these kinds of developments: imagination and initiative, the stimulation of ideas, negotiating and consultancy skills, the building of consent, as well as a need to analyse both the immediate and the longer-term consequences of interdependence. Since the impetus for creating these links or joint ventures may come from either basic unit or institutional level, internal interdependence is also likely to be necessary. To give operational units adequate freedom of manoeuvre in an entrepreneurial environment, partnerships between different levels will need to be created. Both management and leadership could then move from an emphasis on control, direction and command, to a focus on facilitation and the delivery of agreed services.

Finally, the third theme involves a shift in emphasis from 'process' to 'outcomes' in many areas of academic life. It is noticeable in teaching and learning, in performance appraisal, in national initiatives such as NVQs, the competency and capability movements, in student profiling, in the notion of value-added, in the growth of research and development projects and in the emphasis on technology transfer. My earlier assumptions come into play here: financial constraints lead to questions about the value of activities, while links between higher education and wealth creation are likely to be sought in measurable outcomes. Developing, encouraging and proving individual, group and collective worth is likely to form a continuing part of leadership in the future.

Postscript

In this last chapter I have tried both to anticipate events and to remember and examine past events as part of an analysis of leadership in academic settings. Universities and their staff face many different and competing challenges and will continue to be subject to a variety of expectations from different stakeholders. Some of these will no doubt further pressurize traditional values and practices, while others will place a premium on certain features of academic life and organization. Appreciating and maximizing the opportunities that lie ahead and interpreting them in the light of what has gone before depends upon harnessing the individual and collective ingenuity, imagination and initiative that is present in universities. Realizing the full potential of our creative institutions requires leadership that is brave enough to stand and be counted, yet wise enough to listen and learn.

Bibliography

Adair, J. (1968) *Training for Leadership*. Aldershot, Gower.

Adair, J. (1983) *Effective Leadership*. London, Pan.

Adair, J. (1988) *Developing Leaders*. Guildford, Talbot Adair Press.

Adair, J. (1989) *Great Leaders*. Guildford, Talbot Adair Press.

Adams, J., Hayes, J. and Hopson, B. (1976) *Transitions – Understanding and Managing Personal Change*. Oxford, Martin Robertson.

Alban-Metcalfe, B. (1984) Micro-skills of leadership. A detailed analysis of the behaviours of managers in the appraisal interview. In Hunt, J.G., Hosking, D.M., Schriesheim, C.A. and Stewart, R. (eds) *Leaders and Managers: International Perspectives on Managerial Behaviour and Leadership*. New York, Pergamon Press, pp. 179–99.

Alimo-Metcalfe, B. (1993) Women in management: organizational socialization and assessment practices that prevent career advancement, *International Journal of Selection and Assessment*, (2), 68–82.

Allen, M. (1988) *The Goals of Universities*. Milton Keynes, SRHE/Open University Press.

Argyris, C. (1984) Double loop learning in organizations. In Kolb, D.A., Rubin, I.M., and McIntyre, J.M. (eds) *Organizational Psychology* (4th ed.). Englewood Cliffs, NJ, Prentice Hall, pp. 45–59.

Argyris, C. and Schon, D.A. (1974) *Theory in Practice: Increasing Professional Effectiveness*. San Francisco, Jossey Bass.

Argyris, C. and Schon, D.A. (1978) *Organizational Learning: A Theory of Action Perspective*. Reading, MA, Addison-Wesley.

Avolio, B.J. and Bass, B.M. (1988) Transformation leadership, charisma and beyond. In Hunt, J.G., Baliga, B.R., Dachler, H.P. and Schriesheim, C.A. (eds) *Emerging Leadership Vistas*. Lexington, MA, Lexington, pp. 29–50.

Badaracco, J.L. (Jr) and Ellsworth, R.R. (1989) *Leadership and the Quest for Integrity*. Boston, Harvard Business School Press.

Baldridge, J. (1971) *Power and Conflict in the University*. New York, John Wiley & Sons.

Baliga, B.R. and Hunt, J.G. (1988) An organizational life-cycle approach to leadership. In Hunt, J.G., Baliga, B.R., Dachler, H.P. and Schriesheim, C.A. (eds) *Emerging Leadership Vistas*. Lexington, MA, Lexington, pp. 129–49.

Ball, C. (1991) *Learning Pays*. London, Royal Society of Arts.

Ball, C. (1992) *Profitable Learning: Summary Report, Findings and Action Plan*. London, Royal Society of Arts.

Barber, H.F. (1990) Some personality characteristics of senior military officers. In

Clark, K.E. and Clark, M.B. (eds) *Measures of Leadership*. West Orange, NJ, Leadership Library of America, pp. 441–8.

Barnard, C. (1938) *The Functions of the Executive*. Cambridge, MA, Harvard University Press.

Barnett, R.A. (1990) *The Idea of Higher Education*. Milton Keynes, SRHE/Open University Press.

Barnett, R.A. (1992) *Improving Higher Education: Total Quality Care*. Buckingham, SRHE/Open University Press.

Bass, B.M. (1981) *Stogdill's Handbook of Leadership*. New York, Free Press.

Bass, B.M. (1985) *Leadership and Performance Beyond Expectation*. New York, Free Press.

Bass, B.M. (1990) From transactional to transformational leadership: learning to share the vision, *Organizational Dynamics*, 18, 19–31.

Becher, T. (1989) *Academic Tribes and Territories: Intellectual Enquiry and the Culture of Disciplines*. Milton Keynes, SRHE/Open University Press.

Becher, T. and Kogan, M. (1992) *Process and Structure in Higher Education*, 2nd edn. London, Routledge.

Belbin, R.M. (1981) *Management Teams: Why They Succeed or Fail*. London, Heinemann.

Belbin, R.M. (1992) Solo leader/team leader: antithesis in style and structure. In Syrett, M. and Hogg, C. (eds) *The Frontiers of Leadership: an Essential Reader*. Oxford, Blackwell, pp. 267–78.

Bennett, J.B. (1982) Ambiguity and abrupt transitions in the department chairperson's role, *Educational Record*, Fall, 54-7.

Bennett, J. (1983) *Managing the Academic Department: Cases and Notes*. New York, ACE/Macmillan.

Bennett, J.B. (1988) Department chairs: leadership in the trenches. In Green, M.F. (ed.) *Leaders for a New Era: Strategies for Higher Education*. New York, ACE/Macmillan.

Bennett, J.B. and Figuli, D.J. (eds) (1990) *Enhancing Departmental Leadership: the Roles of the Chairperson*. New York, ACE/Macmillan.

Bennis, W. (1989) *On Becoming a Leader*. London, Hutchinson.

Bennis, W. (1992) Quoted in Syrett, M. and Hogg, C. (eds) *Frontiers of Leadership*. Oxford, Blackwell.

Bennis, W. and Nanus, B. (1985) *Leaders: the Strategies for Taking Charge*. New York, Harper & Row.

Bensimon, E. (1989) How college presidents use their administrative groups: 'real' and 'illusory' teams. Paper presented at ASHE, Atlanta, GA.

Bensimon, E., Neumann, A. and Birnbaum, R. (1989) *Making Sense of Administrative Leadership: the 'L' Word in Higher Education*. Washington, DC, ASHE/ERIC Higher Education Report No. 1.

Best, R., Ribbins, P., Jarvis, P. and Oddy, D. (1983) *Education and Care*. Oxford, Heinemann Educational Books.

Biddle, B.J. and Thomas, E.J. (1966) *Role Theory: Concepts and Research*. New York, Wiley.

Birnbaum, R. (1988) *How Colleges Work: the Cybernetics of Academic Organization and Leadership*. San Francisco, Jossey-Bass.

Birnbaum, R. (1989a) Responsibility without authority: the impossible job of the college president. In Smart, J. (ed.) *Higher Education Handbook of Theory and Research, Volume V*. New York, Agathon Press.

Birnbaum, R. (1989b) The Implicit Leadership Theories of College and University Presidents, *Review of Higher Education*, 12, 125–36.

Birnbaum, R. (1989c) Leadership and followership: the cybernetics of university governance. In Schuster, J.H. and Miller, L. (eds) *Governing Tomorrow's Campus: Perspectives and Agendas*. Washington, DC, ACE/Macmillan.

Birnbaum, R. (1989d) The cybernetic university: toward an integration of governance theories, *Higher Education*, 18, 239–53.

Birnbaum, R. (1990) How'm I doing?: how college presidents assess their effectiveness, *The Leadership Quarterly*, 1, 25–39.

Blake, R.R. and Mouton, J.S. (1964) *The Managerial Grid*. Houston, TX, Gulf Publishing Co.

Blake, R.R. amd Mouton, J.S. (1991) *Leadership Dilemmas: Grid Solutions*. Texas, Scientific Methods Inc.

Blake, R.R., Mouton, J.S. and Williams, M.S. (1981) *The Academic Administrative Grid*. San Francisco, Jossey-Bass.

Blau, P.M. (1956) *Bureaucracy in Modern Society*. New York, Random House.

Blau, P.M. (1964) *Exchange and Power in Social Life*. New York, Wiley.

Bolman, L.G. and Deal, T.E. (1984) *Modern Approaches to Understanding and Managing Organizations*. San Francisco, Jossey-Bass.

Boud, D. and de Rome, E. (1983) What counts: Academics' perception of the promotion system. In Moses, I. (ed.) *Tertiary Education in the Eighties: Paths to Reward and Growth*, Research and Development in Higher Education, vol. 6. Sydney, HERDSA, pp. 87–98.

Bowers, D.G. and Seashore, S.E. (1966) Predicting organizational effectiveness with a four-factor theory of leadership, *Administrative Science Quarterly*, 11, 238–63.

Boyatzis, R.E. (1982) *The Competent Manager*. New York, Wiley-Interscience.

Bryman, A. (1986) *Leadership in Organizations*. London, Routledge & Kegan Paul.

Bryman, A. (1992) *Charisma and Leadership in Organizations*. London, Sage.

Burgoyne, J. (1985) Self-Management. In Elliott, K. and Lawrence, P. (eds) *Introducing Management*. Harmondsworth, Penguin, pp. 46–59.

Burgoyne, J. (1988) Management development for the individual and the organization. *Personnel Management*, June, 40-4.

Burns, J.M. (1978) *Leadership*. New York, Harper & Row.

Bush, T. (1986) *Theories of Education Management*. London, Harper & Row.

Bush, T. (ed.) (1989) *Managing Education: Theory and Practice*. Milton Keynes, Open University Press.

Carnall, C. (1990) *Managing Change*. London, Routledge.

Carroll, D. and Cross, G. (1991) *University Stress Survey: Final Report*. London, Association of University Teachers.

Chaffee, E.E. (1984) Successful strategic management in small private colleges, *Journal of Higher Education*, 55(2), 212–41.

Chaffee, E.E. (1985) Three models of strategy, *Academy of Management Review*, 10, 89–98.

Chaffee, E.E. and Tierney, W.G. (1988) *Collegiate Culture and Leadership Strategies*. New York, American Council on Education/Macmillan.

Charlton, D.C. (1992) Developing leaders using the outdoors. In Syrett, M. and Hogg, C. (eds) *Frontiers of Leadership*. Oxford, Blackwell, pp. 454–61.

Clark, B.R. (1970) *The Distinctive College*. Chicago, Aldine.

Clark, B.R. (1983) *The Higher Education System: Academic Organization in Cross-national Perspective*. Berkeley, University of California Press.

Clark, B.R. (1987) *The Academic Profession.* Berkeley, University of California Press.

Clark, K.E. and Clark, M.B. (eds) (1990) *Measures of Leadership.* West Orange, NJ, Leadership Library of America.

Cohen, M.D. and March, J.G. (1974) *Leadership and Ambiguity: the American College President.* New York, McGraw-Hill.

Cohen, M.D. and March, J.G. (1986) *Leadership and Ambiguity: the American College President,* 2nd edn. Boston, Harvard Business School Press.

Collier, K.G. (1982) Ideological Influences in Higher Education, *Studies in Higher Education,* 7(1), 13–19.

Committee of Vice Chancellors and Principals (1985) *Report of the Steering Committee on Efficiency Studies in Universities.* London, CVCP.

Committee of Vice Chancellors and Principals (1993) *Promoting People: a Strategic Framework for the Management and Development of Staff in UK Universities.* London, CVCP.

Conger, J.A. (1989) *The Charismatic Leader: Behind the Mystique of Exceptional Leadership.* San Francisco, Jossey-Bass.

Constable, J. and McCormick, R. (1987) *The Making of British Managers.* London, BIM/CBI.

Cunningham, I. (1981) Self-managed learning and independent study. In Boydell, T. and Pedler, M. (eds) *Management Self-Development: Concepts and Practices.* Aldershot, Gower.

Cunningham, I. (1992) The impact of leaders: who they are and what they do, *Leadership and Organizational Development Journal,* 13(2), 7–10.

Cuthbert, R. (1984) The management process. E324 *Management in Post-compulsory Education,* Block 3, Part 2. Milton Keynes, Open University.

Cuthbert, R. (1992) Management: under new management? in McNay, I. (ed.) *Visions of Post-compulsory Education.* Buckingham, SRHE/Open University Press, pp. 152–61.

Cyert, R.M. and March, J.G. (1963) *A Behavioural Theory of the Firm.* Englewood Cliffs, NJ, Prentice-Hall.

Davies, J.L. (1987) The entrepreneurial and adaptive university: report of the second US study visit, *International Journal of Institutional Management in Higher Education,* 11 (1), 12–104.

Davies, J.L. (1989) The training of academic heads of department in higher education institutions: an international overview, *Higher Education Management,* 1(2), 201–15.

Deal, T.E. and Kennedy, A.A. (1982) *Corporate Cultures: the Rites and Rituals of Corporate Life.* Reading, MA, Addison-Wesley.

de Bono, E. (1984) *Lateral Thinking for Management.* Harmondsworth, Penguin.

Department of Education and Science (1987) *Higher Education: Meeting the Challenge,* Cmd 114. London, HMSO.

Department of Education and Science (1991) *Higher Education: a New Framework,* Cmd 1541. London, HMSO.

Dill, D.D. (1982) The management of academic culture: notes on the management of meaning and social integration, *Higher Education,* 11, 303–20.

Downey, H.K. and Brief, A.P. (1986) How cognitive structures affect organizational design. In Sims, H.P. Jr and Gioia, D.A. (eds) *The Thinking Organization.* San Francisco, Jossey-Bass, pp. 165–90.

Downie, R.S. (1990) Professions and professionalism, *Journal of Philosophy of Education,* 24 (2), 147–59.

Drucker, P. (1988) The coming of the new organization, *Harvard Business Review*, January–February, 45–53.

Duke, C. (1992) *The Learning University: Towards a New Paradigm?* Buckingham, SRHE/Open University Press.

Elton, L. (1988) Accountability in higher education: the danger of unintended consequences, *Higher Education*, 17, 377–90.

Elton, L. and Partington, P. (1991) *Teaching Standards and Excellence in Higher Education: Developing a Culture of Quality*, Occasional Green Paper, no 1. Sheffield, CVCP/USDTU.

Etzioni, A. (1961) *A Comparative Analysis of Complex Organizations*. New York, Free Press of Glencoe.

Etzioni, A. (1964) *A Comparative Analysis of Complex Organizations: On Power, Involvement, and Their Correlates*. New York, Free Press.

Etzioni, A. (1965) Dual leadership in complex organizations, *American Sociological Review*, 30, 688–98.

Faerman, S.R. and Quinn, R.E. (1985) Effectiveness: the perspective from organizational theory, *Review of Higher Education*, 9, 83-100.

Falk, G. (1979) The academic department: chairmanship and role conflict, *Improving College and University Teaching*, 27(2), 79–86.

Fayol, H. (1949) *General Industrial Management*. London, Pitman (first published 1916).

Fiedler, F.E. (1967) *A Theory of Leadership Effectiveness*. New York, McGraw-Hill.

Fiedler, F.E. (1971) Validation and extension of the contingency model of leadership effectiveness: a review of empirical findings, *Psychological Bulletin*, 76, 128–48.

Fiedler, F.E. (1972) Personality motivational systems, and behaviour of high and low LPC persons, *Human Relations*, 25, 391–412.

Fiedler, F.E. (1978) The contingency model and the dynamics of the leadership process. In Berkowitz, L. (ed.) *Advances in Experimental Social Psychological vol 11*. New York, Academic Press, pp. 59–112.

Fisher, J.L. (1984) *The Power of the Presidency*. New York, Macmillan.

Flexner, A. (1930) *Universities: American, English, German*. New York, Oxford University Press.

French, J.R.P. Jr and Raven, B. (1968) The bases of social power. In Cartwright, D. and Zander, A. (eds) *Group Dynamics: Research and Theory*, 3rd edn. New York, Harper & Row.

Garratt, R. (1987) *The Learning Organization*. London, Fontana.

Gibb, C.A. (1969) Leadership. In Lindzey, G. and Aronson, E. (eds) *The Handbook of Social Psychology vol 4*. Reading, MA, Addison-Wesley.

Glendon, A.I. (1992) Radical change within a British university. In Hosking, D.M. and Anderson, N. (eds) *Organizational Change and Innovation: Psychological Perspectives and Practices in Europe*. London, Routledge, pp. 49–71.

Graen, G.B. (1976) Role-making processes in complex organizations. In Dunnette, M.D. (ed.) *Handbook of Industrial and Organizational Psychology*. Chicago, Rand McNally.

Green, M.F. (ed.) (1988) *Leaders for a New Era*. New York, ACE/Macmillan.

Green, M.F. and McDade, S.A. (1991) *Investing in Higher Education: a Handbook of Leadership Development*. New York, American Council on Education.

Greenfield, T.B. (1973) Organisations as social inventions: rethinking assumptions about change, *Journal of Applied Behavioural Science*, 9(5), 551–74.

Greenfield, T.B. (1979) Organization theory as ideology, *Curriculum Enquiry*, 9(2), 97–112.

Greenleaf, R.K. (1973) *The Servant as Leader*. Peterborough, NH, Windy Row Press.
Greenleaf, R.K. (1986) *Servant Leadership: a Journey into the Nature of Legitimate Power and Greatness*. Mahwah, NJ, Paulist Press.
Guildford, P. (1993) *Familiarisation and Training for Lay Members of University Councils: A Compilation of Ideas, Examples and Practices*. Sheffield, CVCP/USDU.
Gunn, L. (1988) Public management: a third approach?, *Public Money and Management*, 8(2), 21–25.
Guttsman, W.L. (1963) *The British Political Elite*. London, Macgibbon and Kee.
Halsey, A.H. and Trow, M. (1971) *The British Academics*. London, Faber & Faber.
Hambrick, D.C. and Brandon, G.L. (1988) Executive values. In Hambrick, D.C. (ed.) *The Executive Effect*. Greenwich, CT, JAI Press.
Hammons, J. (1984) The department/division chairperson: educational leader?, *Community and Junior College Journal*, March, 14–19.
Hampden-Turner, C. (1981) *Maps of the Mind*. New York, Macmillan.
Hampden-Turner, C. (1990a) *Corporate Culture*. London, Economist Books.
Hampden-Turner, C. (1990b) *Charting the Corporate Mind: from Dilemma to Strategy*. Oxford, Blackwell.
Handy, C. (1984) Education for management outside business. In Goodlad, S. (ed.) *Education for the Professions*. Guildford, SRHE/NFER Nelson, pp. 289–96.
Handy, C. (1985) *Understanding Organizations*, 3rd edn. Harmondsworth, Penguin.
Handy, C. (1987) *The Making of Managers: a Report on Management Education, Training and Development in the USA, West Germany, France, Japan and the UK*. London, MSC/NEDC/BIM.
Handy, C. (1989) *The Age of Unreason*. London, Business Books.
Handy, C. (1991) *Waiting for the Mountain to Move*. London, Arrow.
Handy, C. (1993) *Understanding Organizations*, 4th edn. Harmondsworth, Penguin.
Harman, K.M. (1990) Culture and conflict in academic organization, *Journal of Educational Administration*, 27(3), 30–54.
Harvey-Jones, J. (1988) *Making it Happen: Reflections on Leadership*. London, Collins.
Hater, J.J. and Bass, B.M. (1988) Supervisors' evaluations and subordinates' perceptions of transformational and transactional leadership, *Journal of Applied Psychology*, 73, 695–702.
Heider, J. (1986) *The Tao of Leadership*. Aldershot, Wildwood House.
Hersey, P. (1984) *The Situational Leader*. New York, Warner Books.
Hersey, P. and Blanchard, K.H. (1969) *Management of Organizational Behaviour*. Englewood Cliffs, NJ, Prentice-Hall.
Hersey, P. and Blanchard, K.H. (1977) *Management of Organizational Behaviour: Utilizing Human Resources*, 3rd edn. Englewood Cliffs, NJ, Prentice-Hall.
Heywood, J. (1989) *Learning, Adaptability and Change: the Challenge for Education and Industry*. London, Paul Chapman Publishing.
Hofstede, G. (1980) *Culture's Consequences: International Differences in Work-related Values*. Beverley Hills, CA, Sage.
Hollander, E.P. (1978) *Leadership Dynamics*. New York, Free Press.
Hollander, E.P. (1985) Leadership and power. In Lindzey, G. and Aronson, E. (eds) *The Handbook of Social Psychology*, 3rd edn. New York, Random House.
Hollander, E.P. (1987) *College and University Leadership from a Social Psychological Perspective: a Transactional View*. New York, National Center for Post-Secondary Governance and Finance, Teachers College, Columbia University.
Hollander, E.P. and Julian, J.W. (1969) Contemporary trends in the analysis of leadership processes, *Psychological Bulletin*, 71, 387–97.

Homans, G.C. (1950) *The Human Group.* New York, Harcourt, Brace & World.

Homans, G.C. (1961) *Social Behaviour: Its Elementary Forms.* New York, Harcourt, Brace & World.

Honey, P. and Mumford, A. (1992) *The Manual of Learning Styles.* Maidenhead, Peter Honey & Alan Mumford.

House, R.J. (1971) A path-goal theory of leader effectiveness, *Administrative Science Quarterly,* 16, 321–38.

House, R.J. (1973) A path-goal theory of leadership effectiveness. In Fleishman, E.A. and Hunt, J.G. (eds) *Current Developments in the Study of Leadership.* Carbondale, IL, Southern Illinois University Press.

House, R.J. (1984) Power in organizations: a social psychological perspective, unpublished paper, Faculty of Management, University of Toronto.

House, R.J. (1988) Power and personality in complex organizations. In Staw, B.M. (ed.) *Research in Organizational Behaviour, Volume 10.* Greenwich, CT, JAI Press, pp. 305–57.

House, R.J. and Mitchell, T.R. (1974) Path-goal theory of leadership, *Journal of Contemporary Business,* 3, 81–97.

House, R.J., Spangler, W.D. and Woycke, J. (1990) Personality and charisma in the US presidency: a psychological theory of leadership effectiveness. In *Academy of Management Best Paper Proceedings, 1990.* Chicago: Academy of Management.

Hunt, J. (1992) *Leadership: a New Synthesis* London. Sage.

Hunt, J.G., Baliga, B.R. and Peterson, M.F. (1988) Strategic apex leader scripts and an organizational life-cycle approach to leadership and excellence, *Journal of Management Development,* 7(5), 61–83.

Hunt, J.G., Boal, K.B. and Sorenson, R.L. (1990) Top management leadership: inside the black box, *The Leadership Quarterly,* 1, 41–65.

Hurst, D, Rush, J.C. and White, R.E. (1989) Top management teams and organizational renewal, *Strategic Management Journal,* 10, 87–105.

Isenberg, D.J. (1984) How senior managers think, *Harvard Business Review* 62(6), 81–4.

Jacques, E. (1982) *The Form of Time.* New York, Crane Russak.

Jacques. E. (1989) *Requisite Organization.* Arlington, VA, Cason Hall.

Jarvis, P. (1983) *Professional Education.* London, Croom Helm.

Johnson, T.J. (1972) *Professions and Power.* London, Macmillan.

Kakabadse, A. *et al* (1992) Managing senior management teams. In Syrett, M. and Hogg, C. (eds) (1992) *Frontiers of Leadership.* London, Sage.

Kanter, R.M. (1983) *The Change Masters.* New York, Simon & Schuster.

Kaplowitz, R.A. (1986) *Selecting College and University Personnel: the Quest and the Question.* Washington, DC, ASHE-ERIC Higher Education Report no. 8.

Kauffman, J.F. (1980) *At the Pleasure of the Board: the Service of the College and University President.* Washington, DC, American Council on Education.

Keller, G. (1983) *Academic Strategy: the Management Revolution in American Higher Education.* Baltimore, MD, Johns Hopkins University Press.

Kerr, C. (1963) *The Uses of the University.* Cambridge, MA, Harvard University Press.

Kerr, C. (1982) *The Uses of the University,* 3rd edn. Cambridge, MA, Harvard University Press.

Kerr, C. (1984) *Presidents Make a Difference: Strengthening Leadership in Colleges and Universities.* Washington, DC, Association of Governing Boards of Universities and Colleges.

Kerr, C. and Gade, M.L. (1986) *The Many Lives of Academic Presidents: Time, Place and Character*. Washington, DC, Association of Governing Boards of Universities and Colleges.

Kerr, S. and Jermier, J.M. (1978) Substitutes for leadership: their meaning and measurement, *Organizational Behavior and Human Performance*, 22, 375–403.

Kipnis, D. (1976) *The Powerholders*. Chicago, University of Chicago Press.

Kochan, T.A., Schmidt, S.M. and De Cotiis, T.A. (1975) Superior-subordinate relations: leadership and headship, *Human Relations*, 28, 279–94.

Kotter, J. (1982) *The General Managers*. New York, Free Press.

Kotter, J. (1988) *The Leadership Factor*. New York, Free Press.

Kotter, J. (1990) *A Force For Change: How Leadership Differs from Management*. New York, Free Press.

Kouzes, J.M. and Posner, B.Z. (1987) *The Leadership Challenge*. San Francisco, Jossey-Bass.

Kremer-Hayon, L. and Avi-Itzhak, T.E. (1986) Roles of academic department chairpersons at the university level, *Higher Education*, 15, 105–13.

Latcham, J. and Cuthbert, R. (1983) A systems approach to college management. In Boyd-Barrett, O., Bush, T., Goodey, J., McNay, I. and Preedy, M. (eds) *Approaches to Post-school Management*. London, Harper & Row.

Lessem, R. (1991) *Total Quality Learning*. Oxford, Blackwell.

Likert, R. (1961) *New Patterns of Management*. New York, McGraw-Hill.

Likert, R. (1967) *The Human Organization: Its Management and Value*. New York, McGraw-Hill.

Likert, R. and Likert, J.G. (1976) *New Ways of Managing Conflict*. New York, McGraw-Hill.

Lockwood, G. and Davies, J. (1985) *Universities: the Management Challenge*. Guildford, SRHE/NFER Nelson.

Lysons, A.F. (1990) Taxonomies of higher education institutions predicted from organizational climate, *Research in Higher Education*, 31(2), 115–28.

Lysons, A.F. and Hatherley, D. (1991) Cameron's dimensions of effectiveness in higher education in the UK: a cross-cultural comparison. Paper presented at the European Association for Institutional Research, Edinburgh conference.

McCall, M.W., Lombardo, M.M. and Morrison, A.M. (1988) *The Lessons of Experience*. Lexington, MA, Lexington Books.

McCaskey, M.B. (1982) *The Executive Challenge: Managing Change and Ambiguity*. Boston, Pitman.

McCaulley, M.H. (1990) The Myers–Briggs type indicators and leadership. In Clark, K.E. and Clark, M.B. (eds) *Measures of Leadership*. West Orange, NJ, Leadership Library of America.

McClelland, D.C. (1985) *Human Motivation*. Glenview, IL, Scott, Foresman.

McGregor, D. (1960) *The Human Side of Enterprise*. New York, McGraw Hill.

McMahon, L. (1990) Private thoughts on public values, *Health Manpower Management*, 15(3) 15–16.

McNay, I. (ed.) (1992) *Visions of Post-compulsory Education*. Buckingham, SRHE/Open University Press.

March, J.G. and Olsen, J.P. (1979) *Ambiguity and Choice in Organizations*. Bergen, Universitetsforlaget.

Maslow, A.H. (1954) *Motivation and Personality*. New York, Harper & Row.

Meglino, B.M., Ravlin, E.C. and Adkin, S.C.L. (1989) A work values approach to corporate culture: A field test of value congruence process and its relationship to individual outcomes, *Journal of Applied Psychology*, 74, 424–32.

Meglino, B.M., Ravlin, E.C. and Adkin, S.C.L. (1990) Value congruence and satisfaction with a leader: an examination of the role of interaction. Unpublished paper, Riegel and Emory Human Resources Center, College of Business Administration, University of South Carolina, Columbia.

Meindl, J.R. (1990) On leadership: an alternative to conventional wisdom. In Staw, B.M. and Cummings, L.L. (eds) *Research in Organizational Behaviour*, vol. 12. Greenwich, CT, JAI Press, pp. 159–204.

Middlehurst, R. (1989) Leadership development in universities, 1986–1988. Final Report to the Department of Education and Science, University of Surrey (also published in *CORE*, 16(1), 1992, Fiche 3 B01).

Middlehurst, R. (1991) The changing roles of university managers and leaders: implications for preparation and development. Summary Report, CVCP/USDTU.

Middlehurst, R. and Elton, L. (1992) Leadership and management in higher education, *Studies in Higher Education*, 17(3), 251–64.

Middlehurst, R., Pope, M. and Wray, M (1992) The changing roles of university managers and leaders: implications for preparation and development, *CORE*, 16(1), Fiche 5 E11.

Miller, D. and de Vries, K. (1985) *The Neurotic Organization*. New York, Jossey-Bass.

Mintzberg, H. (1973) *The Nature of Managerial Work*. New York, Harper & Row.

Moodie, G.C. and Eustace, R. (1974) *Power and Authority in British Universities*. London, George Allen & Unwin Ltd.

Moran, W.E. (1972) A systems view of university organization. In Hamelman, P.W. (ed.) *Managing the University: a Systems Approach*. New York, Praeger.

Morgan, G. (1986) *Images of Organization*. London, Sage.

Morgan, G. (1988) *Riding the Waves of Change: Developing Managerial Competencies for a Turbulent World*. San Francisco, Jossey-Bass.

Morgan, G. (1991) Paradigms, metaphors and puzzle-solving in organizational theory. In Henry, J. (ed.) *Creative Management*. London, Sage.

Moses, I. (1985) The role of the head of department in the pursuit of excellence, *Higher Education*, 14, 337–54.

Moses, I. and Roe, E. (1990) *Heads and Chairs: Managing Academic Departments*. Brisbane, University of Queensland Press.

Mumford, A. (1989) *Management Development: Strategies for Action*. London, Institute of Personnel Management.

Mumford, A., Robinson, G. and Stradling, D. (1987) *Developing Directors: the Learning Processes*. Sheffield, Manpower Services Commission.

Mumford, A., Honey, P. and Robinson, G. (1990) *Director's Development Guidebook: Making Experience Count*. London, Institute of Directors.

Myers, I.B. and McCaulley, M.H. (1985) *Manual: a Guide to the Development and Use of the Myers–Briggs Type Indicator*. Palo-Alto, CA, Consulting Psychologists Press.

National Advisory Body for Public Sector Higher Education (1987) *Management for a Purpose*. London.

National Association of Teachers in Further and Higher Education (NATFHE) (1992) Managing the university curriculum in the year 2000, Conference Papers. London, NATFHE.

Nelson, P.D. (1964) Similarities and differences among leaders and followers, *Journal of Social Psychology*, 63, 161–7.

Neumann, A. (1990) The thinking team: toward a cognitive model of administrative teamwork in higher education. Teachers College, Columbia University, National Center for Postsecondary Governance and Finance.

Oakland, J. (1989) *Total Quality Management.* Oxford, Heinemann.

Pascale, R.T. and Athos, A.G. (1982) *The Art of Japanese Management.* Harmondsworth, Penguin.

Pedler, M., Burgoyne, J., and Boydell, T. (1991) *The Learning Company.* London, McGraw-Hill.

Peters, T. (1991) *Beyond Hierarchy.* London, Macmillan.

Peters, T. and Austin, A. (1985) *A Passion for Excellence.* London, Fontana/Collins.

Peters, T. and Waterman, R. (1982) *In Search of Excellence.* New York, Harper & Row.

Pettigrew, A., Ferlie, E. and McKee, L. (1992) *Shaping Strategic Change: Making Change in Large Organizations – The Case of the NHS.* London, Sage.

Pfeffer, J. (1977) The ambiguity of leadership, *Academy of Management Review,* 2, 104–12.

Pfeffer, J. (1978) The ambiguity of leadership, in McCall, M. and Lombardo, M. (eds) *Leadership: Where Else Can We Go?* Durham, NC, Duke University.

Pollitt, C. (1990) *Managerialism and the Public Services: the Anglo-American Experience.* Oxford, Blackwell.

Pollitt, C. and Harrison, S. (eds) (1992) *Handbook of Public Services Management.* Oxford, Blackwell.

Quinn, R.E. (1988) *Beyond Rational Management: Mastering the Paradoxes and Competing Demands of High Performance.* San Francisco, Jossey-Bass.

Quinn, R.E. and Cameron, K.S. (1988) *Paradox and Transformation.* New York, Harper & Collins.

Quinn, R.E., Faerman, S.R., Thompson, M.P. and McGrath, M.R. (1990) *Becoming a Master Manager.* New York, Wiley.

Ranson, S., Hinings, B. and Greenwood, R. (1980) The structuring of organizational structures, *Administrative Science Quarterly,* 25(1), 1–17.

Ribbins, P. (1985) The role of the middle manager in the secondary school. In Hughes, M., Ribbins, P. and Thomas, H. (eds) *Managing Education: the System and the Institution.* London, Holt, Rinehart and Winston.

Roberts, W. (1987) *The Leadership Secrets of Attila the Hun.* New York, Warner.

Sadler, P. (1988) *Managerial Leadership in the Post-Industrial Society.* Aldershot, Gower.

Sashkin, M. and Burke, W.W. (1990) Understanding and assessing organizational leadership. In Clark, K.E. and Clark, M.B. (eds) *Measures of Leadership.* West Orange, NJ, Leadership Library of America, pp. 297–326.

Schmidtlein, F. (1991) Commonly accepted organization theories that mislead institutional researchers. Paper delivered at 13th international forum, European Association for Institutional Research, Edinburgh.

Scott, P. (1991) *The Post-modern Challenge.* Stoke-on-Trent, Trentham Books.

Selznick, P. (1943) An approach to a theory of bureaucracy, *American Sociological Review,* 8, 47–54.

Selznick, P. (1957) *Leadership in Administration.* New York, Harper & Row.

Senge, P. (1990) *The Fifth Discipline: the Art and Practice of the Learning Organization.* London, Century Business.

Shattock, M. (1988) Financial management in universities: the lessons from University College, Cardiff, *Financial Accountability and Management in Governments, Public Services and Charities,* 4(2), 99–112.

Sizer, J. (1987) *Institutional Responses to Financial Reductions in the University Sector.* Final Report to the Department of Education and Science, London.

Smith, P.B. and Peterson, M.F. (1988) *Leadership, Organizations and Culture.* London, Sage.

Startup, R. (1976) The role of the departmental head, in *Studies in Higher Education,* 1(2), 233–43.

Stewart, J. (1989) In search of a curriculum for management for the public sector, *Management Education and Development,* 20(3), 168–75.

Stewart, R. (1976) *Contrasts in Management: a Study of the Different Types of Management Jobs, Their Demands and Choices.* London, McGraw-Hill.

Stewart, R. (1982) *Choices for the Manager.* Englewood Cliffs, NJ, Prentice-Hall.

Stewart, R. (1983) Managerial behaviour: how research has changed the traditional picture. In Earl, M.J. (ed.) *Perspectives on Management.* Oxford, Oxford University Press.

Stogdill, R.M. (1948) Personal factors associated with leadership: a survey of the literature, *Journal of Psychology,* 25, 35–71.

Stogdill, R.M. (1974) *Handbook of Leadership.* New York, Free Press.

Stogdill, R.M. and Coons, A.E. (eds) (1957) *Leader Behavior: Its Description and Measurement.* Columbus, OH, Bureau of Business Research, Ohio State University.

Streufert, S. and Nogami, G. (1989) Cognitive style and complexity: implications for I/O psychology. In Cooper, C.L. and Robertson, I. (eds) *International Review of Industrial and Organizational Psychology.* Chichester, Wiley, pp. 93–143.

Streufert, S. and Streufert, S.C. (1978) *Behavior in the Complex Environment.* Washington, DC, Winston.

Streufert, S., Swezey, R.W. (1986) *Complexity, Managers and Organizations.* Orlando, FL, Academic Press.

Symons, J.N. (1991) Leadership: a dialectic. MA Thesis, University of East London.

Szreter, R. (1968) An academic patriciate: vice-chancellors 1966–7, *Universities Quarterly,* 23(1), 17–46.

Tannenbaum, R. and Schmidt, W.H. (1958) How to choose a leadership pattern, *Harvard Business Review,* 36, 95–101.

Tapper, T. and Salter, B. (1992) *Oxford, Cambridge and the Changing Idea of the University.* Buckingham, SRHE/Open University Press.

Tichy, N.M. and Devanna, M.A. (1986) *The Transformational Leader.* New York, Wiley.

Tierney, W.G. (1988) Organizational culture in higher education, *Journal of Higher Education,* 59(1), 2–21.

Toffler, A. (1970) *Future Shock.* London, Bodley Head.

Toffler, A. (1980) *The Third Wave.* London, Pan.

Toffler, A. (1984) *Previews and Premises.* London, Pan.

Tucker, A. (1984) *Chairing the Academic Department: Leadership Among Peers,* 2nd edn. New York, ACE/Macmillan.

Tucker, A. and Bryan, R.A. (1988) *The Academic Dean: Dove, Dragon or Diplomat?* New York, ACE/Macmillan.

Turrill, T. (1986) *Change and Innovation: a Challenge for the National Health Service.* London, Institute of Health Services Management.

Urwick, L.F. (1944) *Elements of Administration.* London, Harper.

Vroom, V. (1964) *Work and Motivation.* New York, Wiley.

Vroom, V. and Yetton, P.W. (1973) *Leadership and Decision-Making.* Pittsburgh, PA, University of Pittsburgh Press.

Watkins, J., Drury, L. and Preddy, D. (1992) *From Evolution to Revolution: the Pressures on Professional Life in the 1990s.* Bristol, University of Bristol.

Weber, M. (1947) *The Theory of Economic and Social Organization.* (tr. A.M. Henderson and T. Parsons). New York: Free Press (first published 1921).

Weick, K.E. (1976) Educational organizations as loosely-coupled systems, *Administrative Science Quarterly,* 21(1), 1–19.

Weick, K.E. (1983) Managerial thought in the context of action. In Srivastva, S. (ed.) *The Executive Mind.* San Francisco, Jossey-Bass, pp. 221–42.

Whetten, D.A. and Cameron, K.S. (1985) Administrative Effectiveness in Higher Education, *Review of Higher Education,* 9(11), 35–49.

Whyte, W.F. (1943) *Street Corner Society.* Chicago, University of Chicago Press.

Willcocks, L. and Harrow, J. (eds) (1992) *Rediscovering Public Services Management.* London, McGraw-Hill.

Williams, P. *et al.* (1992) CVCP Academic Audit Unit Annual Report 1990/1991. London, CVCP.

Wright, P.L. and Taylor, D.S. (1984) *Improving Leadership Performance.* London, Prentice Hall International.

Yukl, G.A. (1981) *Leadership in Organizations.* Englewood Cliffs, NJ, Prentice-Hall.

Yukl, G.A. (1989) *Leadership in Organizations,* 2nd edn. Englewood Cliffs, NJ, Prentice-Hall.

Zaleznik, A. (1977) Managers and leaders: are they different?, *Harvard Business Review,* 55, 67–78.

Index

The Society for Research into Higher Education

The Society for Research into Higher Education exists to stimulate and coordinate research into all aspects of higher education. It aims to improve the quality of higher education through the encouragement of debate and publication on issues of policy, on the organization and management of higher education institutions, and on the curriculum and teaching methods.

The Society's income is derived from subscriptions, sales of its books and journals, conference fees and grants. It receives no subsidies, and is wholly independent. Its individual members include teachers, researchers, managers and students. Its corporate members are institutions of higher education, research institutes, professional, industrial and governmental bodies. Members are not only from the UK, but from elsewhere in Europe, from America, Canada and Australasia, and it regards its international work as amongst its most important activities.

Under the imprint *SRHE & Open University Press*, the Society is a specialist publisher of research, having some 45 titles in print. The Editorial Board of the Society's Imprint seeks authoritative research or study in the above fields. It offers competitive royalties, a highly recognizable format in both hard- and paperback and the worldwide reputation of the Open University Press.

The Society also publishes *Studies in Higher Education* (three times a year), which is mainly concerned with academic issues, *Higher Education Quarterly* (formerly *Universities Quarterly*), mainly concerned with policy issues, *Research into Higher Education Abstracts* (three times a year), and *SRHE News* (four times a year).

The Society holds a major annual conference in December, jointly with an institution of higher education. In 1991, the topic was 'Research and Higher Education in Europe', with the University of Leicester. In 1992, it was 'Learning to Effect' with Nottingham Trent University, and in 1993, 'Governments and the Higher Education Curriculum: Evolving Partnerships' at the University of Sussex in Brighton. Further conferences include in 1994, 'The Student Experience' at the University of York.

The Society's committees, study groups and branches are run by the members. The groups at present include:

Teacher Education Study Group
Continuing Education Group
Staff Development Group
Excellence in Teaching and Learning

Benefits to members

Individual

Individual members receive:

- *SRHE News*, the Society's publications list, conference details and other material included in mailings.
- Greatly reduced rates for *Studies in Higher Education* and *Higher Education Quarterly*.
- A 35% discount on all Open University Press & SRHE publications.
- Free copies of the Precedings – commissioned papers on the theme of the Annual Conference.
- Free copies of *Research into Higher Education Abstracts*.
- Reduced rates for conferences.
- Extensive contacts and scope for facilitating initiatives.
- Reduced reciprocal memberships.

Corporate

Corporate members receive:

- All benefits of individual members, plus
- Free copies of *Studies in Higher Education*.
- Unlimited copies of the Society's publications at reduced rates.
- Special rates for its members e.g. to the Annual Conference.

Membership details: SRHE, 344–354 Gray's Inn Road, London, WC1X 8BP, UK. Tel: 071 837 7880

Catalogue: SRHE & Open University Press, Celtic Court, 22 Ballmoor, Buckingham MK18 1XW. Tel: (0280) 823388